The Pursuit of Justice and Jewish Law

Halakhic Perspectives on the Legal Profession

Second Edition

by

Michael J. Broyde

Yashar Books, Inc.
New York, 2007

THE PURSUIT OF JUSTICE
HALAKHIC PERSPECTIVES ON THE LEGAL PROFESSION
Revised and Expanded Edition

Copyright © 2007 by Michael J. Broyde.

All rights reserved. No part of this book may be used or reproduced in any manner whatsoever without written permission from Yashar Books Inc. except in the case of brief quotations in reviews for inclusion in a magazine, newspaper, or broadcast.

ISBN 978-1-933143-01-0

10 9 8 7 6 5 4 3 2 1

Library of Congress Cataloging In Publication Data

Broyde, Michael J.
 The pursuit of justice and jewish law / by Michael J. Broyde
 p.   cm.
 Includes bibliographical references and index.
 1. Practice of law (Jewish law). 2. Lawyers, Jewish—United States.
 3. Religion and law—United States. I. Title

For information and catalog write to Yashar Books Inc.,
1548 E. 33rd Street, Brooklyn, NY 11234, or visit our website:
www.YasharBooks.com

Contents

Acknowledgments from First Edition vii

Acknowledgments for Second Edition xiii

Overview xi

Chapter One: Introduction 1

General Issues in Legal Practice 5

Chapter Two: Providing Counsel and the Role of the Lawyer . . 7
    The Judge as Advocate. 8
    Lawyers Giving Legal Advice 10
    The Limits of Advocacy. 16
    Conclusion. 18

Chapter Three: Professional Confidentiality 21
    Jewish Law and the Obligation to Help Others. 21
    Professional Confidences and Legal Ethics. 22
    Jewish Law's Perspective on Secular Legal Ethics 23

Chapter Four: Admonition and Collective Responsibility 27
    Admonition as an Obligation 27
    Situations where Admonition is Not Required 29
    How to Admonish 32

In the Courtroom: Litigation 35

Chapter Five: Litigating in Secular Court 37
    The Scope of the Prohibition 38

Conclusion... 43
Chapter Six: Courts and Lawyers........................ 45
    Applying the Prohibitions to Litigate in Secular Courts 45
    The Analysis of Rabbi Klein, and a Response to It........... 46
Chapter Seven: Aiding in a Violation of Jewish Law 49
    An Overview of the Prohibition to Assist
        in a Violation of Jewish Law 49
    Modern Decisors and Issues Involved in Aiding a Person
        to Violate Jewish Law 54
    The Lawyer and Aiding in a Violation of Jewish Law......... 58
Chapter Eight: Secular Law and Secular Court.............. 63
    Bankruptcy Laws: A Paradigmatic Example................ 63
    Public Law..................................... 65
Chapter Nine: Swearing and Oath-Taking 69
    Oaths... 69
    Head Coverings 70
Chapter Ten: Examination of Witnesses 73
    Repeating Harmful Information and Truth-Telling 73
    Truth-Telling in Court 74

Practicing Criminal Law 77
Chapter Eleven: Prosecuting Criminals 79
    Introduction: 79
    Classical Jewish Law and Informing: An Overview 82
    Informing on People When Government is
        Committed to Procedural Justice: Five Opinions
        of Contemporary Decisors 87
Chapter Twelve: Defending One Accused of a Crime......... 117
    Introduction 117
    Assisting the Guilty 119
    Assisting the Guilty: A Second Approach.................. 122

Family Law Issues 125

Chapter Thirteen: Wills and Inheritance **127**
Wills that Bequeath 137
Living Wills 130
Conclusion 131

Chapter Fourteen: Family Law and Child Custody **133**
General Problems in Family Law 133
Child Custody 135
Support Payments 139

Business Law and the Law Business 141

Chapter Fifteen: Usury **143**
Interest Charging: An Introduction 143
Limitations 144
Rabbinically Prohibited Interest 145
Usury and the Lawyer 149

Chapter Sixteen: Negotiations **151**
The Problem of Puffery 151
A Limitation and an Expansion 152

Chapter Seventeen: Arbitration and Compromise **155**
Mandatory Arbitration? 156

Chapter Eighteen: Billing by the Hour **159**
The Role of Custom in Billing Questions 159
Billing Travel Time 162

Chapter Nineteen: Conclusion **165**

Appendix 167

The 1992 New York *Get* Law: A Markedly Less Than Ideal Solution That Creates Many Halakhic Problems **167**
Introduction 168

The Problem with the 1992 *Get* Law 170
Halakhic Considerations............................... 171
The Reality of Divorce................................ 185
Conclusion... 188

Glossary 191

Bibliography 197

**Table of References for the Bible, Talmud,
Post-Talmudic Codes, Commentators and Responsa** 211

Cases, Statutes and Model Codes 219

Subject, Person and Work Index 221

Acknowledgments from First Edition

A number of people have commented on prior drafts of this work, and their assistance is graciously acknowledged: Ms. Daphne Dubin, Esq. of Moses & Singer, Justice Menachem Elon of the Israeli Supreme Court, Rabbi Earl Goldberger of Massachusetts, Rabbi Dr. Norman Lamm, President of Yeshiva University, Rabbi Dr. Emanuel Rackman Esq., Chancellor of Bar-Ilan University, Rabbi Dr. Andrew Schein of AT&T, and Professor Aaron Twerski of Brooklyn Law School. Professor Michael Berger of Emory College closely read a final version of this book, and made many welcomed, corrections. In addition, I benefitted from seeing a manuscript-in-preparation dealing with many of the issues addressed in this article by Professor Steven Resnicoff of De Paul Law School.

I also thank the Atlanta Scholars Kollel and its various members, as well as Congregation Beth Jacob, in whose joint *beit midrash* I have studied for the last four years. During the Spring of 1993, I was privileged to spend afternoons studying topics relating to the mitzvah of admonition with Rabbi Menachem Deutsch and chapter three reflects many of the concepts we developed during that period. So too, I am grateful to the newly-formed Young Israel of Toco Hills, Atlanta, for the opportunity to present some of this material in the course of classes I have given there. The excellent editorial work of Dr. Yaakov Elman of KTAV is most appreciated and has made this a better work, as has the proficient proofreading of Denah Stilerman, Daniel Lasar, and Lisa Krochmal. So too, the bibliographic labors of Dr. Marc Shapiro of Harvard University were of considerable assistance.

Rabbi David Cohen of Congregation Gvul Yavetz, Brooklyn, deserves special thanks, both for his close reading of an earlier version of this book many years ago, and for his insightful help in general. Rabbi Cohen's ongoing open discussions of the issues raised in this book are appreciated.

A special thanks is also due to Rabbi Alfred Cohen, editor of the *Journal of Halacha and Contemporary Society*, who has continuously encouraged my writing in Jewish law, and who published the initial article that led to this book.

I owe a special debt to my teacher, Rabbi Dr. J. David Bleich, Director (*Rosh Kollel*) of the Postgraduate Institute for Jurisprudence and Family Law (*Kollel le-Hora'ah*) of Yeshiva University (where I studied for four years) and a Professor of Law at Cardozo School of Law, for his assistance, both in the preparation of this book, and for the aid and guidance he has provided over many years. Rabbi Bleich and his writings have been a continuous inspiration to this author. The same debt is owed to my teacher Rabbi Mordechai Willig, the Assistant Director of the Institute. I first had the privilege to be a student of Rabbi Willig's fourteen years ago, and many times since then I have benefitted from his erudition.

More generally, an enormous debt is owed to Yeshiva University and its seminary, Rabbi Isaac Elchanan Theological Seminary. I entered Yeshiva University at the age of fourteen and left thirteen years later to start my career in academia. These essentially uninterrupted years of study at Yeshiva University affected me in ways too numerous to list, and I feel indebted to the institution for helping to form me.

Over the last few years, my colleague at Emory, Professor David Blumenthal, has provided me with assistance on many matters—my deepest thanks to him for all of his help, much of which went far beyond the call of duty, over the last four years. So too, Professor John Witte, Jr. of Emory Law School has assisted me in many different ways at various times over the last three years, and his help was greatly appreciated. Finally, Rabbi Howard Jachter has made many valuable contributions to this work, as he has to all of the articles I have written; his assistance is always greatly appreciated. This year marks our tenth year of study together, and I cherish each of them.

This book is a tribute to my parents, Rabbi Dr. Barret Broyde and Dr. Suse Broyde, who spent so much time teaching me how to learn, study, and think. Words cannot express the gratitude I feel to them for the many years they spent providing me with a home and a tradition of the type and caliber so few have the privilege to grow up in. The ideas and values they taught me I can only aspire to reach. Equally important, the contributions of my wife, Channah S. Broyde Esq., whose patience and assistance—and partnership in life—are treasured, have made this book a reality. Without her many years of help and support, this book would not have been written. I can only apologize to her and to our children—Joshua, Aaron, and Rachel—for the time this book has taken away from them.

Finally, following the supplications of an ancient Sage, I thank the Almighty for having set my portion with those who sit in the house of study and pray that I should not err in a matter of *halakhah*.

Michael J. Broyde
May 30, 1995
Rosh Hodesh Sivan, 5755

Acknowledgments for Second Edition

It has been more than ten years since this, my first book, was published. This second edition contains a vastly expanded chapter on the problems of informing (Chapter 11) and hundreds of small changes and revisions. My thanks to Michael Ausubel of Emory University for the hard work he put in to edit this book, as well as Fruma Farkas and Deborah Loubser who helped proofread the galleys.

My thanks to Emory University School of Law for all the gracious research support it has provided and to the Center for the Study of Law and Religion for truly being my research home at Emory Law School. Many times I have said to myself that I would be lost without the help of Prof. John Witte, Jr., as well as Eliza, April, Anita, and Janice of the Center.

I remain deeply indebted to the Beth Din of America and its director, Rabbi Jonathan Reiss, as well as Av Beth Din Rabbi Gedalia Dov Schwartz and Segan Av Beth Din Rabbi Mordechai Willig for allowing me to sit as a *dayan* in the Beth Din. So too, to my congregants in the Young Israel of Toco Hills in Atlanta, I can only express my deep thanks for letting me study Torah with each of you. I have grown in Torah through this interaction. The same is true for my daily learning with the many different members of the Altanta Torah MiTzion kollel. Thank you to each of you, and particular thanks to Rabbi Zev Farber, its new director.

Thank you as well to my colleagues at Emory—particularly to Prof. Michael S. Berger, whose work in the Atlanta Jewish community is of great value. Many of the individuals thanked in the Acknowledgements for the first edition deserve to be thanked again, but space does not permit such.

The first edition of this book was dedicated to my parents, and it thanked my wife Channah S. Broyde and our children Joshua, Aaron, Rachel and Deborah. This edition is dedicated to them.

Michael J. Broyde
October 20, 2007
28 Tishrei, 5767

Overview

This book discusses the many legal and ethical issues Jewish law[1] ponders when Jews consider joining the bar and practicing law as a career. As with all works that consider the intersection of Jewish law and modern life, this book attempts to synthesize the rules of Jewish law and ethics with the requirements of modern law practice. In some areas of law, this can be done without difficulty. In others, some modification of the law practice is needed. Finally, there are some areas where the practice of law is fraught with considerable peril in the eyes of Jewish law. This book hopes to familiarize those new to Jewish law with these issues and to provide some guidance to adherents of Jewish law who practice law.

This book is divided into five basic parts, each of which analyzes a different group of issues within the practice of law. The early chapters (two to four) address general issues that affect all lawyers. The first of these general issues discusses the Sages' admonition not to be like *orkhei ha-dayyanim*, commonly translated as "lawyers." Chapter two discusses one aspect of professional responsibility from the perspective of Jewish law, and the third chapter considers the impact Jewish law's obligation to rebuke a sinner might have on the practice of law as a career.

The second set of chapters (five through ten) addresses many of the issues raised in civil litigation, from the general prohibition of litigating in secular court, to problems of swearing-in witnesses and possibly suborning perjury. The common link each of these chapters has is their relationship to the courtroom process. The next unit (chapters eleven and twelve) discusses issues raised in the practice of criminal law, including both the problems of being a prosecutor and being a defense lawyer. The material in chapters nine and ten are as applicable to this unit as they are to the previous unit.

Chapters thirteen and fourteen discuss three family law issues: willwriting (including living wills), divorce law, and child custody disagreements. The next unit (chapters sixteen through eighteen) discusses issues

---

1 For a brief historical introduction to Jewish law, see the entry "*halakhah*" in the glossary.

related to lawyers' involvement in business law and the problems of negotiation, arbitration and, most significantly, assisting in transactions where interest is being charged in violation of Jewish law. Chapter nineteen addresses some of the practical issues that arise from the common practice of a lawyer's billing by the hour.

The final section contains some general observations on the practice of law and the challenges it poses to those who observe Jewish law.

The details of the interaction of Jewish and secular law are one of the recurring themes of this book. The appendix explores the ramifications in Jewish law, both in the areas of technical Jewish divorce law, as well as in the area of Jewish public policy, of the attempt by New York State in the 1992 *Get* Law, to enact a secular remedy to one particular type of Jewish spousal abandonment.

In addition, a complete glossary, bibliography, and index are included at the end of this work for the benefit of readers who wish to conduct their own research on various issues.[2]

A note on the intellectual history of this work is appropriate. In 1988, Mr. Mordecai Biser wrote an article entitled "Can an Observant Jew Practice Law? A Look at Some Halakhic Problems," and in 1989 I wrote a reply to that article. Regrettably, neither the original article by Mr. Biser nor my reply were then published. In 1990, I turned some of my reply into an independent work which was published in the *Journal of Halacha and Contemporary Society* 20:5–45 (1990) as "The Practice of Law According to Jewish Law." Mr. Biser's format and discussion (whose Jewish law conclusions I do not agree with) provided a framework for many of the issues I discussed. Thus, an intellectual debt is owed to his work, which I would like to acknowledge. In 1994, Mr. Biser's article was published, and reference is made to that article in this book. This book is an expansion and reworking of many of the issues raised in that initial article in the *Journal of Halacha and Contemporary Society* and the still unpublished reply to Mr. Biser's article. The Appendix to this book was published in *Tradition* 29:4, 5–13 (1995).

---

2 A brief notation on the sources cited in this book. For the reader's benefit, this book cites English sources to support propositions that can be readily supported by both English and Hebrew sources. Whenever possible, references to generally available classical sources are also provided. When no specific volume of a multi-volume work is referred to, it is the volume that refers to monetary matters (*Hoshen Mishpat*) that is the source.

Chapter One

Introduction

The practice of law as a profession has received little written analysis through the eyes of Jewish law, although it has been a profession adopted by Jews for many years.[1] This book will survey many of the more common areas of legal practice through the prism of Jewish law. In particular, it will address those areas[2] of practice that are historically perceived to be the most at variance with the requirements of Jewish law.[3]

---

1 Besides this book, and the article that preceded it in the *J. Halacha & Contemporary Society*, the only systemic treatment of the practice of law available can be found in Mordecai Biser, "Can an Observant Jew Practice Law? A Look at Some Halakhic Problems," *The Jewish Law Annual XI:101–135* (1994).

2 The practice of secular law in Israel poses certain additional problems unique to Israel's court system and political circumstances. These issues will not be addressed in this book. For an overview, see R. Eliezer Waldenberg, *Tzitz Eliezer* 12:82 (and the authorities cited therein), and compare with Justice Menahem Elon, *Ha-Mishpat ha-Ivri* (3rd ed., Magnes Press 1988), at 1606–1613. See also, R. Binyamin Zilber, *Az Nidberu* 3:74; R. Ovadia Hadaya, *Yaskil Avdi* 6:8; R. Ezra Batzri, *Sha'arei Ezra* 1:333, and *Ha-Torah veha-Medinah* 1:44 and 7:10. For a discussion of the status of the labor court in Israel, see R. Meir Issaacson, *Mevasser Tov* 1:85. For an excellent review essay, see Eliav Shochatman, "Ma'amad ha-Halakhati shel Batei ha-Mishpat be-Medinat Yisrael," *Tehumin* 13:337–370 (1993).

So too, this book does not address the role of lawyers in a *beit din*. For an excellent analysis of that issue, see Nahum Rakover, *Ha-Shelihut vehaHarsha'ah ba-Mishpat ha-Ivri* (Mosad Harav Kook, 1972), and Aaron Kirschenbaum, "Representation in Litigation in Jewish Law," *Dine Israel* 6:25 (1975).

3 One area not discussed in this book is the general ethical and halakhic issues associated with running any business, including a law practice. There are many excellent works that address this significant issue. Chapter eighteen does however, address some of the issues involved in hourly billing.

One thing is absent from this introduction: a historical review of the problems associated with Jews practicing law and functioning as lawyers. The reason for this absence is that relatively little has been written discussing the systemic involvement of Jews as lawyers in a secular legal system from a Jewish law perspective. The problems posed are unique to modern (western) democracies where Jews have been free to involve themselves in the secular legal system in any manner. In pre-emancipation times, Jewish involvement in the secular legal system was rare and was certainly not systemic. Frequently, when such involvement was favored, it was to protect a specific "Jewish" interest.[4] The notion that any given Jew would engage in an ongoing enterprise involving the practice of secular law merely as a way to earn a livelihood was essentially unheard of until the early part of the nineteenth century. As noted by the *Encyclopedia Judaica*:

> Jews were generally prevented from practicing law in most countries in which they settled until early in the 19th century. In some countries their exclusion was based on the belief that law was largely ecclesiastical law and hence unsuitable for non-Christians ...while in many other countries it was believed that membership of the legal profession was a mark of distinction not to be conferred on an alien race to whom citizenship and political rights had not been granted.[5]

Even when Jews were granted the legal right to practice law and remain faithful to their religion, many barriers, cultural and otherwise, remained. Rather "many of the Jews who set out to become lawyers in a Christian society found it necessary to become Christians before they could be accepted as lawyers."[6] It was only in the United States, Great Britain, and the British colonies, that Jews could function as lawyers without intense pressure to abandon the Jewish faith.

---

4 "Lawyers," *Encyclopedia Judaica*, 10:1491.

5 Ibid., at 1490–1491.

6 Ibid, at 1491. It is interesting to note that the iconography of the secular "Justice," which is discussed in Appendix A of Judith Resnik, "Managerial Judges," *Harvard L.R.* 96:374, 446 (1982), most likely has within it some origins in the medieval Jewish-Christian polemics. Historically, the image of "Justice" was depicted as a "large female figure, draped in Greco-Roman robes. She carries scales and sword, and her eyes are covered with a blindfold." The classical depiction of "justice" in medieval Christian Europe was without the blindfolds. Blindfolds were a symbol

The plight of the religiously-observant lawyer was even more difficult, and it was not until well into the current century that one encountered more than a handful of observant Jews practicing law.[7] Indeed, it is only in the last thirty years, with the resurgence of fidelity to, and study of, Jewish law that observant Jewish lawyers have become aware of these issues and responsa have been written directly addressing this issue.[8]

The fact that this activity is without direct historical precedent in Jewish law does not necessarily mean that Jewish law or ethics frowns on it.[9] Rather, like all changes in society or technology,[10] one must seek to

---

used to denigrate Judaism and Jewish justice to which the "new revelation" was not visible. The addition of the blindfolds to the iconography of "Justice" after the emancipatibn most likely has its origins in the abandonment of Christian iconography as the sole image of justice; see Andrew Simmonds, "The Blindfolds of Justice," *American Bar Association J.* 63:1164 (1977).

Interestingly, a number of nineteenth century Jewish law works from eastern European countries note the problems confronted by Jewish courts, whose services were apparently being solicited by the general Christian population, because the Jewish courts heard cases "blindly" and impartially (and apparently the local secular courts did not); see R. Hayyim Cohen, *Divrei Geonim* 52:15 and 77:19.

7   For a discussion of the cultural factors which perhaps directed Jews in the direction of secular law as a source of a livelihood, see Jerold S. Auerbach, *Rabbis and Lawyers: The Journey from Torah to Constitution* (Indiana University Press, 1990). For a discussion of what exactly makes a "Jewish lawyer," see Sanford Levinson, "Identifying the Jewish Lawyer: Reflections on the Construction of Professional Identity," *Cardozo L.R.* 14:1577, 1600–1611 (1993), and Jerome Hornblass, "The Jewish Lawyer," *Cardozo L.R.* 14:1639 (1993).

8   It is worth noting that all of the responsa cited in this book that deal directly with the practice of law in America are no more than thirty-five years old. So too, Agudath Israel of America's conference on "The Legal Profession Today: A Torah Perspective" of November 5, 1989 in New York City, represents the first such conference on this topic.

9   But see Biser, "Practicing Law," at 108.

10 For more on Jewish law's responses to changes in technology, see "Electricity," *Encyclopedia Talmudit* 18:155–190, and 641–781 (Jerusalem, 1988); R. Shlomo Zalman Auerbach, *Minhat Shlomo* ch. 9–13 (Jerusalem, 1986); Howard Jachter and Michael Broyde, "Fire, Light and Electricity in Positive Commandments According to Jewish Law," *J. Halacha & Contemporary Society* 25:119–127 (1993), all of which discuss ritual changes caused by changes in technology; and Michael Broyde, "The Definition of Fire in Halacha: A Theoretical Discourse with Some Practical Insights" (distributed by *Rabbinical Council of America*, October 1993), which discusses changes in technology as reflected in the definition of "fire" according to Jewish law.

apply the principles used by Jewish law to modern life and times to determine the correct position Jewish law takes on an issue. Indeed, most likely, the absence of historical precedent within Jewish law more likely reflects the development of secular law in Christian Europe[11] and its decision to deprive Jews of the right to participate in the secular legal system.[12]

---

11 "Secular" courts have never really developed in Islamic countries and this is clearly reflected in Jewish law's discussion of them; for more on this, see note 5 of chapter five.

12 For more on this, see *Rabbis and Lawyers*, at chapters 1–2, and *Encyclopedia Judaica*, at 1490–1491.

General Issues in Legal Practice

The next thee chapters discuss issues related to all lawyers' conduct. The opening chapter discusses the Talmud's admonition concerning *orkhei ha-dayyanim*, which is generally translated as lawyers. The next chapter discusses an area of tension between legal ethics and Jewish law; finally, the third section discusses the obligation to rebuke one who sins and how that affects the practice of law.

Chapter Two

Providing Counsel and the Role of a Lawyer

Introduction

This chapter will explore the consequences of advice-giving within the Jewish tradition. In particular, it will discuss the concept of "arrangers of the law" (*orkhei ha-dayyanim*), and the various restrictions imposed by Jewish law on one who advocates for or gives advice to another. However, before one even considers this topic, one must understand the basic elements of how a Jewish court (*beit din*) should function. Unlike the common law model of a court of law, with its emphasis on the referee or umpire model of justice,[1] Jewish law directs that its judges adopt a more activist model of justice. In a Jewish law court, judges ask questions of

---

1 See e.g., Steven Flanders, "Blind Umpires," *Hastings L. J.* 35:505 (1984). It is interesting to note that *Ethics of the Sages* 1:8 is cited by Judith Resnik, "Managerial Judges," *Harvard L.R.* 96:374 (1982), as a justification for the concept of neutral or referee-type judges. After citing Rabbi Samson R. Hirsch's commentary to *Ethics of the Sages* 1:8, which states:

> Should you be called upon to function as a judge, do not be like the legal advisers who offer to place their juridical knowledge at the service of the litigating parties... [Y]ou must remain silent and abstain from interference in the arguments.... Do not by even so much as a gesture seek to influence either prosecution or defense.

Resnik asserts that this is one of the bases for umpire theory of judging, which contrasts with the managerial theory she advocates. *Ethics of the Sages* 1:8 at its core addresses the impartiality of the judge and not the balance between the inquisitorial and referee models of judging. As noted above, Jewish law mandated that a judge function in an inquisitorial mode and yet remain impartial.

witnesses, cross-examine the parties, collect evidence, and make findings of both fact and law.[2] Lawyers are not needed, and frequently are discouraged. In short, Jewish law adopts an inquisitorial model of justice.

In such a system, lawyers are not required in order for the court to fairly decide a matter, and parties need not solicit a lawyer's advice in order to insure a fair hearing. Indeed, *Ethics of the Sages* (*Pirke Avot*) 1:8 states:

> Judah ben Tabai states: Do not act like lawyers [lit: arrangers of the law; *orkhei ha-dayyanim*]; when litigants are in front of you they should be considered as guilty; once they have been dismissed from the court, they should be in your eyes as innocent, provided that they accepted the judgment.[3]

This chapter is an explanation of the various rules and interpretations derived from *Ethics of the Sages* (*Avot*) 1:8, with a particular emphasis on how the mandates of *Avot* 1:8 should affect the conduct of lawyers. The thrust of this chapter is that *Avot* 1:8 has two different components to it. The first is directed to judges and compels them to treat litigants in an evenhanded manner, even when they think one of the parties is at fault. The second component is directed to advocates and lawyers and instructs them to be careful in providing and formulating legal advice.

The Judge as Advocate

As noted above, Jewish law envisions courts running along the inquisitorial model, whereby judges direct the trial and the court. Litigants would not normally need to be represented by lawyers, advocates, or other representatives, and certainly not by individuals who would help the litigant formulate claims of law or fact in a Jewish court (*beit din*). Indeed, part of the job of the judge is to evaluate the credibility of the unrehearsed testimony of the various witnesses. Rabbi Jacob ben Asher, writing in his code, *Arba'ah Turim* (*Tur*), explains that the prohibition of being a lawyer (*orekh din*) applies to judges generally, and is most applicable when they help a litigant formulate his testimony or claim in front of the judge. Such help is normally prohibited and is only permitted when

---

[2] R. Joseph Karo, *Shulhan Arukh, Hoshen Mishpat* 17:5–9.

[3] *Ethics of the Sages* 1:8.

the litigant wishes to save himself with a proper claim, but because of his anger his claim is not formulated or it is confused because of misunderstanding. In that case it is permitted to help him understand the beginnings of his claim since it states, "one must open the mouths of those who are mute."[4] One has to be very careful in this matter lest one be like one of the lawyers [*orkhei din.*][5]

The almost identical language is quoted by Rabbi Karo in the *Shulhan Arukh*,[6] as well as by numerous other authorities.[7] It is clear that Jewish law does not allow judges to function as advocates for one party, and treats any such transference of roles as unethical, unless the circumstances are such that the party is actually incapable of pleading its case.[8]

It is true that Jewish law calls for litigant-appointed judges—a system where each party chooses a judge, and those two judges pick a third judge—and that such a system contains within it some form of advocacy by the judges. Indeed, the Jerusalem Talmud notes that each judge in such a case endeavors to find support for his party's interest.[9] However, as noted by Rabbenu Asher, these judges are completely bound to function as judges according to Jewish law and may not deviate in any way from the norms of judicial conduct found in Jewish law. They certainly are not lawyers or advocates in the classical sense of the word.[10]

---

4 Proverbs 31:8.

5 R. Jacob ben Asher, *Tur, Hoshen Mishpat* 17:9. He adds that Rabbenu Asher (*Rosh*) felt that even this limited help was not allowed. For more on this, see R. Jonah Landsofer, *Me'il Tzedakah* 53. For an explication of this based on the biblical verses, see the commentary of R. Barukh Epstein, *Torah Temimah*, Exodus 22:7–8.

6 *Shulhan Arukh, Hoshen Mishpat* 17:9.

7 See e.g., R. Yehiel Mikhel Epstein, *Arukh ha-Shulhan, Hoshen Mishpat* 17:13; R. Jacob Lorberbaum, *Netivot ha-Mishpat* 17:16; *Halakhah Pesukah* (Makhon Harry Fishel, 1991); and *Kovetz ha-Poskim* (Makhon Kovetz haPoskim, 1975) commenting on 17:9.

For a discussion of when precisely a judge (*dayyan*) may assist a litigant, see R. Jacob Reisher, *Shevut Yaakov* 1:64 and R. Benyamin ben Mattityahu, *Binyamin Ze'ev* 50.

8 See R. Jacob Lorberbaum, *Netivot ha-Mishpat* 9:16.

9 *Sanhedrin* 3:1.

10 *Rosh*, commenting on *Sanhedrin* 3:2; see also R. Yehiel Mikhel Epstein, *Arukh ha-Shulhan, Hoshen Mishpat* 13:1–4, who discusses this issue.

This aspect of the rules found in *Ethics of the Sages* 1:8 is, at a certain level, obvious, and is codified into the codes of Jewish law, not only as ethical rules, but as rules of law also.[11] A judge must conduct himself with impartiality and neutrality and cannot take the role of advocate of either side. Indeed, modern American law codifies this into its legal code also. As it states in the canon of legal ethics that governs American judges:

> A judge must perform judicial duties impartially and fairly. A judge who manifests bias on any basis in a proceeding impairs the fairness of the proceeding and brings the judiciary into disrepute. Facial expression and body language, in addition to oral communication, can give to parties or lawyers in the proceeding, jurors, the media and others an appearance of judicial bias. A judge must be alert to avoid behavior that may be perceived as prejudicial.[12]

Lawyers Giving Legal Advice

The second situation addressed by *Ethics of the Sages* 1:8 is the more common one of a lawyer giving advice to clients (or a person giving legal advice to friends or relatives). Maimonides, in his commentary on *Ethics of the Sages* states:

> *Like lawyers:* These are people who teach others what to claim until these others are experts.... When the judge states such, they teach you to reply such; when the opponent claims such, they teach you to reply such, as if they are setting forth the law.[13]

Similar sentiments are expressed by Rabbi Menahem Meiri in his commentary. He states:

---

11 See also *Shevuot* 30b-31a for similar ideas, which are codified in detail in *Shulhan Arukh, Hoshen Mishpat* 17.

12 Canon of Judicial Ethics, Canon 3(b)(5).

13 Maimonides, commenting on *Ethics of the Sages* 1:8; see also R. Menahem Mendel Kirschbaum, *Menahem Meshiv* 1:54.

Do not make oneself like a lawyer: These are the people who organize the claims of either the plaintiff or the defendant.... Similar to this is the incident involving Rabbi Yohanan (*Ketubot* 52b) where he taught a legal claim to one of his relatives and regretted it, and he [Rabbi Yohanan] stated that he made himself like one of the lawyers, since anyone who does this teaches another to lie and to negate the truth.[14]

The source for these interpretations can be found in an incident recounted in the Talmud. The Talmud states:

The relatives of Rabbi Yohanan had to support the wife [widow] of their father who required continuous medical treatment. They came in front of Rabbi Yohanan who advised them to arrange for a contract with a doctor for medical care for the woman's whole life for a fixed price. Rabbi Yohanan later stated that we have made ourselves like lawyers (*orkhei ha-dayyanim*). Initially, [the Talmud asks], why did Rabbi Yohanan think [that it was permitted for him to help these people with advice]: since it states from one's relatives one should not turn away"[15] [i.e., one should help one's relatives]; in the end he thought that this conduct was unbecoming of an eminent scholarly person.[16]

In order for the episode's legal significance to be understood, a certain background in Jewish family law is needed. According to Jewish law, a widow must be supported by the estate of her husband unless she sues for her payment due according to her *ketubah*.[17] The heirs may not compel

---

14 *Ha-Meiri*, commentary on *Ethics of the Sages* 1:8. Rabbi Shlomo Yitzhaki (*Rashi*), commenting on *Ethics of the Sages* 1:8, advances a similar explanation.

15 Isaiah 58:7.

16 *Ketubot* 52b. Who precisely is an eminent scholarly person is beyond the purview of this paper; it is clear however, that by no means is a typical lawyer such a person; see generally *Encyclopedia Talmudit* 1:175–180, for a discussion of the parameters of this status.

17 *Shulhan Arukh, Even ha-Ezer* 93:1–2.

her to receive this payment in lieu of support from the estate.[18] Along with the various expenses the estate must bear to support the widow, Jewish law mandates that a woman's continuing medical expenses are chargeable against the estate of her husband generally, and not against the wife's entitlement from the estate. On the other hand, fixed-cost contracts for medical care are considered expenses that may be deducted from the wife's *ketubah* payment.

Rabbi Yohanan's advice to the heirs was very simple and was designed to reduce the heirs' total payout from the estate. Instead of paying for medical care as needed, they should seek to purchase a contract for medical care, which they then can deduct from the widow's entitlement in the estate. In a situation where the heirs to the estate are not the same as the heirs to the widow's estate, there can be significant repercussions to this choice.[19]

A simple example illustrates this. In an estate of $100,000—with the woman's *ketubah* payment equalling $20,000, medical care costing $1,000 a year, and a lifetime contract for medical care for the widow costing $20,000—if the widow lives twenty years and right before her death institutes an action for payment of her *ketubah*,[20] the estate will be worth only $80,000, and it will still have to make a $20,000 payment to the widow (or her heirs). If on the other hand, the estate purchases a contract for fixed medical care for $20,000, the estate will still only be worth $80,000 at the time of the widow's death, but all of that money will belong to the heirs.

This is exactly the kind of advice lawyers routinely dispense, and the Talmud indicates that giving a person completely legal advice on how to avoid an expense or cause the expenses to fall on others—a central activity for a lawyer—is considered conduct unbecoming for an eminent scholarly person and perfectly proper for a relative.[21]

---

18 Ibid.

19 *Shulhan Arukh, Even ha-Ezer* 79:1–2.

20 For more on this, see *Shulhan Arukh, Even ha-Ezer* 96:1–2.

21 Unlike the legal mandates found in the second section of this chapter dealing with judicial ethics, a claim could be made that the issues involved in advice-giving that do not suborn perjury are within the field of those ethical mandates typically limited to *Ethics of the Sages*, and not part of the classical legal rules of Jewish law. Thus, these issues are left out of *Rambam*'s code, as well as the *Tur, Shulhan Arukh* and *Arukh ha-Shulhan*. While it is true that R. Joel Sirkes (*Bah*) on *Hoshen Mishpat* 17

The Talmud does not address the propriety of such advice-giving by a non-relative who is also not an "eminent scholarly person," and it is this status that the typical lawyer has. Indeed, the balance between these two poles is the subject of some disagreement. Rabbi Joel Sirkes (*Bah*) states that to give a person truthful legal advice prior to litigation that minimizes risk or exposure is perfectly permissible for one's relatives, providing that one is not an eminent scholarly person.[22] No one else may give such advice in anticipation of litigation. On the other hand, Rabbi Yom Tov Lipman Heller states that it is permissible to give truthful legal advice to anyone, relative or not, providing that the advisor is not an eminent scholarly person, and, for such a person, giving advice is prohibited even for relatives.[23] Rabbi Shabtai ben Meir Hacohen (*Shakh*), quoting Rabbi Joshua Boaz, writing in the *Shiltei Giborim*, agrees that giving legal advice to people that is deleterious to the interests of another person is completely permissible—whatever the relationship between the advisor and the advisee—providing that the one giving the advice is not also a judge (*dayyan*) in the case or an eminent scholar.[24]

Rabbi Abraham David Botatshats, writing in *Kesef ha-Kodashim*, adds a level of understanding to this rule. He states that it is only problematic to give advice that involves a certain amount of underhandedness or trickery. However to simply tell people the complete mandates of Jewish law is absolutely permissible, and even laudatory, in all situations, relatives or otherwise.[25] The essence of his argument is that the providing

---

and R. Abraham Hirsch Eisenstadt, *Pithei Teshuvah*, *Hoshen Mishpat* 17:15, do both discuss these issues, it is unclear from their discussions if the mandate is technically halakhic or not; R. Yehiel Mikhel Epstein, *Arukh ha-Shulhan*, for example, limits his discussion to the case of judges, and not lawyers or advisors.

22 R. Joel Sirkes (*Bah*), commenting on *Shulhan Arukh*, *Hoshen Mishpat* 17:9. This is agreed to by R. Israel Wolf, *Sha'ar ha-Mishpat*, *Hoshen Mishpat* 17:9 and *Halakhah Pesukah*, commenting on 17:9.

23 R. Yom Tov Lipman Heller, *Tosafot Yom Tov*, commenting on *Ethics of the Sages* 1:8. He notes that Rabbi Shlomo Yitzhaki (*Rashi*) appears to disagree with this approach.

24 *Hoshen Mishpat* 66:82, quoting *Shiltei Giborim* on *Ketubot* 52b, and *Shakh*, *Hoshen Mishpat* 123:32; this is also agreed to by R. Hayyim Palache, *He-Hafetz Hayyim* 102:5.

25 R. Abraham David Botatshats, *Kesef ha-Kodashim*, commenting on *Hoshen Mishpat* 17:9.

of pure data about Jewish law's position on any given topic should always be permissible.[26]

The crucial question for lawyers, however, is why a relative may give this kind of legal advice. Certainly it is not because relatives (or lawyers) are excused from Jewish law's mandate of honesty and integrity. Rather, as can be implied from some early authorities,[27] the reason is that relatives are already involved in the dispute as they are family, and thus they, by definition, stand to gain from the enrichment of the family member they are advising. To give advice to a person that helps one person but harms another and is of no consequence to the advisor one way or another, is perceived as ethically improper. Simply put, why meddle in another's dispute to the benefit of one and the detriment of another?[28]

However, in any situation where the advisor also gains from the advice, it is completely permissible to give it. As proof to this, one sees that Jewish law allows the assignment of claims to a representative who would press the claim in court only in a case where the "agent" had actually purchased a real stake in the litigation (and thus was like a relative in that he had an interest). Indeed, while the rules relating to appointing another as one's agent to press a claim are detailed and complex, the fact is that Jewish law permits such representation both as a matter of Jewish law and on an ethical level.[29] As noted by many authorities, the lessons of *Ketubot* 52b (quoted above) and Rabbi Yohanan are limited to situations

---

26 In this author's opinion, this line of reasoning has much merit to it. The mandate not to be an advocate has to be limited to "advocacy," which is quite different than the providing of information, which is almost always a fulfillment of the biblical mandate of studying Jewish law, and thus difficult to imagine as prohibited merely because someone might misuse the legal concepts that one is presenting.

27 See R. Solomon ben Meir (*Rashbam*), *Bava Batra* 174b (s.v. *eizehu*).

28 Of course, if one were to involve oneself in such a dispute to either do justice or to make peace, that would be permissible and laudatory. Here we are referring to involving oneself solely to aid one side with no just or pious motives; see comments of R. Yom Tov Ishbili (*Ritva*) to *Ketubot* 52b where this distinction is found.

29 See Nahum Rakover, *Ha-Shelihut ve-ha-Harsha'ah ba-Mishpat ha-Ivri* 85–179 (Mosad Harav Kook, 1972), and R. Ezra Batzri, *Dinei Mamonot* 1:256–265. Interestingly, classical American legal ethics absolutely prohibited this type of representation, called champerty; see Charles Wolfram, *Modern Legal Ethics* (1985), at 490–491.

where free advice is given solely for the sake of gratuitously aiding one and harming another.[30]

Based on this analysis, there are a number of modern authorities who suggest that a lawyer who is paid to provide legal advice[31] has the same status as a relative—the advisor and the recipient both gain from this activity and it is in the best interest of both of them that the advice be legal and work properly.[32] It is precisely this rationale that has been developed to defend the institution of *to'en*, the term commonly given to an advocate in a *beit din*.[33] Indeed, over the course of many years, it has become the established norm within Jewish law that one may send a representative to a *beit din* hearing in one's stead or to help press one's claim.[34] One is hard-pressed to distinguish between the duties of a *to'en* or representative and that of an ethical litigator; in both cases advice to hide testimony would be improper.

---

30 This is first found in R. Azaryah Figo, *Giddulei Terumah*, commenting on R. Samuel ben R. Isaac ha-Sefardi, *Sefer ha-Terumot* at 300, and is cited as correct by R. Hayyim Benveniste, *Knesset ha-Gedolah, Hoshen Mishpat* 123 (*Tur*, 123); R. Shimon ben Solomon, *Matteh Shimon, Hoshen Mishpat* 123:4; and R. Ezra Batzri, *Dinei Mamonot* 1:440.

31 This analysis would imply that a lawyer working on a case *pro bono* (and without compensation for his time from another source, as an associate in a law firm is) may not function as an advice-giver in the same manner as one who is paid; see also text accompanying note 36 of this chapter for some limitation on this.

32 This position is tentatively advanced by R. Ezra Batzri, *Dinei Mamonot* 1:440, and by R. She'ar Yashuv Cohen, "Ma'amad Orkhei Din ba-Halakhah," *Torah she-Be'al Peh* 22:64 (1981). See also Dov Frimer, "The Role of a Lawyer in Jewish Law," *J. Law & Religion* 1:297, 304 (1983). For similar assertions, see R. Abraham Nissim Ashkenazi, *Nehmad le-Mareh* 3:100; R. Jonah Landsofer, *Meil Tzedakah* 53; and R. Samuel Aboab, *Devar Shmuel* 41 and 43.

33 In Ezra Batzri, *Dinei Mamonot* 1:439–441. See also R. Kalfon Moshe ha-Cohen, *Shoel ve-Nishal, Hoshen Mishpat* 5:2, and sources cited in note 34. Indeed, the use of these *to'anim*/lawyers has become absolutely common in the *beit din* system.

34 For a general discussion of these issues, see Nahum Rakover, *Ha-Shelihut ve-ha-Harsha'ah ba-Mishpat ha-Ivri*, 85–179 (Mosad Harav Kook, 1972), and R. Ezra Batzri, *Dinei Mamonot* 1:256–265. It is beyond the scope of this chapter to discuss how one goes about appointing such a representative in Jewish law. It is important to note that there is little discussion of the halakhic or ethical problems of such representation or advisement, indicating that having such help is perceived as permitted, in accordance with the ruling of *Shakh*, or with the analysis of Batzri and others, that paid representatives are like family for the purposes of these rules.

In addition, it is possible to distinguish between advice as to how to order one's affairs when there is no litigation pending and advice given in anticipation of litigation. It would appear to this author that the former is always permissible, as the various authorities limit *Ethics of the Sages* 1:8 to cases in which litigation is pending—i.e., one is advising people how to triumph in their disputes.[35] If this analysis is correct, lawyers who work on transactional matters to facilitate a business deal between two clients or to restructure the business of a single client, are not governed by the mandate of *Ethics of the Sages* 1:8.

Even more generally, a case can be made that the ethical strictures against being a lawyer or advisor (*orekh din*) are limited to cases where the parties are Jewish and committed to the Jewish legal system. In a case where the underlying legal framework properly is secular law, and the secular law contains no restrictions on advice-giving by lawyers, there should be no problem in a lawyer providing advice of any kind.[36]

The Limits of Advocacy

Advocacy, however, does have limits in the Jewish tradition. One must make certain that the advice given is legal and proper and is not taken as an invitation to suborn perjury or to engage in otherwise illegal activity. As noted by no less an authority than Rabbi Hayyim Benveniste, writing in the *Knesset ha-Gedolah* over three hundred years ago, scholars must be discreet in their legal advice, lest it be misused and understood as a form of suborning perjury.[37]

However, the countervailing factors sometimes favoring advocacy and representation need to be mentioned. Rabbi Solomon ben Adret (*Rashba*)

---

35 See *Halakhah Pesukah* 17:9 and comments of *Rashi*, *Rambam*, and *Meiri* discussed above, all of which focus on the role of an advocate in assisting a litigant to deceive the court or *beit din*.

36 This type of argument can be found in a more expansive form in the name of Rabbi Schwab in Biser, "Practicing Law," at n. 135. This is also found in Rabbi Shammai Gross, *Shevet Kehati* 3:322. A more detailed discussion of the uses of secular law for Noahides can be found in chapters four and seven.

37 R. Hayyim Benveniste, *Knesset ha-Gedolah*, *Hoshen Mishpat* 17:19 (*Hagahot ha-Tur*); see also R. Mordecai ben Judah Halevi, *Darkhei Noam*, *Hoshen Mishpat* 42.

was asked in a responsum what he thought of the practice of appointing an advocate to plead on behalf of a party in a case. He replied:

> After you have reviewed the opinions of the various early authorities, I need not state for you that this is the opinion of this authority and this is the opinion of that authority. Rather, my opinion is that a plaintiff cannot appoint an advocate who will plead specific facts on his own knowledge, since one who does not know the truth cannot possibly recount what happened.... Nonetheless, there are cases where even the Jewish court (*beit din*) pleads the case of a person, such as the case of opening the mouths of the mute.[38] In any situation where the *beit din* sees that the person is not pleading properly because of ignorance [it is proper to allow an advocate].... It all depends on the circumstances and upon one's innermost intentions; for Torah which is true favors that which is true.... Nonetheless, to appoint an advocate to plead whatever he thinks proper [without regard to the truth] is wrong.[39]

Rabbi Adret's analysis is even more true in a situation like the modern American legal system This modern legal system functions on the assumption that all people do, in fact, employ lawyers on significant legal matters (such as the purchase of a house), that court—and the government bureaucracy generally—is bewildering to a non-lawyer, and that special legal skills are needed simply to insure justice. This is true for nearly all civil and criminal matters.

This insight is particularly valid when combined with the fact that a lawyer does not plead facts on behalf of a person, but only arranges the case and honestly pleads the law. Lawyers are precluded from presenting facts or testimony in a case. Lawyers advance legal arguments or organize facts presented by others. Indeed, Rabbi Shimon Schwab has been cited as ruling that the strictures against being an "arranger of the law" (*orekh din*) are completely inapplicable in the American legal system.[40] The basis of such a rule can perhaps be found in the fact that in an inquisitorial legal

---

38 Proverbs 31:8.

39 R. Shlomo ben Adret, *Teshuvot ha-Rashba* 2:393. See also the comments of R. Baruch Epstein, *Torah Temimah* on Exodus 22:8.

40 See Biser, "Practicing Law," at n. 135.

system, like that envisioned by Jewish law, lawyers—even when permitted—detract from the system. In an adversarial system of justice that is the essence of the common and American law, it is precisely through zealous advocacy that truth is supposed to emerge. This approach is even more valid when a lawyer advises a client about the legal repercussions of his actions *prior* to the possibility of any litigation.[41]

In short, in twentieth century America, a person when confronted with a significant issue of modern law—because of its complexity, both procedural and substantively—is often like the mute in Rabbi Adret's responsum. American law and economic life is sufficiently complex that absent such legal advice, a person engaging in business can hardly function.[42]

Conclusion

Ethics of the Sages (*Avot*) 1:8 contains within it two distinctly different admonishments: The first is directed toward judges. It directs them to treat litigants with fairness and equality. This mandate is codified by Jewish law, and a violation of it by a judge casts doubt on the fairness of the process. The second mandate is directed toward lawyers and is ethical in nature. It is understood in different ways by different authorities. Some maintain that it prohibits strangers from giving legally proper advice on how to best order one's affairs if that advice negatively affects others. Most rule that *Avot* 1:8 only prohibits that type of advice from being given when it is done by one not benefiting from offering it or by an eminent scholar; however, in the case of a lawyer, paid advisor, or relative, such advice is permissible.

In sum, it appears to this writer that Jewish law permits a lawyer, who is not an eminent scholar (*adam hashuv*), to give truthful legal advice which is to the detriment of another, for pay, to clients. Three rationales can be advanced to support this ruling:

1) Many authorities rule that advice-giving by non-relatives who are not eminent scholars is always permitted.

---

41 See note 35.

42 Indeed, that perhaps is precisely the type of advice permitted by R. Abraham David Botatshats in *Kesef ha-Kodashim*; see text accompanying note 25.

2) A number of scholars rule that paid lawyers have the status of relatives who always may advise.

3) In modern American law a person without a lawyer is analogous to the mute in the time of the Talmud, and incapable of advancing his truthful legal claim. In such cases, Jewish law allows the person to seek the assistance of one who will help him arrange the case.

Of course, it is prohibited for an advisor to give advice that is illegal, that would inhibit a court or *beit din* from reaching the proper result, or that encourages perjury.[43]

---

43 The intentional providing of advice to violate the law transgresses the biblical prohibition of "placing a stumbling block in front of a blind person" (Leviticus 19:14). This is the classical case of a violation; *Sefer ha-Hinnukh*, Negative Commandment 232. R. Hezekiah di-Medini, *Sedei Hemed* 9:36 (p. 6), discusses whether one violates a biblical or rabbinic prohibition when one advises a person to violate secular law. The analytical basis for the opinion that one violates only a rabbinic prohibition when the underlying prohibition is only rabbinic—such as secular law enforced through *dina de-malkhuta dina* (the law of the land is the law)—is that the aider cannot violate a biblical prohibition if the principal is not also in violation. The alternative, which labels all counseling in violation of Jewish law as biblical violations of placing a stumbling block in front of a blind person, maintains that giving bad advice is prohibited, and advising or aiding a person who is doing a rabbinically forbidden action is a form of bad advice and thus biblically prohibited.

American law prohibits a lawyer from suborning perjury in any way, shape, or form; see *Model Rules of Professional Responsibility* Rule 3.4 ("A lawyer shall not ...falsify evidence, counsel or assist a witness to testify falsely, or offer an inducement to a witness that is prohibited by law.").

Chapter Three

Professional Confidentiality

Jewish Law and the Obligation to Help Others

Jewish law requires one to inform a Jew of harm that might befall him and which could be avoided[1]; this is based on the verse: "Do not stand by while your brother's blood is being shed."[2] As has been noted by many,[3] this obligation applies not only to saving lives, but also to preventing monetary losses. Thus, if there had been no secular regulation of this area and no contract between the lawyer and the client, a lawyer who learned that his client was planning to cause monetary loss through impropriety would be halakhically obligated to inform the potential victim, and thus prevent the loss.[4]

---

1 The analysis developed in this section is similar to the analysis first advanced in Biser, "Practicing Law," at 118–121, and was developed initially in my unpublished reply to his article; see the Acknowledgment section of this book.

2 Leviticus 19:16. At least in the case of physical harm, the intent of the one who is harming others is not relevant according to many authorities; see R. Elijah of Vilna, *Be'ur ha-Gra, Orah Hayyim* 425:10. Rather the crucial issue is whether harm actually results.

3 See Aaron Kirschenbaum, "The Bystander's Duty to Rescue in Jewish Law," *Journal of Religious Ethics* 8:204–226 (1980).

4 To understand why Jewish law does not fully accept the inviolability of a professional confidence, see R. J. David Bleich, *Contemporary Halakhic Problems* II:74–80; R. Yaakov Breisch, *Helkat Yaakov* 3:136; and R. Eliezer Waldenberg, *Tzitz Eliezer* 13:81.

Professional Confidences and Legal Ethics

The bar, like many professions in common-law countries, has developed internal rules regulating the conduct of lawyers. Many of these regulations are innocuous, and address either purely professional issues (e.g., politeness) or issues of substance whose results are in harmony with Jewish law (e.g., prohibition of theft). One rule, however, has created quite some controversy and poses a dilemma for Jews in that it conflicts with the obligation to prevent even financial harm from befalling a fellow Jew when possible. That rule is the requirement that a lawyer keep confidential information given to him by a client even if others will be harmed through the lawyer's silence. Two versions of this regulation are in force in the United States of America, depending on whether the state has adopted the Model Rules or the Model Code.[5]

The Model Rules state:

(a) A lawyer shall not reveal information relating to representation of a client....

(b) A lawyer *may* reveal such information to the extent the lawyer reasonably believes necessary:
(1) to prevent the client from committing a criminal act that the lawyer believes is *likely to result in imminent death or substantial bodily harm;*[6]

The Model Code adopts a different formulation of the lawyer's obligation to keep confidences. It states:

(c) A lawyer *may* reveal:
(3) The intention of his client to commit a crime and the information necessary to prevent the crime;[7]

---

5 Two distinct systems of regulations exist. They are called the "Model Rules" and the "Model Code" of the American Bar Association (ABA). The Model Code was endorsed by the ABA in 1969 and the Model Rules in 1982. They differ in many ways. In theory, each state develops its own regulations guiding professional conduct; however every state, except California, bases its regulations on either the Rules or the Code.

6 Model Rule, Rule 1.6 (emphasis added).

7 Model Code DR 4–101 (emphasis added). Subparagraphs one and two are not relevant, and thus have been left out.

Neither the Model Rules nor the Model Code require the revelation of information that damages a person. However, the Model Code permits such conduct at least in a case of fraud or other criminal activity. Thus, a person bound by Jewish law could fulfill the mandates of Jewish law and still be in conformity with the mandates of legal ethics under the Model Code.[8]

However, it is apparent that the professional regulations advocated by the Model Rules, and accepted in those states that have adopted them, are incompatible with the obligations of a Jew to prevent harm from befalling a fellow Jew where possible.[9]

Most states, including New York, New Jersey, and California,[10] have simply declined to adopt the Model Rules on this issue and instead enforce the Model Code's test, which allows for disclosure of confidences to protect a person from financial loss caused by fraud or other criminal activity by a client. Thus, the secular obligation is no longer in absolute tension with the requirements of Jewish law in those states that have adopted the Code.[11] Furthermore, this appears to be the current trend in the United States.[12]

Jewish Law's Perspective on Secular Legal Ethics

In those jurisdictions that have adopted the Code as the basis for their law, the only conflict between Jewish law and secular legal ethics that actually occurs is when the intent of the client to harm is not sufficiently clear as to meet the standard of the Model Code ("reasonably believes"), but suf-

---

8 It would be difficult to imagine a case where Jewish law mandates disclosure and yet no secular statute is violated.

9 See generally Gordon Tucker, "The Confidentiality Rule: A Philosophical Perspective with Reference to Jewish Law and Ethics," *Fordham Urban L.J.* 13:99 (1984), where this point is made.

10 See e.g., David Fried, "Too High a Price for Truth: The Exception to the Attorney-Client Privilege for Contemplated Crimes and Frauds," *North Carolina L.R.* 64:443 (1986); and Gerald Lynch, "The Lawyer as Informer," *Duke L.J.* 1986:491 (1986).

11 They are not, however, in harmony either.

12 See *Annotated Model Rules of Professional Conduct*, Rule 1.6 (ABA 1984); *People v. Fentress*, 425 N.Y.S.2d 485 (Sup. CT. 1980).

fices for Jewish law (which perhaps requires only "more likely than not").[13] In that narrow case, or in a state that has adopted the Model Rules as the basis for its decisions, a direct conflict occurs.

In such a situation a lawyer must tread gingerly. The obligation to rescue a fellow Jew from harm is a very serious one. However, there is no obligation to rescue one from harm if the rescuer will suffer significant financial harm. As Rabbi Alfred Cohen has stated:

> Our research shows that the majority of halakhic authorities accept the position that a person whose livelihood depends upon maintaining the confidentiality of revelations made to him, need not jeopardize his position by telling those secrets. Although keeping silent might violate the negative *mitzvah* [commandment] of not standing by and allowing another Jew to be harmed, yet as long as he is not violating the commandment by *doing* any action and, were he to act he would endanger his own livelihood, then he is permitted to remain silent.[14]

When a lawyer knows that he will be disciplined by his fellow lawyers and thus lose his ability to earn a living, most agree that the obligation to rescue is suspended.[15] For the same reason, the obligation to rescue is also

---

13 Jewish law would require that one act under the assumption that a harm will occur in any case in which it is plausible that such harm might occur, as this case involves a biblical obligation, which in a case of uncertainty is resolved in favor of fulfilling the obligation. See also R. Alfred Cohen, "Privacy: A Jewish Perspective," *J. Halacha & Contemporary Society* 1:53, 74–78 (1981).

14 R. Alfred Cohen, "Privacy," at 84; see also R. Alfred Cohen, "Professional Confidence," at 74–78.

15 See R. Tzvi Hirsch Eisenstadt, *Pithei Teshuvah, Yoreh Deah* 157(4); *Sefer ha-Hinnukh, Mitzvah* 585; R. Joseph Teomim, *Peri Megadim, Orah Hayyim* 656; R. Moshe Schreiber, *Hatam Sofer, Hoshen Mishpat* 176; and R. Elijah of Vilna, *Be'ur ha-Gra, Yoreh Deah* 157:5. An additional reason can be advanced when a lawyer breaches a confidence to avoid purely financial harm to another. Nothing is gained when one person saves another a sum of money when the act of saving costs an equally significant sum. See Aaron Kirschenbaum, "The Good Samaritan: Monetary Aspects," *J. Halacha & Contemporary Society* 17:83, 84–87 (1989); see also *Shulhan Arukh, Hoshen Mishpat* 375:1–3.

suspended in a case where a lawyer will not be disciplined but will lose a significant percentage of his clients (as his particular clients do not wish the services of a lawyer who reports clients' legal violations to the authorities). Lawyers concerned with Jewish law should, however, realize that the Model Rules enforce a regulation that can be contrary to Jewish law, and should work to see it changed—at the very least—to mandate disclosure in cases of harm to a third party.

In addition, there is the issue of the lawyer's agreement (explicit or implicit) with the client not to reveal the client's information improperly. Indeed, the essence of that agreement is to conduct oneself according to the secular legal rules. People would not discuss their legal problems absent such an agreement, and it is part of every private lawyer's contract with a client. Particularly when the client's violation poses no threat to the physical integrity of another, it is quite possible that the lawyer's contract binds him to keep silent.[16]

In a case of future physical harm to another, in this author's opinion, a lawyer should report whatever plans of a client needed to prevent the violent act, since it is unlikely that such a person will, in fact, be disciplined or otherwise suffer a serious loss, and thus his silence cannot be justified by a fear of loss of livelihood. It appears that such disclosure would be compelled by Jewish law. (However, it is important to add that a survey of the various casebooks and hornbooks, as well as Westlaw reports, shows no occasion where a lawyer was disciplined for disclosing information improperly when Jewish law would compel the disclosure.)[17]

---

16 R. Alfred Cohen, "Professional Confidences," at 74–78, advances various reasons why Jewish law might not, even in the face of loss of life, require the breaching of a confidence. It is unclear to what extent Jewish law would actually accept the "policy" reasons advocated by Cohen in the context of the practice of law. One could limit such privacy considerations to cases of prior, rather than future, misdeeds. Certainly, the arguments advanced by Cohen have merit when the stakes are only financial.

17 The obligation to obey the secular law because it is the law of the land (see note 12 of Chapter Eight) is inapplicable to disciplinary rules, since they do not have the status of "law" in America. One additional possibility needs to be addressed. In a situation where the lawyer can violate his professional obligation without being detected, and doing so would fulfill the biblical commandment of not standing by while one's neighbor's blood is shed, it would appear to this writer that this violation is obligatory according to Jewish law. Such situations are very contextual, however.

Chapter Four

Admonition and Collective Responsibility

You must not hate your brother in your heart, admonish your neighbor so that you incur no guilt because of him.
—LEVITICUS 19:17

Admonition as an Obligation

Jewish law obligates its adherents to engage in admonition (*tokhahah*) when one sees a Jew violating Jewish law.[1] One is compelled to persuade the person to cease the violation. So too, when one sees people unintentionally violating Jewish law, one must tell them what Jewish law requires so that they can correct their ways. This obligation is known as collective responsibility (*arevut*).[2] These two obligations affect the way one practices

---

1 This commandment is limited to Jewish sinners. None of the classical commandments designed to deter sinning by Jews (except the biblical prohibition of facilitating sin (*lifnei ivver*), which will be discussed in chapter seven) is generally thought applicable to gentiles. Thus, there is no obligation of *tokhahah* (to admonish) toward a gentile who sins; see generally *Sanhedrin* 75a and *Rashi ad locum*. So too, there is no notion of *arevut* (cooperative activity) that compels collective responsibility; see generally Aaron Kirschenbaum, "Covenant with Noahides compared with Covenant at Sinai," *Dinei Israel* 6:31, at n. 37. For more on the obligation to seek observance of Noahide law, see my article, "The Obligation of Jews to Seek Observance of Noahide Laws by Gentiles: A Theoretical Perspective," in volume six of *Orthodox Forum Proceedings* entitled *Tikkun Olam: Jewish Responsibilities to Society*, D. Shatz and C. Waxman, eds. (Jason Aronson, 1997), 103–143.

2 *Arevut* and *tokhahah* perhaps have different intellectual roots. This will be dealt with further in this chapter.

law, as Jewish lawyers too are obligated in the duties imposed through collective responsibility and the obligation to admonish. These issues are particularly pressing in the context of obligations found within Jewish law that are generally foreign to the Western ethical model. How should a lawyer respond to a client's request for assistance in a transaction that strikes most people as completely ethical, but clearly violates Jewish law? A classic example of this occurs in the area of lending with interest to a Jew—a transaction common in modern society—but yet clearly in violation of Jewish law.[3]

Within certain limits, which will be discussed, Jewish lawyers are obligated to encourage clients to observe Jewish law. The scopes of these obligations to show people the right path however, are not quite as broad in practice as they appear in theory. In circumstances where admonition will not be effective, many rule that Jewish law does not require that one engage in that (ineffective) admonition. This situation arises in three different forms. The first involves a Jewish person who is so far removed from Jewish law that a rebuke given will be completely ineffective, because the person rejects Jewish law as a basis for making moral decisions.[4] The second involves a person who is completely involved in Jewish law, has contemplated his actions, and has decided that they are in compliance with Jewish law.[5] The third involves a person generally observant of Jewish law but who is so involved in the prohibited activity that he is engaging in, that he is unlikely to accept admonition at that time.[6]

---

3 For a discussion of other issues related to interest-paying, see chapter fifteen.

4 For example, a person who is born Jewish and converts to a different religion which permits the charging of interest to a Jew. It is a wasted admonishment for a lawyer to tell him that such a transaction is prohibited according to Jewish law and that he should desist from that activity.

5 For example, a Jew who lends money to a corporation and charges interest on that loan, based on the ruling of those authorities discussed in chapter fifteen in the text accompanying note 4, will not accept the admonition as he thinks his actions are completely permissible.

6 It is usually difficult for people to publicly admit the error of their ways, and the process of admonition at the time of the violation will only cause a hardening of their resolve. For a clear exposition of this principle, see R. Solomon ben Adret (*Rashba*), *Responsa* 5:238; and R. Judah ha-Hasid, *Sefer Hasidim* 413 (as quoted by *Magen Avraham, Orah Hayyim* 608:3).

Situations where Admonition is Not Required

In general, one is not obligated to admonish a person who has completely left the path of observance and has no ideological fidelity to Jewish law at all. This is stated quite unambiguously by Rabbi Yehiel Mikhel Epstein, who writes:

> You should know that the obligation to admonish is only applicable to a Jew who is generally committed to Jewish law but who has been overtaken by desire to commit [this sin]. In such a case, admonition applies; concerning those who completely deny the words of the Sages, the obligation of admonition does not apply.[7]

Thus, a lawyer who is confronted with a Jewish client who is completely indifferent to Jewish law and who wishes to act in violation of Jewish law, is under no obligation to admonish that client. This is even more so when the violation is of a law that appears to be without any rational basis to a person unconnected to Jewish tradition, as in such a case the person will certainly not accept the admonition. In the event that a client wished to violate this type of law, nothing is gained by rebuke.

Rabbi Yehuda Amital, in his essay *Rebuking a Jew: Theory and Practice*, indicates that this ruling is to be tempered with the ruling of those various authorities (generally accepted) who maintain that modern day Sabbath violators are to be treated as kidnapped children (*tinokot shenishbu*) and not as apostates or intentional violators.[8] This author believes that these two rulings are not at all in tension. The obligation to admonish is limited to the category of people who are known as "your neighbors" or "brothers." The status of people as "lost children" is much broader and includes people who are not one's "neighbors" or "brothers." They are referring to the scope of different concepts.[9]

---

7 *Arukh ha-Shulhan, Orah Hayyim* 608:7. Similar sentiments are expressed by *Mishnah Berurah* 608, *Be'ur Halakhah* s.v. *aval*. For a discussion of this principle in some detail, see R. Eliezer Waldenberg, *Tzitz Eliezer* 17:37.

8 See R. Yehuda Amital, "Rebuking a Jew: Theory and Practice," in *Jewish Tradition and the Non-Traditional Jew* (J. J. Schachter, ed), at 119, 125–126.

9 For more on this distinction, see Michael Broyde & Michael Hecht, "The Gentile and Returning Lost Property According to Jewish Law: A Theory of Reciprocity," in *Jewish Law Annual* 13:225–254 (1996). This article argues that the over-arching theory which explains distinctions based on religion in Jewish financial law is reciprocity.

As will be explained in chapter seven, there are many authorities who rule that it is permitted to directly assist a person in a violation of Jewish law when that person is a consistent and unrepentant violator of that prohibition of Jewish law—even if otherwise observant.[10] In this author's opinion, these authorities would also rule that one is excused from the obligation to admonish such a person. This ruling must flow logically from their ruling that one may actually assist such a person in his sin. That these authorities maintain that one may assist these violations, but—while assisting—one must admonish them, is farfetched.[11]

So too, a client who has considered the Jewish law associated with a particular activity, and has decided that the action or question does not violate Jewish law, need not be admonished. Four reasons can be advanced to support this ruling. First, many authorities rule that one is excused from any obligation to admonish in a situation where one is certain that the one being rebuked will not listen.[12] Such is the case here.[13] Second, a number of authorities explicitly rule that there is no obligation to admonish in any situation where the apparent sinner thinks his conduct is in fact permissible according to Jewish law.[14] Third, it is quite possible that this case would fall under the rubric of "better to let them sin unintentionally than to make

---

10 *Shakh* and *Dagul me-Revavah*, discussed in chapter seven in the text accompanying notes 19 to 23.

11 A close examination of the *Dagul me-Revavah* indicates this to be true. Such a conclusion is agreed to by R. Feinstein also; see *Iggerot Moshe, Yoreh Deah* 1:72.

12 *Sefer Mitzvot Gedolot, Mitzvah* 11; *Rashi, Yevamot* 65b; *Meiri, Yevamot* 65b; *Sefer Yereim ha-Katzar* 37; R. Elijah from Vilna, *Be'ur ha-Gra, Orah Hayyim* 608:4; *Sefer ha-Hinnukh* 239; as well as perhaps Rambam, *Sefer ha-Mitzvot, Aseh* 205 (and see *Deot* 6:7); For additional information, see R. Amital, "Rebuking a Jew," at note 2.

A number of authorities reject this ruling; see *Yereim* 223; *Sefer Mitzvot Katan* 114; *Ritva* to *Yevamot* 65b; and *Rema, Orah Hayyim* 608:2. However, in my opinion, a case could be made that even these authorities are only requiring admonishment for an intentional violation and not for a person who actually thinks his conduct is permitted (*omer mutar*). A close examination of the language of the *Yereim* would lead one to that conclusion.

13 *Mishnah Berurah* (*Sha'ar ha-Tziyyun* 608:13) indicates that these lenient authorities are to be relied on as one side of a *sefek sefeka*, a case of double doubt. That is being followed here.

14 See *Mordecai, Betzah* 689, commenting on *Betzah* 31a; and Rabbenu Hannanel, cited in *Teshuvot Rashi* 20.

them sin deliberately."[15] In addition, one must consider the possibility that this person's halakhic advice concerning his actions is, in fact, correct, and the action is permitted according to Jewish law.[16]

The third case involves a lawyer dealing with a generally observant client who is now engaged in a violation of Jewish law. If the violation is unintentional, and if pointed out, would be corrected,[17] it is unquestionable that a lawyer—as a Jew—must inform the person of the mandates of Jewish law.[18] In the case of the intentional violation, there clearly is an obligation in such a case for a lawyer to advise a client of the requirements of Jewish law, if the person would cease the violation once it is pointed out to him.[19] Thus, for example, a lawyer should remind religiously observant clients of the need to use a *heter iska*[20] in transactions that involve the payment of interest.

However, where a lawyer is fearful of the consequences of his admonition on his livelihood, rather than of his advice not being heeded, the rule

---

15 *Mutav sheyihyu shogegim ve'al yiheyu mezidim*; Rema, *Orah Hayyim* 608:2. Of course, this assumes that the person's consultation with Jewish law is genuine and sincere. For more on this, see R. Yehudah Hertzel Henkin, "Mutav Sheyihyu Shogegim Ve-al Yiheyu Mezidim be-Zeman ha-Zeh," *Tehumin* 2:272–280 (1991).

16 Thus, for example, as explained in Michael Broyde & David Hertzberg, "Enabling a Jew to Sin: The Parameters," *J. Halacha & Contemporary Society* 19:5–33 (1990), at 30–31, it would not only be permissible to not admonish such a person, it would be permissible to actually assist the person.

17 Otherwise one enters into the area of better to let an unintentional violation occur than to force an intentional one; Rema, *Orah Hayyim* 608:2.

18 See R. Abraham Boorstein, *Avnei Nezer* 461:4. For more on this concept and a discussion of whether the unintentional violator and the process of admonishment is actually a form of a *tokhahah* or *arevut*, see R. Nachum Rabinovitch, "All Jews are Responsible for One Another," at 177–204.

19 See *Mishnah Berurah* 608:5. Indeed, this is the classical case where admonishment is required.

20 A *heter iska* recasts a prohibited interest bearing loan into a permissible partnership. A *heter iska* is easy to use, completely solves nearly all halakhic problems and poses no additional expense or difficulty; but see Steven Resnicoff, "A Commercial Conundrum: Does Prudence Permit the Jewish Permissible Venture [*Heter Iska*]?", *Seton Hall L.R.* 20:77–129 (1989). Ya'ir Goldstein, Esq. of the New York City Corporation Council office writes that "at least one prestigious Midwestern law firm regularly uses *heter iska*s in transactions involving Jewish clients regardless of whether the client is observant" (letter on file with the author).

may be different. For example, a lawyer working in a law firm fears that his admonition will be reported to his superiors, or in the case of a lawyer who is self-employed, that his client will give heed to the admonition in this case, but will find another lawyer in the future to handle his cases. In such a situation it might be appropriate to rely on the ruling of Rabbi Moshe Isserles (*Rema*) that:

> One is not obligated to spend money to engage in admonition, and thus the custom is not to rebuke sinners in situations where one fears that they will commit reprisals on our body or our livelihood.[21]

While this rule is not to be liberally applied to exclude admonishment in all cases of possible harm, it is a well-accepted halakhic ruling that might be applicable in many circumstances, particularly in economically troubled times when clients are quick to leave attorneys, or when a law firm would dismiss an associate for raising a religious issue with a client.[22]

How to Admonish

What has been left out of this discussion is the details of how to admonish in a situation where such admonishment is called for.

This is unquestionably the most difficult issue in this context. A lawyer who seeks to convince a client to observe the strictures of Jewish law should be aware that the manner of such a conversation is crucially

---

21 *Rema, Yoreh Deah* 334:48; see also *Rema, Yoreh Deah* 328:12. Equally applicable are remarks of *Taz* 334:23. A claim could be made that perhaps *Mishnah Berurah* (608:7) does not agree with this, as he cites only danger to one's body as limiting the obligation. On the other hand, he clearly refers to the remarks of *Rema* in *Yoreh Deah* 334:48 in his discussion and it would not be the style of Rabbi Kagan in the *Mishnah Berurah* to disagree with *Rema* without citing numerous other authorities; see also remarks of *Pithei Teshuvah, Yoreh Deah* 334:19 and *Arukh ha-Shulhan, Yoreh Deah* 334:42.

22 In addition, one can add, as an additional factor to this approach, the ruling of *Birkhei Yosef*, cited in *Be'ur Halakhah, Orah Hayyim* 608 s.v. *mohin be-yadayim* that there is no obligation ever to engage in *tokhahah* when one cannot compel a person to listen to one's words.

important and varies based on the needs of the client and the moral posture of the one admonishing. Rabbi Yehuda Amital quotes a story concerning Rabbi Israel Salanter that is worthy of reflection before one engages in admonishment. He states:

> Rabbi Israel Salanter arrived in a port city in Germany [and] discovered that those Jewish merchants who had business at the port would load and unload their goods on the Sabbath as on any other day. He delivered an inspiring sermon on the practice of the Sabbath which was perfectly suited to his audience. He concluded the sermon by saying that "while loading and unloading at the port is necessary, writing is not," and the merchants accepted his suggestion and refrained from writing on the Sabbath. After several Sabbaths, Rabbi Salanter offered another sermon in that synagogue and told his audience that "removing one's goods [at the dock] is essential, but surely loading is not," and the merchants accepted this as well. A while later, he again delivered the sermon and spoke of the prohibition of unloading also, and thus the Jews were slowly brought to observe the Sabbath properly.[23]

Admonition is to be performed with care lest it not accomplish its goal,[24] or even worse, distance people from Judaism.[25]

---

23 R. Amital, "Rebuking a Jew," at 129, citing Dov Katz, *Tenuat ha-Musar* (5th ed.) 1:184.

24 For more on this issue, see R. Norman Lamm, "Loving and Hating Jews as Halakhic Categories," *Tradition* 24:2 (1989), at 98–122.

25 See R. David ha-Levi, *Turei Zahav* (*Taz*), *Yoreh Deah* 334:1, and remarks of *Shakh* as found in *Nekudat ha-Kesef* commenting on it.

In the Courtroom: Litigation

The next six chapters discuss issues related to litigation. Chapters five through eight contain a detailed discussion of the prohibition to litigate civil cases in secular court, as well as a discussion of the rules related to assisting another in sin. Chapters nine and ten review various issues involved in actually testifying in court, such as oath-taking and examining witnesses.

Chapter Five

Litigating in Secular Court

As a general proposition, Jewish law prohibits Jews from engaging in litigation in secular (governmental) courts, and requires that all litigation be conducted in front of a Jewish court (*beit din*).[1] Indeed, a Jew who improperly summons to secular court a Jew who wants to go to *beit din*, and triumphs in the lawsuit and collects an amount in excess of what he would collect according to Jewish law, has committed an act of theft.[2] While much has been written about the history of the prohibition to litigate in secular court (*issur arkhaot*) and the critical role this prohibition has played in continuing the development of Jewish law as a practical and autonomous system of law,[3] the scope of the prohibition can be summarized in four distinct rules.

---

1 See generally *Hoshen Mishpat* 26. Whether this prohibition is biblical or rabbinic is of some dispute; see *Kovetz ha-Poskim*, *Hoshen Mishpat* (1979) (hereinafter *Kovetz*) 3:26(1) (p. 176). R. Joshua Falk-Cohen assumes it is rabbinic; see R. Joshua Falk-Cohen, *Sefer Meirat Enayim* (hereinafter *Sema*), *Hoshen Mishpat* 26:11.

2 See R. Akiva Eiger, commenting on *Hoshen Mishpat* 26:1; R. Israel Meir Mizrachi, *Peri ha-Aretz*, *Hoshen Mishpat* 1:13; and R. Ovadia Yosef, *Yabia Omer*, *Hoshen Mishpat* 2:1. The words "who wants to go to *beit din*" are not found in the classical codes. An examination of the commentaries on *Hoshen Mishpat* 26 indicates that one who litigates in secular court has violated Jewish law–even in a case where all the parties actually want to litigate in court and not *beit din*. However, the violation of Jewish law is not the prohibition of "taking money improperly," but rather a violation of the rules relating to litigating in secular court; see *Sema* commenting on *Hoshen Mishpat* 26:1 and *Kovetz ha-Poskim* on *Hoshen Mishpat* 26:1.

3 See R. Simcha Krauss, "Litigation in Secular Courts," *J. Halacha & Contemporary Society* 2:35 (1982), and Menachem Elon, *Jewish Law: History, Sources, Principles* 50–51, 1914–1917 (JPS, 1994). The following discussion will concentrate on the impact of this prohibition on lawyers and the practice of law.

The Scope of the Prohibition

1. *In order for there to be a prohibition of litigating in secular court,[4] both the plaintiff and the defendant must be Jewish.*

As noted by many authorities, there is no difference between the courts of idol worshipers, non-Jewish monotheists, and secular courts in applying this rule.[5] On the other hand, it matters not at all what the religious faith of a particular judge is for determining whether the prohibition of litigating in secular court (*arkhaot*) applies. As noted by Rabbi Abraham Isaiah Karelitz (*Hazon Ish*), the prohibition certainly applies to litigating a case in front of a Jewish judge who is part of a secular or gentile legal system.[6] The crucial issue, according to Rabbi Karelitz, is whether a system of law, other than Jewish law, is employed. If any system of law (as distinguished from the rules of fairness that are present in any person) is used, Rabbi Karelitz feels that such a structure presents a "system of law" to whom fidelity by Jewish litigants raises a problem.[7]

In this author's opinion, however, even Rabbi Karelitz would only advance this rule when the judge is duty bound by precedent to follow such rules; an arbitrator who chooses to follow a particular legal system's rules in any particular case because its rules appear logical to him does not present a litigating in secular court (*arkhaot*) problem, since it is only

---

4 The precise definition of the term "court" as distinct from "arbitration panel" requires further analysis; see also chapter seventeen.

   On the question of the propriety of sitting as a judge in a secular court system, see R. Yitzhak Isaac Liebes, *Beit Avi* 2:144, who rules that being such a judge is permissible. See also R. Ovadia Hadaya, *Yaskil Avdi*, *Hoshen Mishpat* 6:8; R. Hayyim Menahem, *Ve-Samah Lev* 2:60; R. Moshe Feinstein, *Iggerot Moshe*, *Hoshen Mishpat* 1:8; R. Menasheh Klein, *Mishneh Halakhot* 7:255, 3:214; and Eliav Shochatman "Ma'amad ha-Halakhati shel Batai ha-Mishpat be-Medinat Yisrael," *Tehumin* 13:337–370 (1993).

5 Almost all authorities agree that the prohibition of *arkhaot* applies to all types of non-Jewish courts; see e.g., R. Shimon Duran, *Tashbetz* 4:6 (prohibition applies to Muslim courts); *Kovetz ha-Poskim* 26:1 (in the name of many authorities); *Arukh ha-Shulhan*, *Hoshen Mishpat* 26:1–3; but see Rabbi Shlomo Yitzhaki (*Rashi*) commenting on Exodus 21:1.

6 *Sanhedrin* 15(4) (essays at the end of *Hoshen Mishpat*).

7 See also R. Ovadia Yosef, *Yehavveh Da'at* 4:65 (in footnote **) where similar sentiments are expressed in the name of Rabbis Tzvi Pesach Frank, Yitzhak Isaac Herzog, and others.

because he thinks those rules fair that he chooses to follow them, and he can abandon them whenever he wishes.⁸

Although Rabbi Shimon Duran states that the prohibition of litigating in secular court applies even when a gentile litigant wishes to litigate in a Jewish court, his opinion has been generally rejected by most authorities as not the normative opinion of Jewish law.⁹ Even if one were to accept Rabbi Duran's position, a lawyer may assume that a gentile would not consent to use a *beit din* to arbitrate his disputes, and the Jew may proceed to use a secular court unless the gentile advises him that he wishes to use a Jewish court (*beit din*). The gentile litigant would have to affirmatively indicate that he wishes to litigate in a Jewish court.¹⁰

2. *Whenever the defendant refuses to go to a Jewish court, one may, after seeking rabbinic permission, summon him to secular court.*

Since the immediate post-talmudic era (of the scholars called *geonim*)¹¹ more than a thousand years ago, it has been accepted that a plaintiff may litigate in secular court if the defendant will not appear before a *beit din*. This ruling is cited in the name of numerous *geonim*¹² and even though this rule is not found explicitly in the Talmud,¹³ it appears in all the codes. Rabbi Karo, writing in the *Shulhan Arukh*,¹⁴ states the rule as follows:

> If the hand of the gentiles is strong and that of the litigant weak [i.e., one cannot force the defendant to litigate in *beit din*] and one cannot reclaim one's money in a Jewish court, one must summon

---

8 For proofs to this proposition see the discussion in chapter seventeen (accompanying note 4) and that note itself concerning administrative courts and arbitration.

9 *Kovetz ha-Poskim*, at 178–180; R. Shimon Duran, *Tashbetz* 2:290.

10 See R. Hayyim Cohen, *Divrei Geonim* 52:15 and 77:19, and R. Yehoshua Pinhas Bombach, *Ohel Yehoshua* 2:115 both of whom adopt this rule. For a discussion of the status of an apostate, see also *Tashbetz* 1:61.

11 Seventh to tenth century scholars living in Babylonia.

12 Quoted in R. Asher ben Yehiel (*Rosh*), *Bava Kamma* 8:17, in the name of Rav Palti Gaon; see also R. Joseph Karo, *Beit Yosef* commenting on *Tur*, *Hoshen Mishpat* 26:2, where such a ruling is also quoted in the name of Rav Sherira Gaon.

13 Rather it is derived from a discussion in *Bava Kamma* 92b by a number of *geonim*.

14 R. Joseph Karo, *Shulhan Arukh*, *Hoshen Mishpat* 26:2; see also comments of *Rema* on ibid.

the person [to *beit din*]; if the defendant will not come [to *beit din*] one may be given permission from *beit din* and save one's possessions from the defendant through secular court.

Although little has been written on this topic, a number of rabbinic authorities are of the opinion that permission to litigate a claim in secular court may be given by even a single rabbi, and in certain circumstances, by a single rabbi to cover a whole category of cases.[15] Furthermore, some have argued that one may presume that a non-observant Jew would never use a Jewish court (*beit din*) under any circumstances, and thus no rabbinic permission is ever needed before litigating in secular court with such a person.[16] Indeed, Rabbi J. David Bleich writes:

> [T]here may be grounds for relaxation of that prohibition [to litigate in secular court] in cases in which the defendant is entirely non-observant. There are sources indicating that Jews are required to summon, not only fellow Jews, but also non-Jews to rabbinic courts rather than institute proceedings before secular courts. In practice this is not done, goes the argument, only because of a strong presumption to the effect that such a summons would be ignored. When such a summons is ignored the rabbinic court customarily grants a *ketav seruv*, i.e., leave to resort to a secular

---

15 See e.g., *Kovetz ha-Poskim* at 250–251. See also R. Moshe Schreiber, *Hatam Sofer, Hoshen Mishpat* 1:1; R. Betzalel Stern, *Be-Tzel ha-Hokhmah* 4:371; and R. Shalom Mordecai Shwadron, *Maharsham* 4:105, for a further discussion.

16 R. Abraham David Botatshats, *Kesef ha-Kodashim, Hoshen Mishpat* 26:1. For a similar result, see R. Hayyim Cohen, *Divrei Geonim* 77:9. R. Moshe Sternbuch (*Teshuvot ve-Hanhagot* 1:795, revised edition) advances a rationale that would extend this principle. He explores the possibility that a litigant who is not generally observant of Jewish law and would not accept them when they are to his detriment, is not entitled to selectively accept Jewish law's legal rules when they are to his benefit. According to this principle, even if a *beit din* were to hear the case, it is possible that secular law would actually provide the legal rules of decision. He bases his analysis of this topic on whether the rule that an apostate has the same status as a gentile is to be applied even in financial situations which are to the detriment of the apostate. For more on this, see R. Yehudah Amichai "A Gentile who Summons a Jew to *Beit Din*," *Tehumin* 12:259–265 (1991).

court. Hence it is argued, since it is known in advance that the non-Jew will not heed the summons, there already exists constructive leave to proceed before a secular forum.[17] ...It seems to me that a similar line of reasoning might be applied in situations involving Jews totally unmindful of the obligations imposed by Jewish law. I state this not as a definitive *p'sak halakhah* [normative rule of Jewish law] but as a *limud zekhut* [possible reason] for those plaintiffs—and their attorneys—who do not at least attempt to have their disputes adjudicated by rabbinic courts.[18]

Thus, there are significant rationales found in Jewish law that explain the common custom of refraining from summoning one to a Jewish court who most likely will decline to attend. Indeed, this explains the infrequency with which Jewish courts actually issue written leave to resort to secular court; in most cases, that ability is presumed.

3. *A litigant who wishes to go to a Jewish court solely as a means of delay, and will not abide by an unfavorable decision of the* beit din, *is not considered as one who will go to Jewish court.*[19]

---

17 Rabbi Bleich cites "*Tashbetz* IV, no. 6 and *Divrei Ge'onim* 52:15. Cf. also *Orhot ha-Mishpatim* 46:2."

18 Rabbi J. David Bleich, "A Letter to a Student about a Jewish Law School," dated 10 Tevet 5748/January 5, 1987, at 2–3 (on file with this author). He adds:

> Any recovery accepted on the basis of a decision of a secular court in excess of that which would have been ordered by a *beit din* constitutes extortion in the eyes of Jewish law.

See also note 1 and note 16 of this chapter for a discussion of the crucial issue of what law a *beit din* would apply when a person is completely unobservant (for if a *beit din* would apply secular law in such a case, almost definitionally the award given by a secular court will not exceed that which should have been given by a *beit din*).

19 This is a very common event. A litigant who will not sign a binding arbitration agreement which would allow a Jewish court to enforce its judgments in secular court might be considered as if he will not follow the decision of the Jewish court. Many authorities do not require that one first engage in an unnecessary and non-binding Jewish court proceeding before one litigates in secular court; see R. Yosef Elijah Henkin, *Kol Kitvei ha-Rav Henkin* (New York, Ezras Torah, 1989), at 171–179.

On the other hand, the decision to seek a preliminary injunction before going to a *beit din* is not a form of using the secular courts in violation of Jewish law.[20]

Another way in which a plaintiff or defendant occasionally misuses a *beit din* occurs through the mechanism in which each side chooses its own judge and the two judges choose the third one.[21] In many circumstances, as already noted by the earliest authorities, an unscrupulous person will choose as his "judge" a person who will not decide the case except in his favor, and who will not consent to the choice of the third judge unless that judge also will decide the case in the backer's favor.[22] Such behavior by these "judges" unquestionably violates Jewish law, and adherents to Jewish law are not obligated to participate in a proceeding with such judges under any circumstances.[23]

4. *A Jewish defendant may litigate in a secular court when the plaintiff improperly summons him into secular court in violation of Jewish law. Thus, from the perspective of a lawyer, the prohibition is only to represent plaintiffs who improperly commence litigation and not defendants.*[24]

The reason for this rule is obvious. A Jewish defendant may litigate in secular court once improperly summoned for the same reasons that one may summon a defendant to secular court who refuses to allow a Jewish court (*beit din*) to decide a case.[25]

---

20 R. Moshe Feinstein, *Iggerot Moshe, Hoshen Mishpat* 2:11 and R. Ezra Batzri, *Dinei Mamonot, Dayyanut* 1:5(11) (It is ideally proper to first receive permission from *beit din*).

21 In Hebrew, *zebla*, an acronym for *ze borer lo ehad* ("this one picks one").

22 *Rosh* commenting on *Sanhedrin* 3:2; *Arukh ha-Shulhan, Hoshen Mishpat* 13:1–7.

23 *Shulhan Arukh, Hoshen Mishpat*, chs. 7–8 (prohibition to litigate in front of unfit judges).

24 See R. Ovadia Yosef, *Yehavveh Da'at* 4:65; and R. Gedaliah Felder, "Secular Courts," *Sefer ha-Yovel le-Rav Yosef Dov Halevi Soloveitchik* (Mosad HaRav Kook, 1984), 399, 408–411. Rabbi J. David Bleich, in a letter to a student, note 18 in this chapter, states "Most significantly, a Jew may always defend himself in a secular court even though the plaintiff may transgress in bringing suit in that forum."

25 Counterclaims may also be pressed if, as in most legal systems (see e.g., Fed. R. Civ. Proc. 13), they are waived if not presented. Even permissive claims, after rabbinic permission is sought, may be presented, since the plaintiff in such a case will only very rarely consent to a *beit din* deciding other claims.

Conclusion

The cumulative effect of the four rules discussed above is that a Jewish plaintiff in a civil action may not seek to litigate an action with a Jewish defendant who agrees to go to a Jewish court. Obviously, any time a client may properly litigate in secular court, a lawyer may represent that client.

It is important to note that sometimes determining who is the actual "defendant" is quite difficult. It would appear that the identity of the "real party in interest" is determinative for the purposes of the prohibition of litigating in secular courts, and the "named party," if it does not control the litigation, is halakhically irrelevant. When an insurance company fully compensates a defendant for a loss and controls theft litigation, the identity of the named party is not relevant.[26] Although one contemporary authority disagrees,[27] it seems that there should be no prohibition for an attorney to represent a gentile in a legal dispute. The logic of permitting such representation is apparent: in any situation in which the litigant may himself properly go to secular court, there is no prohibition for a lawyer to represent him there. Since the gentile litigant may go to secular court, a Jewish lawyer may represent him.[28]

So too, it should be permissible to aid one gentile in his legal disputes with another, because gentiles are not obligated to observe Jewish law or

---

[26] For responsa that discuss this issue, and recognize the insurance company as a real or primary litigant, see R. Eliezer Waldenberg, *Tzitz Eliezer* 18:67; R. Moshe Preschel, *Va-Yeshev Moshe* 22; R. Yekutiel Asher Zalman Enzel, *Mariaz Enzel* 72; R. Hayyim David HaLevi, *Mekor Hayyim* 1:22; R. Menasheh Klein, *Mishneh Halakhot* 2:11; and perhaps R. Moshe Sternbuch, *Teshuvot ve-Hanhagot* 1:822; but see R. Yaakov Blau, *Pithei Hoshen* 1:6 (n. 12) (Jerusalem, 1982), which perhaps can be limited to Jewish insurance companies. This is particularly true in jurisdictions that have "direct action" statutes. In case of partial indemnification or where the insurance company and the named defendant's legal interests are not identical, this might not be the case.

[27] R. Menasheh Klein, *Mishneh Halakhot* 7:255, 3:214.

[28] See also chapter six for a further discussion of this issue. See also R. Yehoshua Pinhas Bombach, *Ohel Yehoshua* 2:115; R. Saul Dweck, *Emet me-Aretz* 46, and *Ha-Torah ve-ha-Medinah* 7:89.

in fidelity to Jewish court (*beit din*).[29] The primary rationale for the prohibition of litigating in secular court is that Jews should use Jewish law and Jewish courts to decide their disputes, and that a decision not to do so undermines the validity of Jewish law. Such a rationale is obviously inapplicable in a dispute where one of the parties is not bound to use *beit din* or Jewish law as the basis for resolving his or her disputes.

Thus, Jewish law prohibits a Jew from initiating litigation in secular court against a fellow Jew who might consent to having this matter heard in a *beit din*.

---

29 Felder, "Secular Courts," at 410. This is true even if one accepts Nahmanides' opinion (commenting on Genesis 34:13) as understood by R. Moshe Isserles, *Responsa of Rema* 10, that the Noahide commandment of laws (*dinim*) incorporates Jewish commercial law into Noahide law, since it certainly does not incorporate the obligation to use a Jewish court. Most authorities do not accept Nahmanides' opinion as understood by Rabbi Isserles; see e.g., Maimonides, *Melakhim* 10:10, and commentary of R. Abraham Isaiah Karelitz, *Hazon Ish* ad loc. R. Isser Zalman Meltzer, *Even ha-Azel, Hovel u-Mazek* 8:5; R. Yom Tov Ishbili (Ritva), Responsa 14 (quoted in *Beit Yosef, Hoshen Mishpat* 66:18); *Tosafot, Eruvin* 629a (s.v. *"ben noah"*); R. Yehiel Mikhel Epstein, *Arukh ha-Shulhan he-Atid, Melakhim* 79:15; R. Naphtali Tzvi Yehuda Berlin, *Ha'amek She'alah* 2:3; R. Abraham Isaac Kook, *Etz Hadar* 38, 184; R. Tzvi Pesach Frank, *Har Tzvi*, Orah Hayyim II, *Kuntres Milei di-Berakhot* 2:1; R. Ovadia Yosef, *Yehavveh Da'at* 4:65; and R. Yitzhak Yaakov Weiss, *Minhat Yitzhak* 4:52:3. For a more complete analysis of this issue see Nahum Rakover, "Jewish Law and the Noahide Obligation to Preserve Social Order," *Cardozo L.R.* 12:1073, 1098–1118, and App. I & II (1991).

Chapter Six

Secular Courts and Lawyers

Applying the Prohibition to Litigate in Secular Courts

So far, this work has only discussed the prohibition of being the plaintiff in a secular-court lawsuit. What, however, is the status of an attorney who represents a person in court? For a lawyer, it is important to focus on the prohibition of litigating in secular court *as it applies to lawyers and not to litigants*. A careful reading of *Hoshen Mishpat* 26, where the rules on this topic are given, indicates that the prohibition applies only to the *litigants* whose decision it is to use the secular courts. It would seem thus that the status of the lawyer is only that of a facilitator to the litigants. The lawyers themselves have not violated the prohibition of litigating in secular courts, as noted by Rabbi Ovadia Yosef and others.[1] A lawyer who aids one in a lawsuit violates only the Jewish law prohibition of aiding another in a violation of Jewish law (referred to in Jewish law as the prohibition of *lifnei ivver*) and not the central prohibition of litigating in secular court.

---

1 R. Ovadia Yosef, *Yehavveh Da'at* 4:65 (in footnote **). For further support for this ruling, see also text accompanying note 31 of chapter seven. That one who assists in improper litigation only violates the prohibition to assist, and not the primary prohibition, is also apparent from a dispute among the codifiers as to whether one can be a witness in secular court in a dispute that actually should be heard in *beit din*; see R. Israel Wolf, *Sha'ar ha-Mishpat* 26:1; R. Moshe Isserles, *Responsa of Rema* 52. Both sides only discuss whether such conduct is prohibited on *lifnei ivver* grounds. No one argues that the substantive prohibition of litigating in secular court is violated by a facilitator.

The Analysis of Rabbi Klein, and a Response to It

Rabbi Menasheh Klein advances a rationale for ruling to the contrary and mandating that the substantive prohibition of litigating in secular court applies to a lawyer as well as the client.[2] Rabbi Klein maintains that because in the common law's legal tradition the client remains in the background and is typically invisible in court, the prohibition of litigating in secular court should apply primarily to lawyers. He thus prohibits a Jew from functioning as a lawyer in any situation in which a Jewish court (*beit din*) could—in theory—hear the case.

His analysis can be criticized in a number of ways.[3] First, there are no textual proofs in the Talmud that the prohibition applies to anyone other than the litigants, since it is the client/litigant who decides where a lawsuit should be brought and who can prevent a violation of the prohibition of litigating in secular court (*arkhaot*) from occurring by choosing *beit din* as the forum. The lawyer does not (and cannot) make that decision.[4] Second, the wording of this ruling in all of the significant codes inclines one in that direction, since the primary prohibition is expressed in terms of being *judged* by secular (gentile) courts. As Maimonides states:

> All who *are judged* by non-Jewish law or in their courts, even if their law is similar to Jewish law are regarded as having reviled, cursed, and rebelled against the laws of Moses, our teacher.[5]

So too, Rabbi Karo, writing in *Shulhan Arukh*, posits:

---

2 R. Menasheh Klein, *Mishneh Halakhot* 7:255 and 3:214. In combination with his opinion that gentiles also must bring matters to *beit din*, the permitted scope of activity for a lawyer is very small.

3 For an example of some of this criticism, see R. Shammai Gross, *Shevet Kehati* 3:322, who rules that one may be a lawyer for a gentile.

4 In American law, the decision to submit a case to a *beit din* can only be made by mutual agreement between the parties; the attorneys have no formal role in that decision. So too, litigation is captioned around the name of the defendant and the plaintiff; lawyers are listed only as representing a party. Cases are settled by the parties and parties can hire and fire attorneys, not the other way around.

5 Maimonides, *Sanhedrin* 26:7 (emphasis added).

> It is prohibited to be judged before gentile judges and in their courts; this is true even if the law applied is the same as the law used by Jewish law. Even if both litigants wish to be judged by them it is prohibited. Anyone who goes to be judged before them is evil and it is as if this person has mocked and rebelled against the laws of Moses our teacher.[6]

The Talmud also emphasizes only the prohibition to be "judged" in secular court when it states:

> Rabbi Tarfon states: In regards to places where one finds courts of gentiles [lit: idol worshippers], even though their law is identical to Jewish law, *one is prohibited to appear before them as a litigant*, as it states "These are the laws that I place before you;" before you and not before gentile courts.[7]

The use of the phrase "to be judged" in these sources seems to limit the prohibition to being a litigant—the person who is being judged. A survey of the responsa literature found on this prohibition reveals no other works which extend the prohibition to anyone other than the litigants. While there is discussion of the status of various court personnel and witnesses, that discussion inevitably focuses on the problems of assisting in a violation by a litigant; no one applies the central prohibition of litigating in secular court to these cases.[8]

One could seek to support Rabbi Klein's ruling by arguing that he is only incorrect in the typical fee arrangement, where the lawyer is paid by the hour or case, independent of result. However, in a case where the lawyer is paid on a contingency fee basis, one could claim that the lawyer certainly is a principal in the case, as he has a stake in the outcome. In this author's opinion, that argument too is incorrect. According to classical Jewish law, a lawyer would actually purchase a portion of the case as a

---

6 *Hoshen Mishpat* 26:1.

7 *Gittin* 88b (emphasis added).

8 See R. Rafael Alkova, *Karnei Re'em, Hoshen Mishpat* 88:1; R. Shabtai ben Yonah Cohen, *Shai la-Moreh, Edut* 2:1; and R. Meir Ben Zion Chai Uzi'el, *Mishpetei Uzi'el Hoshen Mishpat* 13.

form of compensation, and would then sue in his own name, as well as that of the client's.[9]

Such a lawyer is a principal in a case. In American law the lawyer, even in a contingency fee case, is not the named plaintiff, does not control the crucial decisions in the litigation, and remains only capable of carrying out the client's wishes as to how and where to litigate the case. The client is the "real party in interest"—the lawyer is not.[10] A contingency fee affects only the method of payment (and nothing else). The prohibition of litigating in secular courts would only apply to the plaintiff even in contingency fee cases.

Thus, even where all of the litigants are Jewish, and are acting improperly in bringing the lawsuit in secular court, it would appear that the plaintiff's lawyer is only violating the prohibition to assist or aid in an improper lawsuit, rather than acting as a principal[11] in such a violation.[12]

---

9   For more on this, see Aaron Kirschenbaum, "Representation in Litigation in Jewish Law," *Dine Israel* 6:25 (1975).

10 As considered in note 26 of chapter five, when discussing the status of insurance companies, there certainly can be cases where the "real party in interest" is not the named party. What it takes to do that, however, would be control over the litigation process (which is typically demonstrated when an insurance company indicates to the named defendant—that it is nominally defending—that he should hire his own lawyer). A lawyer on a contingency fee still must defer to the client in all significant matters. However, a lawyer who is also the executor of an estate, and who thus controls the litigation as the executor, would be the principle, in this author's opinion.

11 As a general rule, Jewish law accepts that there is no agency for a violation of the law (*ein shaliah li-devar averah*). One could claim based on this principle that whoever files the papers violates the law, no matter under whose direction this is undertaken. That would be a mistake. Jewish law does not accept the principle that there is no agency for a violation of the law when the agent and principal are not both equally bound by the legal rule. Thus, for example, in a case where one person hires another person to rob another, it is the robber who is liable and not the one who hires the robber. However, in a case where the law does not detect the conduct of the agent, but is only directed to the principal, it is clear that the violation does not fall on the agent; see comments of *Rema* on *Hoshen Mishpat* 348:8 as well as commentaries *ad locum*.

12 The next chapter will discuss the parameters of *lifnei ivver* to determine if it is ever inapplicable to lawyers.

Chapter Seven

Aiding in a Violation of Jewish Law

An Overview of the Prohibition to Assist in a Violation of Jewish Law

Having established that when it is prohibited for a litigant to use the secular courts, the prohibition upon the attorney who represents the plaintiff is not one of resorting to secular court, but rather of aiding another in committing a violation, it is important to note that there are many situations in which it is permissible to aid another person in committing a violation even though it is unquestionably prohibited to commit the violation oneself. Jewish law has a separate and distinct prohibition to aid another in illegal activity (commonly called *lifnei ivver*). This prohibition is derived from Leviticus, which states:

> You shall not curse a deaf person and before a blind person (in Hebrew, *lifnei ivver*) you shall not put a stumbling block; you shall fear your God, I am the Lord.[1]

These laws are especially important to the life of a lawyer, as lawyers, more than most professionals, are frequently directed by clients to assist them in a violation of Jewish (or for a gentile, Noahide) law. This chapter will discuss the approaches taken by Jewish law in assisting another in a violation of Jewish law.[2]

---

1 Leviticus 19:14.

2 The material discussed in this chapter is relevant to each of the following chapters, as well as the chapter concerning litigation in secular court.

According to talmudic law, there are two distinctly different components to this prohibition—both of which are relevant to lawyers. The first prohibits giving ill-intentioned advice. The second (and more common aspect) encompasses aiding a violation of Jewish law.

The "bad advice" aspect of this prohibition is not the primary focus of either the Talmud or its commentaries.[3] Rather, the Talmud advances a more expansive definition of the prohibition of placing a stumbling block in front of a blind person by defining "blindness" broadly. The Talmud quotes the following statement:

> Rabbi Nathan said: From where do we know that one may not extend a cup of wine to one who swore not to drink wine [a *nazir*] nor a limb of a live animal to a Noahide [who, like all others, may not eat such flesh]? The source is from the verse "before a blind person thou shalt not put a stumbling block."[4]

Since the Talmud does not distinguish between an intentional and an unintentional violation in this regard, it may be inferred that this conduct is prohibited even when the one who may not drink wine or eat flesh from a living animal is aware that these actions are prohibited. Support for this inference can also be found in the Talmud's assertion[5] that a father may not strike his grown child because the child may retaliate physically—an act which is a capital offense.[6] The Talmud bases its opinion on the verse

---

3 This aspect of the prohibition prevents a lawyer from knowingly giving a client advice not in the client's interest. Maimonides maintains that this was the primary purpose of the prohibition. He states regarding *lifnei ivver*:

> By this prohibition we are forbidden to give misleading advice. Thus, if one asks your advice on a matter which he does not really understand, you are forbidden to mislead or deceive him; you must give him what you consider the correct guidance. The prohibition is contained in His words, "before a blind person thou shalt not put a stumbling block," on which the *Sifra* says: "If one is 'blind' in a matter, and asks you for advice, do not give him advice which is not suitable for him." (*Sefer ha-Mitzvot*, Negative Commandment 299.)

For further analysis of this issue, and a general survey of the rules related to *lifnei ivver*, see Michael Broyde & David Hertzberg, "Enabling a Jew to Sin: The Parameters," *J. Halacha & Contemporary Society* 19:5 (1990).

4 *Pesahim* 22b.

5 See *Moed Katan* 17a and *Kiddushin* 29b.

6 See Exodus 21:15, which lists striking one's parents as a capital offense.

in Leviticus 19:14 concerning tripping a blind person (*lifnei ivver*), even though the child is fully aware of the consequences of his action.

In the Talmud's discussion in *Bava Metzia* one sees yet further application of this prohibition. Biblical law proscribes both charging and paying interest. In addition to the standard prohibitions,[7] the Talmud states that all people who participate in or facilitate this transaction—including the guarantor, witnesses, and even the scribe of the document—violate the prohibition of assisting in a violation (*lifnei ivver*).[8] The concept that even the ancillary and supportive participants are in violation of this prohibition broadens our understanding of the scope of the prohibition even further. The participation, as a scribe or witness, in such a transaction violates the prohibition only because, by enabling the transacion to occur, one is deliberately helping "blind" people to sin. A "blind" person thus includes one who voluntarily sins as a result of an intentional "stumbling block."

From the above sources it becomes clear that "blindness" is not limited to cases where the sinner is blinded by ignorance or naïveté, but also encompasses cases where the person is blinded by a desire to violate the law. Thus the Biblical verses concerning tripping a blind person (*lifnei ivver*) prohibit aiding in any violation of the law. It not only prohibits one from maliciously misguiding another, but also prohibits cooperating with one who is misguided by his own material needs or improper sense of law.

However, there are certain cases where there is no violation of the *lifnei ivver* prohibition. The Talmud quotes Rabbi Nathan's statement (as recited above) and limits its application to an instance of "two sides of a river."[9] Thus, when one who cannot drink wine is on one side of a river and wine is on the other side so that he cannot obtain the wine without assistance, then, and only then, is the person who gives it to him in violation of the prohibition to assist (*lifnei ivver*). On the other hand, if the wine and the one who may not drink it are on the same side of the river, no biblical prohibition is violated when one assists that person in procuring the wine. The assumption is that the prohibition will be violated in any case.[10]

---

7   See Exodus 22:24 and Leviticus 25:36–37.

8   *Bava Metzia* 75b.

9   In Aramaic *trei ibrei d'nahara*; see *Avodah Zarah* 6b.

10 The Talmud, in *Avodah Zarah* 14a, also states that it is permitted to aid an aider (*lifnei de-lifnei ivver*), i.e., help a person whose action is itself only prohibited because he is an aider. The early authorities (*Rishonim*) limit this rule to situations where the first recipient of the aid is not himself obligated in the prohibition of *lifnei ivver*

These talmudic statements served as the basis for deductions by the early commentaries which focused on one particular aspect of the prohibition, namely, aiding one who wishes to violate the law, and who can do so unaided or with the assistance of those not falling under the prohibition. From the perspective of a lawyer, this is a crucial question. Typically, if one lawyer does not aid a plaintiff or defendant, another lawyer will. From a practical economic perspective, almost all transactions in which a lawyer will participate involve "one side of the river" (i.e., others will aid the litigant if this lawyer does not).

On this issue, the early authorities (*Rishonim*) may be divided into three groups. The first maintains that one may never aid a person who is attempting to violate the law, even if another will aid him if one declines. The prohibition applies whether or not the next person who aids him is also obligated to observe the law. Thus, those who hold this position reject the approach taken in *Avodah Zarah* 6b and make no distinction between one or two sides of the river. This is generally thought to be the position of Maimonides. Although he does not state so explicitly, it can be inferred from a number of his comments. First, in his enumeration of the commandments,[11] Maimonides does not limit the scope of the rule to situations where others cannot help. Secondly, he never quotes this limitation in any of the instances when he deals with assisting others in sin in his primary work, the *Mishneh Torah*.[12]

(*i.e.*, a non-Jew); see *Tosafot, Avodah Zarah* 15a, 22a and Rabbenu Nissim, *Avodah Zarah* 15a. The rationale for this is that *lifnei ivver* prohibits aiding in the commission of a prohibited act–even if the prohibited act is itself only a violation of *lifnei ivver*; see R. Joseph Babad, *Minhat Hinnukh* 231:2. For example it is permitted under this rationale to sell wine to a non-Jewish wine salesman who is then going to sell it to a *nazir*. Others have developed a different understanding of when *lifnei ivver* does not apply; see *Hiddushei Anshei Shem, Avodah Zarah* (page 4a in Rif pages) 1; and R. Moshe Feinstein, *Iggerot Moshe, Orah Hayyim* 4:79 and *Yoreh Deah* 1:68.

11 See note 3 of this chapter.

12 Maimonides would maintain that the statements by Rabbi Nathan in *Avodah Zarah* 6b represent only his opinion, and was not accepted by most of the *Amoraim*. To support this he would cite the fact that this limitation of Rabbi Nathan is not quoted in the Talmud in any other place.

This understanding of Maimonides is found in R. Joseph Babad, *Minhat Hinnukh*, Negative Commandment 232:3, R. David Tzvi Hoffmann, *Melammed le-Ho'il* 1:34, and others. Thus, in all likelihood, Maimonides maintains that a biblical violation occurs in all circumstances. It is possible that Maimonides maintains that there is never any rabbinic prohibition of *lifnei ivver*; see R. David ben Solomon ibn Zimra, *Teshuvot Radvaz* 5:215 (1579).

The second position is taken by Rabbenu Nissim (*Ran*). He states that even though, according to biblical law, the prohibition of assisting in a violation (*lifnei ivver*) is transgressed only when the aider's assistance is necessary for the commission of the prohibited act, rabbinic law prohibits this assistance even when the facilitator's assistance is not needed.[13] Rabbi Judah Rosanes adds to this position and states that in order for assisting an action to become permissible, the assistance must have been either not really needed, or available either from a gentile, or a person otherwise not obligated in the commandment of *lifnei ivver*, rather than by a different Jew who would then be violating this law himself.[14]

The third position is taken by *Tosafot*.[15] *Tosafot* rules that the biblical prohibition of assisting in a violation of Jewish law encompasses only situations of "two sides of the river" (i.e., when the sinner requires the help of the aider to accomplish his goal). Furthermore, *Tosafot* states that in "one side of the river" situations (i.e., where the principal can execute the prohibited act himself or with the assistance of others) there is no prohibition to help him—either according to biblical or rabbinic law.[16] According to *Tosafot*, this type of conduct is permitted.

Thus, three approaches can be found with regard to aiding one who wishes to sin. Maimonides maintains that the biblical prohibition is always violated by aiding. Rabbenu Nissim (*Ran*) believes that biblical law is violated only when others cannot also execute the act; in all other situations the aider violates only rabbinic law. *Tosafot* maintains that when there are others who can—and will—aid the violator or he could act alone, neither rabbinic nor biblical law is violated.

---

13 See Rabbenu Nissim, commenting on *Avodah Zarah* 6b.

14 Rabbi Judah Rosanes, *Mishneh le-Melekh, Malveh ve-Loveh* 4:2. Rabbi Rosanes' approach is based upon his understanding of *Tosafot* (*Hagigah* 13a, s.v. *"ein mosrim"*) that "one side of the river" (*had ibra de-nahara*) refers only to situations where the principal can do it on his own or through the assistance of a non-Jew.

15 *Tosafot*, commenting on *Avodah Zarah* 6b s.v. *"minayin."*

16 Obviously, if one accepts *Tosafot*'s framework, then the ability of the principal alone to execute the complete act unassisted would remove the prohibition of aiding him, as the sinner himself is his own aider. Perhaps even *Ran* accepts this rule. See Nahmanides quoted by *Ran*, *Avodah Zarah* 6b–7a.

Modern Decisors and Issues Involved in Aiding a Person to Violate Jewish Law

The classical codifiers of the law have taken a number of approaches to this topic. Rabbi Joseph Karo, writing in *Shulhan Arukh*, when discussing whether one can sell items to a non-Jew which might be used in his (idolatrous) religious practice, apparently adopts the approach of Maimonides (or at least *Ran*) and concludes that it is prohibited to aid a person in the commission of a sin, although others will aid him if one does not.[17]

Rabbi Isserles (*Rema*) in his glosses does not agree with this position. He quotes the position of *Tosafot* that when others can aid the sinner, it is permissible for any other individual to aid him as well. Additionally, he quotes the position of *Ran*, that this is prohibited according to rabbinic law. He concludes:

> The tradition is in accordance with the first opinion (*Tosafot*); pious people [literally, spiritually elevated people] should conduct themselves in accordance with the second opinion (*Ran*).[18]

The classical commentary of the *Shakh* adds yet another rule.[19] He states that when dealing with a person whom one is not obligated to prevent from sinning,[20] all authorities[21] agree that if others will aid him if the prospective facilitator does not, or if he can do the whole act himself, it is entirely permissible to aid him. The basis of the rabbinic prohibition to aid sinners is to separate them from sinning. Thus, according to *Shakh* it is permissible to aid a non-Jew or a Jew with no fidelity to Jewish law[22]

---

17 See *Yoreh Deah* 151:1.

18 *Rema*, *Yoreh Deah* 151:1. It is most unlikely that *Rema* was referring to Maimonides as the basis for the second opinion; *Ran* is a more likely candidate, since even *Tosafot* in other places in the Talmud maintains that *Ran* is correct (see also note 25 of this chapter). However, the source notes for *Rema* provide no guidance as they were not written by *Rema*; see R. Hayyim Hezekiah di Medini, *Sedei Hemed, kelalei ha-Poskim* 14.

19 R. Shabtai Meir HaCohen (*Shakh*), *Yoreh Deah* 151:6.

20 I.e., either an apostate or a non-Jew. For more on aiding a gentile in sinning, see the end of this chapter.

21 *Ran* and *Tosafot*.

22 See text accompanying note 7 of this chapter.

when others can aid them, since there is no obligation to prevent such a person from sinning. It is only in the case of generally observant Jews, according to the *Shakh*, that the two opinions of Rabbi Isserles (*Rema*) are relevant.

Rabbi Ezekiel Landau adds his own insight to the opinion of *Shakh*.[23] He states that according to *Shakh*, any time a person knowingly violates a particular rule, that person is to be classified as a Jew with no fidelity to Jewish law for the purposes of the prohibition to assist this person in a violation. Thus, according to this opinion, a lawyer can aid even an apparently religious Jew in an improper lawsuit provided that the religious Jew knows he is violating Jewish law.

Thus, in summary, four positions are taken in the codes and commentaries:

(1) One may never aid a person in committing a violation of Jewish or Noahide law and all such assistance is a biblical violation (Maimonides and Rabbi Karo).

(2) It is rabbinically prohibited to aid another person in sinning when others will aid him if the prospective facilitator does not. This is prohibited according to biblical law when no one else can (*Ran*).

(3) It is permitted to aid another person in sinning if others will do so if the prospective facilitator does not (*Tosafot* and *Rema*).

(4) It is permitted to aid in a violation when one is not obligated to separate the violator from sinning (*Shakh* and Rabbi Landau).

Among the latter commentaries, it appears that only a single decisor accepts as normative the approach of Maimonides.[24] All other decisors agree that when others can provide the services or goods needed, there can be no biblical violation. Thus, a lawyer is almost always faced with at most a rabbinic prohibition, since in the current legal market it is extremely rare that a single lawyer is the unique supplier of a service within a given geographic area. Hence, most authorities discuss the approaches of *Tosafot*, *Ran*, and *Shakh* all of whom rule that many of the forms of assistance provided to one who is seeking to violate Jewish law is not biblically prohibited. While it is difficult to summarize the numerous opinions offered among the later commentaries, it appears that most Ashkenazic decisors

---

23 R. Ezekiel Landau, *Dagul me-Revavah*, commenting on *Yoreh Deah* 151.

24 See R. Yair Hayyim Bacharach, *Havvot Yair* 137.

rule that *Tosafot*'s position, or *Shakh*'s further addition to *Ran*'s rule, is generally considered an acceptable approach to adopt, although some maintain it appropriate to be strict in this matter, and some even prohibit relying on these liberalities.[25]

When the client is a gentile, and the violation is one of Noahide law,[26] the vast majority of authorities permit one to assist in this violation as there is no obligation to prevent a gentile from sinning.[27] While it is true that R. Menachem Mendel Schneerson writes that:

---

25 See generally, Michael Broyde & David Hertzberg, "Enabling a Jew to Sin: The Parameters," *J. Halacha & Contemporary Society* 19:5, 17–30 (1990) for a more complete discussion of the permissibility of relying on the opinions of *Rema*, *Tosafot*, and *Shakh*. Among the classical codifiers, R. Mordecai Yaffe, *Levush*, *Yoreh Deah* 151:3, R. Shmuel mi-Purdah, *Beit Shmuel*, *Even ha-Ezer* 5:18, and R. Shmuel Halevi Kalin, *Mahatzit ha-Shekel*, *Orah Hayyim* 163:2, all accept the opinion of *Rema*. R. Hayyim Yosef Azulai, *Birkei Yosef*, *Yoreh Deah* 151, appears to accept *Shakh*'s approach. While *Shakh* does not himself distinguish between an underlying act as a biblical or rabbinic violation when he excludes apostates from the obligation of rebuking, many authorities only accept *Shakh* when the prohibited act itself is only a rabbinic prohibition; see R. Yosef Teomim, *Peri Megadim*, *Eshel Avraham*, *Orah Hayyim* 163(2). Others, however, appear not to accept *Tosafot*'s or *Shakh*'s approach but embrace *Ran* as the better approach. Thus, R. Elijah of Vilna, *Yoreh Deah* 151:8, accepts *Ran* as correct. He appears to do so based upon the fact that, in other places in the Talmud, *Tosafot* themselves explicitly accept *Ran*'s approach. R. Abraham Gumbiner, *Magen Avraham*, *Orah Hayyim* 347:4, as well accepts the approach of *Ran*.

R. Feinstein rules that it is permissible to accept the approach of *Shakh* and *Dagul me-Revavah*, at the very least in a case of financial need; see *Iggerot Moshe*, *Yoreh Deah* 1:72 and *Even ha-Ezer* 4:61(2). For a different formulation of when one may assist in a violation (in the context of practicing medicine), see R. Abraham S. Abraham, *Nishmat Avraham* 4:86, 93–94.

26 The Talmud (*Sanhedrin* 56a) recounts seven categories of prohibition: idol worship, taking the Lord's name in vain, murder, prohibited sexual activity, theft, eating flesh from a living animal, and the obligation to enforce laws. The precise scope of Noahide law is beyond the purview of this book; for more on this, see Aaron Lichtenstein, *The Seven Laws of Noah* (2nd ed., New York 1986), and *Encyclopedia Talmudit*, s.v. "*ben noah*" 3:348–362.

27 For more on this issue, see my "The Obligation of Jews to Seek Observance of Noahide Law by Gentiles: A Theoretical Perspective."

From all of the above, it is clear that anyone who has in his ability to influence, in any way, a Noahide to keep the seven commandments, the obligation rests on him to do so, since that was commanded to Moses our teacher. Certainly, one who has connections with Noahides in areas of commerce and the like, it is proper for him to sustain the connection in order to convince and explain to that person, in a way that will reach that person's heart, that the Almighty commanded Noahides to keep the seven commandments.[28]

Most authorities rule that this approach is not mandated by Jewish law, although it certainly is morally laudatory to conduct oneself in such a manner.[29] Of course, even these authorities agree that in a case where the violation of Noahide law cannot occur without the assistance of this Jewish lawyer, no assistance is permitted, as that is a "two sides of the river" case and a biblical violation of the prohibition to enable a violation of Jewish law (*lifnei ivver*).

---

28 R. Menachem Mendel Schneerson, *Sheva Mitzvot Shel Benei Noah, Hapardes* 59:9 7–11 (1985). In a previous paragraph he stated:

> In *Responsa Tashbetz* (3:133) it states that even in a case where there is no prohibition of *lifnei ivver* such as one side of the river cases, still it is prohibited to assist Noahides who wish to sin, since "we are obligated to separate them from sin."

29 This approach—which rules that there is no obligation to prevent sinning by a Noahide or convince a Noahide to cease sinning—is accepted by nearly all authorities, including *Magen Avraham, Orah Hayyim* 347:4; *Gra, Yoreh Deah* 151:8; *Levush, Yoreh Deah* 151:3; *Beit Shmuel, Even ha-Ezer* 5:18; *Mahatzit ha-Shekel, Orah Hayyim* 163:2; *Dagul me-Revavah, Yoreh Deah* 151; and *Birkei Yosef, Yoreh Deah* 151. (R. Feinstein, *Iggerot Moshe* 3:90 states that this conclusion is obvious, "proper and true.") Indeed, it is important to realize that a number of authorities reach the conclusion that it is permitted to assist a Noahide while it is prohibited to assist an unobservant Jew. This is based on their observation that there is no obligation to separate a Noahide from sinning; indeed, this approach is used to harmonize apparently inconsistent talmudic texts using this Noahide/*mumar* (heretic) distinction to separate the various cases; see comments of *Gra* and *Magen Avraham* cited above.

That this conduct is morally laudatory can be seen from the remarks of Rabbi Judah HeHasid, who states in *Sefer HeHasidim* 1124 that "when one sees a Noahide sinning, if one can correct him, one should, since God sent Jonah to Nineveh to return them to his path."

The Lawyer and Aiding in a Violation of Jewish Law

When a lawyer litigates a case that ought to be heard by a Jewish court (*beit din*), he is at most violating only the prohibition of "placing a stumbling block in front of a blind person." If the attorney is willing to rely on the well accepted opinions of *Tosafot*, *Rema*, *Shakh*, and Rabbi Landau, discussed above, then this prohibition is inapplicable, and thus he may represent a Jewish plaintiff in any situation where the client[30] will go to secular court with a different attorney if this attorney declines to represent him. This is only true, however, if the lawyer does not assist in the decision to use secular court.

This analysis is explicitly adopted by Rabbi Gedaliah Felder. After concluding that it is certainly permissible to represent a gentile in his legal disputes, Rabbi Felder adds:

> Even if both litigants are observant Jews, and thus when they are litigating in secular court one of them is certainly acting improperly...it is not prohibited for a lawyer to represent them, since if this lawyer declines, another will act. It is no different from that which *Rema* writes (*Yoreh Deah* 151) that when they can purchase their [prohibited] goods elsewhere, it is permitted for a religious Jew to provide them.[31]

Another example of this can be found in the *Responsa Meshiv Ba-Halakhah* written by the Kollel Lehoraah of Monsey, New York. The following question was posed to them:

> Two Jews had a monetary dispute and went to court to settle their differences. Each one hired a lawyer. [May the lawyer work for the parties?]

The Kollel answered in part:

> If both the complainant and the respondent are not observant of Jewish law and there are other lawyers available who would and

---

30 Who is improperly going to secular court.

31 R. Gedaliah Felder, "Secular court," at 410.

could take the case, then the Jewish lawyer may let himself be hired to represent either of the parties to the case....If both the complainant and the respondent are observant, and yet both want to resolve their differences in court, then certainly the two parties to the lawsuit are violating a prohibition, but the lawyer may assist and represent either side if there is another lawyer available.[32]

In essence, the Ashkenazic understanding of Jewish law would generally permit this representation by a lawyer.

To a person who follows Sephardic norms of Jewish law, this issue is much more complex. It seems to this author that the crucial question then becomes whether the prohibition involved in litigating in secular court is biblical or rabbinic.[33] In situations where the underlying prohibition is only rabbinic in nature, one sees numerous Sephardic halakhic authorities who permit this assistance in all cases.[34] On the other hand, once a biblical prohibition is involved, Rabbi Ovadia Yosef, as well as other Sephardic authorities, and Rabbi Karo himself rule strictly.[35] Indeed, as would logically flow from this position, such authorities as Rabbi Yosef show great hesitancy in relying on *Shakh* and Rabbi Landau. On the other hand, particularly in the responsa of Rabbi Yosef, one could limit these strictures to the land of Israel, where the participants are essentially all Jewish, and thus the problem of assisting in a violation of Jewish law is made more complex, since when one Jew declines to assist in a sin, another Jew will do so.[36] That would indicate that there would be little difference in America between those who follow Sephardic norms and those who follow the Ashkenazic tradition.

In addition, there might be a distinction between the lawyer who is actually litigating the case in court and signing the briefs[37] and one who is associated with producing documents for the lawyer who is actually

---

32 *Kovetz Meshiv ba-Halakhah* 10:9–10 (Hebrew pages) and 6–10 (English pages), (1993).

33 See note 1 of chapter five.

34 See R. Ovadia Yosef, *Yehavveh Da'at* 3:38, based on R. David Ibn Zimra (*Radvaz*) 5:215 (1579) and the authorities cited therein.

35 See *Yehavveh Da'at* 3:67.

36 See *Yehavveh Da'at* 3:38 and 3:67. For why this factor is significant, see text accompanying note 14 of this chapter.

37 In those jurisdictions where no one formally signs briefs or pleadings, it would be that lawyer who bears responsibility for their content.

arguing in court. The lawyer whose job is limited to drafting legal documents related to litigation, but who does not sign these documents or argue the case, is only aiding one whose sole violation is that he is assisting another in a violation. While most authorities are of the opinion that assisting another who is assisting in a violation (in Hebrew, *lifnei delifnei*) is prohibited when both aiders are Jewish,[38] in this case where the primary aider's conduct is itself proper according to some authorities, it very likely is permitted to aid him even if the secondary aider would not himself rely on those opinions.[39]

Thus, for example, it would appear to be permissible for a lawyer to represent an estate and seek to probate a secular will. According to these opinions, the lawyer could do so even if the rightful heirs (according to Jewish law) sought to contest the will, and argue that its use violates Jewish law (for reasons explained on page 128). The lawyer's Jewish law defense to his activity is that he is merely aiding the actions of the heirs in the will, who can easily seek different counsel for this task should this lawyer decline. In addition, the lawyer could make reference to Rabbi Feinstein's opinion (discussed on page 130) that this form of a will is valid according to Jewish law, and thus the lawyer's conduct is completely proper.

However, it should be noted that a distinction must be made between representing a litigant who wishes to (improperly) use the secular courts in litigation against one who desires to use a Jewish court (*beit din*), and representing a litigant in a case where neither of the parties wishes to use *beit din*. Once one side in litigation actually seeks to have the dispute adjudicated in *beit din*, and *beit din* accepts jurisdiction and orders both

---

38 See "Enabling Sin," at 12 n. 8. Even this limited problem is inapplicable to a situation where the client is engaging in an activity which is permitted according to Jewish law, but discouraged by the force of Jewish custom or historical precedent. An example of this occurs when one represents a client who wishes to initiate a lawsuit during the (first nine days of the) Hebrew month of *Av* against one whom Jewish custom discourages such suits to be brought during that period (because of the range of tragedies that historically have befallen the Jewish community then); see *Shulhan Arukh, Orah Hayyim* 551:1 for more on this. A lawyer may represent such a client, as bringing the lawsuit does not violate Jewish law, and the lawyer is merely assisting in the "violation" of a custom and if this lawyer declines to do so, others will represent the client.

39 Ibid, at 30–31. On a broader level, Rabbi Bleich writes, in "A Letter to a Student," (see chapter five at note 18), that the prohibition of causing another to sin (*lifnei ivver*) "construed in a technical halakhic sense, simply does not apply to transmission of information. In technical terms, it seems at worst to be a *lifnei de-lifnei* [a secondary aiding problem]."

parties to appear, it is a violation of the Jewish court's order to assist the recalcitrant litigant in pursuing a prohibited secular remedy.[40] In such a case it would be prohibited for anybody—lawyer or layman—to assist a litigant in defying the Jewish court and using the secular courts. In cases where neither litigant actually desires to use *beit din*, this limitation is inapplicable.

The application of pressure (social and economic) on individuals who refuse to abide by the decision of a Jewish court (*beit din*) is an integral component of Jewish law and the imposition of sanctions as a method of enforcing the ruling of a *beit din* is a recurring theme in Jewish law.[41]

---

40 Very frequently *beit din* will order the recalcitrant litigant into some form of excommunication; see R. Moshe Isserles (*Rema*), commenting on *Shulhan Arukh, Hoshen Mishpat* 26:1; and *Kovetz ha-Poskim* at 217–218. This order typically prohibits business associations with such a person; see *Shulhan Arukh, Yoreh Deah* 334. At the least, this order encompasses assisting a person in circumventing *beit din*'s ruling.

41 See for example *Yoreh Deah* 334:43 and *Hoshen Mishpat* 1:5, 1:6, 2:1, 8:5, 11:1, 11:5 (*Rema*), 16:3, 18:3, and 100:3. The argument that Jewish law no longer allows for such penalties, sometimes advanced by those unfamiliar with Jewish law, is unquestionably incorrect in light of these criteria. For more on this, see my "Forming Religious Communities and Respecting Dissenter's Rights: A Jewish Law Approach to a Tort Law Problem" in *Religious Human Rights in the World Today: Legal and Religious Perspectives* (Martinus Nijhoff, 1995).

Chapter Eight

Secular Law and Secular Court

One other issue must be addressed in a discussion of the prohibition of litigating in secular courts (*arkhaot*): the type of litigation to which it applies. Public causes of action (i.e., those types of actions created by secular governments under the rubric of "the law of the land is the law,") and which aid the government in its task of governing) may be permissibly litigated in secular court. The scope of this rule is limited in criminal cases and will be discussed in chapters eleven and twelve, but it has applications in many other areas of the law as well. One may unquestionably litigate against the government or its (coincidentally Jewish[1]) agents, such as the Securities and Exchange Commission, the Environmental Protection Agency, or the Internal Revenue Service, or engage in any litigation where the primary cause of action was created by the secular government and involves public litigation in order to "make the world a better place"[2] and not to resolve individual disputes (even if individual disputes are incidentally resolved).

Bankruptcy Laws: A Paradigmatic Example

Classifying such litigation is not always easy. For example, one might argue that declaring bankruptcy is a private, rather than public, action and therefore improper or ineffective under Jewish law to the extent it diminishes the rights of the Jewish creditors. However, there is a responsum by

---

1 Thus, for example, the writ of mandamus is sought against a named person, and not the government; however, it is clear that the government is the real party in interest in a mandamus action, and not the particular judge.
2 See e.g., *Shulhan Arukh*, *Hoshen Mishpat* 369:8 and *Sema*, *Hoshen Mishpat* 269:21.

Rabbi Feinstein, one of the premier decisors of the modern era, to the contrary, indicating that it is permissible to avail oneself of the secular bankruptcy laws, and that such laws are valid according to Jewish law as "the law of the land." The rationale for his opinion is that bankruptcy was instituted by the government not only to protect an individual debtor or creditor, but to further a general government interest in the organized economy and to encourage investment. Thus, when the secular government allocates the debtor's assets in a manner contrary to that used by Jewish law,[3] a Jew (and a Jewish court) must honor this division, even to the extent of returning money already in his control. Rabbi Feinstein states:

> Thus, the laws promulgated by the government in the case of one who indebted himself, does not have the ability to pay back his debts (bankruptcy) and is a debtor to many creditors [are valid]. The government regulations which appoint a commission of three people to divide the money and property among all creditors in proportion to the money owed to them are proper. *It is prohibited for any creditor to seize property for himself because this is one of the laws applicable to all in the country and thus falls under the rubric of "the law of the land is the law"*[4] as the Rema states. This is even more true in a corporation which involves gentiles [as creditors.][5]

While Rabbi Feinstein does not explicitly state that the discharge of an individual's contractual debts in bankruptcy prevents a Jewish court (*beit din*) from ordering future repayment, he indicates this when he says "It is prohibited for any creditor to seize property for himself [without permission from the Bankruptcy Court]." After the assets are distributed, no further permission will ever be given—in American law[6]—to seize future

---

3 As explained in *Ketubot* 93a and *Shulhan Arukh, Hoshen Mishpat* 104.

4 Emphasis added.

5 R. Moshe Feinstein, *Iggerot Moshe, Hoshen Mishpat* 2:62.

6 Actually this might not be necessarily true. The questioner in that responsum resided in Switzerland. In Switzerland, a bankrupt debtor receives no discharge for unsatisfied debts. Creditors holding claims related to pre-petition debts receive a certificate stating the amount unpaid. The creditor, however, is stayed from collecting on the debt as long as the debtor has not been able to gain "new fortune." Therefore, "in Swiss practice, the defense of not having gained 'new fortune' effectively prevents creditors from collecting on their claims," Ulrich Huber, "Creditor Equality in Transnational Bankruptcies," *Vanderbilt Journal of Transnational Law* 19:741, 762 (1986).

monies of the debtor. Rabbi Feinstein expresses no doubt that this is correct in the case of a corporation (which never receives new capital after a bankruptcy liquidation, and rarely after a bankruptcy reorganization) due to the presence of shareholders.[7]

Public Law

While it is possible to disagree with Rabbi Feinstein's analysis concerning bankruptcy law, there are many areas of the law[8] where the government's

---

7 One could understand this responsum as an application of *Shakh's* opinion (*Hoshen Mishpat* 73:39) that in any case in which Jewish law is silent, secular law (*dina de-malkhuta*) provides the mandatory answer (R. Abraham Isaiah Karelitz, *Hazon Ish*, *Hoshen Mishpat* 16, thought this wrong), or that if the case involved common commercial practice, *beit din*, when hearing the case, should assume that the parties have made a condition of accepting the secular law. A careful reading of the responsum indicates that the approach of the *Shakh* was not what was intended. Even if the *Shakh's* approach were accepted, only the mechanism, and not the result, would change; see e.g., R. Yaakov Blau, *Pithei Hoshen* 1: ch. 4 (n. 63) (discussing whether bankruptcy is incorporated through this mechanism) and n. 72 (discussing whether statutes of limitations are incorporated through this mechanism).

For an analysis of rent control regulations similar to Rabbi Feinstein's analysis of bankruptcy, see R. Yosef Elijah Henkin, "The Law of the Land is the Law," *Hapardes* 17:54 (1954), reprinted in Rabbi Yosef Elijah Henkin, *Kol Kitvei ha-Rav Henkin* 2:174–177.

8 R. Moshe Sternbuch, *Teshuvot ve-Hanhagot* 2:701, agrees with this result as does R. Menasheh Klein, *Mishneh Halakhot* 6:277. Two authorities are occasionally quoted as disagreeing, when in fact no disagreement need be present. *Minhat Eleazar* 3:31 (by R. Hayyim Eleazar Shapira), while it does deal with bankruptcy, is discussing a situation where the nation's own bankruptcy laws allow for future collection. So too, *Avnei Tzedek*, *Hoshen Mishpat* 2 (by R. Yekutiel Teitelbaum), deals only with the limited issue of whether debt forgiveness has occurred, and not the relationship between *dina de-malkhuta* and secular law. For more on the issue of bankruptcy, see Steven Resnicoff, "Bankruptcy—A Viable Halachic Option?" *J. Halacha & Contemporary Society* 24:5–54 (1992). This author is aware of only one published responsum which unambiguously rules secular bankruptcy to be unavailable to an individual according to Jewish law; see R. Yaakov Breish, *Helkat Yaakov* 2:160. From the perspective of a lawyer, it is sufficient that the client's conduct be tenably within the normative parameters of Jewish law in order to allow the lawyer to unquestionably assist the client; to the extent a violation of Jewish law is occurring when bankruptcy is filed it is by the debtor. The lawyer merely assists.

purpose is to benefit society as a whole and not to create rules of individual dispute resolution even though such rules have incidentally been created. For example, the United States Environmental Protection Agency, in the process of seeking funds to pay for environmental cleanup of toxic waste dumps, can reorder the priority of liens on a property so as to insure adequate funds to pay for a cleanup. This type of reorganization frequently affects the rights of private parties.[9] Once a plan of this type is approved, a strong claim could be made that Jewish law recognizes the reorganization of the obligations even between the original Jewish landowner and Jewish lienholder for the same reasons explained in Rabbi Feinstein's responsum concerning bankruptcy. Furthermore, in such a case a Jew may litigate in secular court against the government or its agents (even if the specific agent is Jewish) to enforce his societal, rather than individual, rights—even if the outcome of the case affects the private rights of other Jewish parties. The reverse is true as well; a lawyer may work for the government to defend the government in any situation in which the government is acting in accordance with Jewish law's understanding of its proper role. In a situation where the government is acting improperly, unjustly, or beyond its mandate, such a case is analogous to assisting in an improper litigation, which is discussed in chapter seven.

Thus, there are vast areas of law that are simply outside the scope of the prohibition to litigate in secular court. Besides those "hard cases"

---

9 See 42 U.S.C. §9607–08. So too, any litigation which requires the plaintiff to function as a *qui tam* (*qui tam pro domino rege quam pro se simpos sequitur* "who brings the action as well for the King as for himself") litigant may be brought in secular court. This conclusion is buttressed by the realization that one who sues *qui tam* does not act in his own name, but in the name of the government. For more on this, see Evan Caminker, "The Constitutionality of *Qui Tam* Actions," *Yale L.J.* 99:341, 343 (1989), which states: "Congress recently revitalized the *qui tam* framework in the False Claims Act.... [T]he Act has authorized both public law enforcement officers and all private citizens to sue *on behalf of the United States* to recover damages and civil penalties for such fraudulent acts and to share in the recovery" (emphasis added).

Rabbi J. David Bleich, in a personal communication to this author, questions the correctness of this rule, and notes that it is quite possible that a *qui tam* litigant, while not in violation of the prohibition of litigating in secular court, would be in violation of other aspects of Jewish law if the scope of the government's action was not in fact subsumed under the rubric of a proper application of the "law of the land" (*dina demalkhuta*).

mentioned above, there is little doubt that such fields as tax law, immigration law, federal labor law, administrative law, and many others, may unquestionably be litigated in secular court against the government.[10]

The scope of the powers of the secular government under *dina de-malkhuta dina* ("the law of the land is the law"), while a critical issue to Jews, is a topic whose analysis is beyond the scope of this book.[11] Suffice it to say, however, that a lawyer may not assist a client in an action which is prohibited by the law of the land, and accepted by Jewish law as a proper application of the *dina de-malkhuta* principle, since the lawyer's conduct would normally also violate the law of the land.[12] So too, any time Jewish law recognizes as valid the authority of the secular government's laws and its authority to regulate conduct of Jewish citizens, it is permitted to aid that government in civil enforcement.[13]

---

10 Rabbi Bleich states:

  Moreover there are many areas of law entirely outside the ambit of the prohibition of [litigating in secular court] *lifneihem ve-lo lifnei arkhaot shel akum*. Immigration law and tax law are but two such examples.

  R. J. David Bleich, "A Letter to a Student," chapter five, at note 18.

11 For a complete analysis of these issues, see Shmuel Shilo, *Dina de-Malkhuta Dina* (1974). Undoubtedly, which theory one accepts as the basis for binding secular law affects the scope of its incorporation.

12 In fact there might be situations in which *dina de-malkhuta* is inapplicable, but a lawyer might nonetheless not aid a violation of the secular law because of his special promise (taken at the time of admission to the bar) to uphold the law (a promise which Jewish law might recognize as binding); see R. Eliezer Waldenberg, *Tzitz Eliezer* 13:81. In this case, even though the citizen's actions violating the law are halakhically permitted, the lawyer's conduct would be prohibited; see R. Alfred Cohen, "On Maintaining a Professional Confidence," *J. Halacha & Contemporary Society* 7:73, 78–81 (1984).

13 For more on this, see chapter 11 and R. Moshe Feinstein, *Iggerot Moshe, Hoshen Mishpat* 1:92.

  Sema (*Hoshen Mishpat* 369:21), quoting a responsum of Rabbi Adret, which is quoted in part by *Darkei Moshe*, asserts that the obligation to obey the law of the land is limited to pronouncements from the king (executive) and not pronouncements from the courts. This author is inclined to think that such a distinction is unworkable and irrelevant in the structure of current American government, with the legislative branch making law, the president/governor enforcing law and the judiciary interpreting law. Unlike other legal systems, both extant and throughout history, in America nearly all judicial opinions are now attempts to interpret legislative enactments, and not classical common law pronouncements of law absent any legislative intent. In a government so created, the distinction of *Rashba*—based essentially on the source of authority—is very difficult to apply. Except for the few areas of un-codified common law, all power is legislatively based, and all remaining judicial pronouncements are interpretations of those pronouncements. It would be difficult to argue that the statutes themselves are binding, but the interpretations of them advanced by the courts—which the legislator authorized to produce binding interpretation—are not binding.

Chapter Nine

Swearing and Oath-Taking

Oaths

According to Jewish law, a Jew should avoid taking verbal oaths (even where the Lord's name is not used)[1] as part of his or her daily life, and it has become accepted that one who is pious declines to take oaths, even if such action causes the loss of money owed.[2] Accordingly, Jewish tradition directs that, when possible, it is better to "affirm" rather than "swear." The Federal government, all fifty states within the union, as well as all other common law countries accept that an "affirmation" without any invocation of a deity has the same legal effect as an "oath," and secular courts allow all who desire to affirm rather than swear.[3] Thus, a lawyer should

---

1 Any time a person uses the language "I swear," even if the Lord's name is not mentioned, an oath has been taken. "I affirm" is not considered an "oath" according to Jewish law; see *Shulhan Arukh, Yoreh Deah* 237:1–3. Adding the phrase "so help me God", at the end of an affirmation changes the statement from an affirmation into an oath according to Jewish law. Written oaths are not generally recognized by most halakhic authorities as a form of oath or testimony; see *Shulhan Arukh, Hoshen Mishpat* 28:11 and 236:1; R. Eliezer Waldenberg, *Tzitz Eliezer* 7:50; but see R. Moshe Schreiber, *Hatam Sofer, Yoreh Deah* 220, 227. Nonetheless, it is the better practice to avoid even written oaths.

2 See *Gittin* 35a; Maimonides, *Shevuot* 12:12; *Shulhan Arukh, Orah Hayyim* 156:1. One of the significant influences Jewish law has had on the secular law in Israel is the abolition of the practice of swearing in witnesses. Unlike other common law countries, witnesses are not required to recite an oath or affirmation prior to giving testimony in Israel; see Laws of the State of Israel, XXXIV p. 231.

3 See generally, "Oaths and Affirmations," *Am. Jur. 2d* 58:1043 §3 ("No distinction is drawn between an oath and an affirmation"). For example, the Constitution of the

"affirm" rather than swear whenever an "oath" is required. So too, it is not problematic for a lawyer to subpoena a witness to testify (truthfully) even if the witness might choose to swear rather than affirm at the beginning of his testimony, as truthful swearing is only discouraged and not forbidden and, more significantly, the witness can choose to affirm and avoid any oath. Placing a person in a situation where he might violate Jewish law if he wishes, but he can easily choose a permitted alternative, is not a transgression of the prohibition to assist in a violation of Jewish law (*lifnei ivver*).[4]

Head Coverings

A related issue is taking an affirmation (or when permitted, an oath), by a man[5] not wearing a head covering, either a *kippah* (*yarmulke*) or some other head covering. First, one must establish when it is permissible for men to go without a head covering generally. A number of modern authorities have addressed this issue. The consensus is that if it is needed for functioning in business or in order to retain one's livelihood, it is permitted for a man to go without a head covering (perhaps only so long as the Lord's name is not invoked).[6] Indeed, a long list of esteemed decisors dating back nearly a thousand years can be found which label the wearing of a head covering during daily activity (other than prayer) as a proper custom, an

---

United States, in deference to those whose religious practice prohibits swearing, states that the President of the United States, when he takes his oath of office, may choose to affirm rather than swear; see United States Constitution Art. 2 §1.

4 R. Yaakov Ettlinger, *Binyan Tziyyon* 1:15; R. Moshe Schreiber, *Hatam Sofer, Yoreh Deah* 19. This assumes that the oath is not in the name of a particular deity, but rather uses the generic "god." For a rationale why it might be permitted to accept an oath by a gentile even in the name of a specific deity, see R. Moshe Feinstein, *Iggerot Moshe, Yoreh Deah* 1:71. As to the status of assisting a person in doing something permitted by law, but prohibited by tradition, see R. Ovadia Yosef, *Yehavveh Da'at* 1:10; 3:38.

5 For a discussion of the obligation of women to cover their hair, see my "Tradition, Modesty and America: The Obligation of Women to Cover their Hair," *Judaism* 40:79–87 (1991).

6 For a survey of the different approaches, see R. Yaakov Hayyim Sofer, *Kaf ha-Hayyim* 2:n. 13–16; R. Yehiel Mikhel Epstein, *Arukh ha-Shulhan, Orah Hayyim* 2:10.

For a list of decisors who do not require a head covering (except perhaps during prayer) see R. Moshe Feinstein, *Iggerot Moshe, Orah Hayyim* 3:2, 2:25, 4:2, *Hoshen*

expression of humility and fear of Heaven, but not technically required according to Jewish law.[7]

The question of taking an oath or affirmation bareheaded has been addressed by a number of authorities. While some prohibit such oaths,[8] most allow them if it is absolutely necessary, since, according to technical Jewish law, a head covering is not required even in those circumstances.[9] This is even more true in America since an "oath" (or affirmation) which does not mention any god can be taken.[10] One interesting response to this question was given by Rabbi David Tzvi Hoffmann. He stated that a head covering is not absolutely required to take an oath, and he recounts that the general tradition among German Jews was not to wear a head covering while engaged in any non-Jewish activities. He states:

> From the comments of Rabbi Elijah of Vilna on *Orah Hayyim* 8:2, it appears that there is no prohibition even to use the Almighty's name while one is bare headed, but is only prohibited as a form of pious conduct.... Here in the community of *Frankfurt am Main* in

---

Mishpat 1:93, *Yoreh Deah* 2:33, 2:40(24); R. Azriel Hildesheimer, *She'elot u-Teshuvot Rabbi Azriel* 2:253; R. Tzvi Pesah Frank, *Har Tzvi* 3; R. Ovadia Yosef, *Yabia Omer*, *Orah Hayyim* 4:15, 52; R. Ovadia Yosef, *Yehavveh Da'at* 4:1 and R. Ovadia Hadaya, *Yaskil Avdi*, *Orah Hayyim* 1 (appendix).

For a more general survey of this topic that also confirms the conclusion found in the text, see Eric Zimmer, "Men's Headcovering: The Metamorphosis of this Practice," in *Reverence, Righteousness and Rahamanut: Essays in Memory of Rabbi Dr. Leo Jung* 325–351 (J. J. Schacter, ed., Northvale, 1992).

7   Maimonides, *Deot* 5:6; R. Abraham b. Nathan ha-Yarhi, *Sefer ha-Manhig* 1:84, 87 (Jerusalem, 1978); R. Judah ben ha-Rosh, *Zikhron Yehudah* 20 (Berlin, 1846); R. David Abudarham, *Abudarham ha-Shalem* 41 (Jerusalem, 1963); R. Eliezer ben Joel ha-Levi, *Sefer Raavyah* 2:145 (Jerusalem, 1966); R. Moshe Isserles, *Darkei Moshe*, *Orah Hayyim* 8:4 (Jerusalem, 1993); and R. Shlomo Luria, *She'elot u-Teshuvot Maharshal* 72 (Lemberg, 1859).

8   See R. Yitzhak Wolf, *Nahalat Binyamin* 30.

9   See R. Hayyim Benveniste, *Knesset ha-Gedolah*, *Yoreh Deah* 157, and R. David Tzvi Hoffmann, *Melammed le-Ho'il* 2:56, for a list of authorities who permit this.

10 This is analogous to the insights of Rabbi Feinstein in regard to bare headed "prayer" in the public schools where he states that "the rulers of our nation are accommodating and do not wish to impose their faith on citizens of different faiths. They therefore wrote a document of a non-sectarian nature...and thus there is no problem with reciting it bare headed;" Rabbi Moshe Feinstein, *Iggerot Moshe*, *Orah Hayyim* 2:25.

the school started by the Rabbinic giant Rabbi Samson Raphael Hirsch (where I [Rabbi Hoffmann] taught for two and a half years) the students study their secular studies bareheaded, and it is only while studying Judaica that they cover their heads. (This is also the tradition in the Hamburg schools.) This was all done under the direction of Rabbi Hirsch.[11]

Thus, the consensus opinion is that an affirmation (or oath) may be taken bareheaded if such is needed.[12]

It is worth noting that while Rabbi Hoffmann permits such oaths, he advises witnesses that they should request permission from the judge to cover their head while taking an oath. In the United States such permission will be granted and, when possible, should be requested.[13]

---

11 R. David Tzvi Hoffmann, *Melammed le-Ho'il* 2:56.
12 Such a conclusion is also found in R. Yehiel Mikhel Epstein, *Arukh ha-Shulhan, Orah Hayyim* 2:10.
13 See 42 U.S.C. § 2000bb-1 ("The Religious Freedom Restoration Act"). However, it is important to understand that the reason most lawyers wish to go barehaded has changed from the time of Rabbi Hoffmann, in that the pressures that are felt are social in nature and not legal. Rabbi Hoffmann himself, in this same responsum, recognizes the permissibility of going bare headed merely as a mark of respect, and notes that such was the practice in certain circumstances of Rabbi Samson Raphael Hirsch.

Chapter Ten

Examination of Witnesses

Repeating Harmful Information and Truth-Telling

Lawyers, like all Jews, are prohibited from speaking falsely or derogatorily about people without just cause. Three distinctly different things are forbidden: making unflattering, but true, remarks about a person for no reason; recounting to a person gossip heard about him; and knowingly communicating false, negative statements about another.[1] Many lawyers, for whom giving advice is a central part of their professional life, must know when it is permissible (or prohibited) to repeat negative comments heard about another. The details of when this type of conduct is prohibited and when it is mandated have been addressed numerous times and are beyond the scope of this book.[2] In order for a lawyer to repeat damaging information about another, most authorities mandate that a five-part test must be satisfied. These five parts are:

(1) The lawyer must not exaggerate the truth;

(2) The lawyer must be motivated by a desire to aid the client;

(3) The least damaging means must be employed;

---

1 In Hebrew, the first is called *lashon hara*; the second, *rekhilut* and the third, *motzi shem ra*; see Maimonides, *Deot* 7:1–7, where these distinctions are cleady articulated. For the classical work on this, see generally, R. Israel Meir Kagan, *Hafetz Hayyim*.

2 For a general discussion of giving advice within the rubric of activity discouraged because of the mandate of *Avot* 1:8, see chapter two of this book.

(4) The lawyer must instruct the client not to repeat this information to others; and

(5) The lawyer must contemplate his course of conduct considerably and only recount information that needs to be repeated.[3]

Truth-Telling in Court

One particular issue, however, is unique to lawyers. When may one, in the process of litigation, expose a person's prior misdeeds to undermine the credibility of his testimony? It is accepted that a lawyer may, in the process of cross-examining a witness, subject the witness to questioning if such questioning seeks to demonstrate that the witness is not telling the truth or the complete truth, even if (or because) that embarrasses the witness.[4] However, it is prohibited for a lawyer to undermine the credibility of a witness whom the lawyer knows is telling the truth, in order to cast false doubt on the truthfulness of the testimony. That would seem to be a violation of the Bible's commandment of "distancing oneself from falsehood,"[5] as well as embarrassing another in public for no valid reason.[6] Many violations of these rules also violate the Code of Professional Responsibility for lawyers, which prohibits the presentation of evidence designed to mislead the jury, judge, or other litigants.[7]

A lawyer may not cooperate with a client's desire to present a defense which falsely exonerates the client in a civil matter.[8] Thus, when a client

---

3 R. Israel Meir Kagan, *Hafetz Hayyim*, *Rekhilut* 9:1–15 and *Lashon Hara* 10:1–17. There is no requirement of personal knowledge, and reliable hearsay may be repeated.

4 To rule to the contrary would prevent truth-seeking in many court proceedings, since pronouncement of a verdict frequently reveals one of the litigants to be a liar.

5 Exodus 23:7.

6 *Sotah* 10b; see also *Bava Metzia* 58b. *Shevuot* 30b-31a recounts examples of the obligation to distance oneself from falsehood (*midvar sheker tirhak*) in a legal proceeding. It is possible that it may be permitted to cast false doubt on the truthfulness of a portion of a person's testimony, if that is needed to undermine the viability of other sections of his testimony which actually are false. For similar cases, see *Shulhan Arukh*, *Hoshen Mishpat* 4:1 and 28:11.

7 Model Code of Professional Responsibility DR7–102 (A)(4).

8 A false defense is presented when a client seeks to deny liability based upon the plaintiff's inability to prove his case in a court of law or through the client's committing perjury.

comes to a lawyer and states that he is being sued for refusing to repay a loan, and the client states that he did in fact borrow the money from the plaintiff, but the whole transaction was oral and the plaintiff cannot prove the occurrence of the loan, a lawyer may not present this defense in court since the client must actually deny the loan to triumph at law. So too, it would appear that in a civil matter a lawyer cannot seek a demurrer and then summary judgment to permanently dismiss a case based on a failure of proof on the issue of liability if he knows that money is actually owed.

On the other hand, perhaps a lawyer can aid a client in a "false defense" if the client should, in fact, factually triumph and cannot prove his "true" defense, but can win on a false defense. However, this is true only if no perjury in actual court testimony is involved, as perjury is prohibited under nearly all circumstances.[9]

Indeed, while American law has no *migo*-like[10] alternative pleadings, and once one starts formal hearings, one must always state the truth, there are many situations where a lawyer could assist a client in a false defense

---

For a discussion of these issues in the context of criminal law, see chapters eleven and twelve.

9   For example, assume "A" lends "B" money without witnesses or documentation, and "B" repays the loan in the same manner. In Jewish law, if "A" sues "B" alleging that "B" never repaid the loan, "B" could present the alternative defense that he never borrowed the money (if no perjury were involved) if the true defense would not triumph at law; see *Shulhan Arukh, Hoshen Mishpat* 4:1–2.

The classical common law example of this phenomenon is referred to as the "Case of the Kettle" and involves a plaintiff who sought damages for a kettle which he claimed the defendant had borrowed and cracked while using. The defendant is supposed to have pleaded in reply to the allegation that: "(1) he did not borrow the kettle; (2) the kettle was never cracked; and (3) it was cracked when he borrowed it." For more on this, see Gregory Hankin, "Alternative and Hypothetical Pleadings," *Yale L.J.* 33:365, 369, 373–77 (1933).

10 Unlike Jewish law, American law lacks the institution called *migo*, which allows a defendant to assert a false, but provable, claim in court as just that—a false but provable claim, whose viability should allow a defendant to triumph. The mechanism of *migo* in financial cases is commonly misunderstood by beginning students of Jewish law. Essentially, *migo* is a sophisticated pleading in the alternative, in which a defendant states that since he has a legally provable defense that would allow him to triumph in court if he wished to disregard the ethical obligation of justice, that false defense, coupled with defendant's sincere claim that he has a truthful defense (that he cannot prove) is sufficient in Jewish law to allow the defendant to triumph. (For example, if "A" borrowed $100 from "B" without any loan documentation and repaid the loan in the same way, then when "B" sues "A" for payment of the loan, "A" would

where the client maintains that an unprovable—but true—defense is present. That occurs at the vast negotiations stages of litigation, where claims are frequently settled based on the apparent (but perhaps incorrect) strength of an opponent's claim. At that stage, one could assist in a false defense designed to reach the just result.[11]

---

claim that he already paid the loan. The court should believe him on that unprovable claim, because he has a very strong *migo* claim—that he never borrowed the money—which, if he were to assert, would allow him to prevail.)

It is important to realize (and this is commonly overlooked) that in order for a *migo* claim to be valid, the false claim must be one that the defendant would triumph with if the case and the false defense were actually litigated in court. If the *migo* claim can be defeated by the plaintiff through the presentation of evidence, then it is of no value. Jewish law essentially rewards the defendant for his honesty in labeling his provable defense as false, by allowing him to press it anyway. The common law tradition in that case simply encouraged perjury. For more on this, see R. Oded Lipa Levfar, *Mishpetei ha-Migo*.

(The term *migo* is also used in the Talmud in reference to a different type of pleading. There are cases where Jewish law permits a person, in the area of ritual or personal law, to assign themselves a status that does not reflect their actual status. Thus, a person who asserts that he is divorced is treated with the strictures of one who actually is divorced even if a review of the record would lead one to conclude that this claim is false. In this situation, while the Talmud uses the same term (*migo*), it is referring to a completely different type of pleading issue, unrelated to the alternative fictitious pleading in civil cases addressed here. For more on this fundamental distinction, see the approbation of Rabbi Shimon Briesh, printed at page i of *Mishpetei ha-Migo*.)

11 The material in chapters nine and ten (which deal with oath-taking and examining witnesses) are equally applicable to the next unit (criminal law) as they are to this unit dealing with civil litigation.

Practicing Criminal Law

Three distinct issues are involved in a Jewish law discussion of an attorney practicing criminal law: When is it permissible to inform upon a person for committing a crime and to serve as a witness at the trial? May one prosecute criminals? May one represent a person who has been accused of a crime, and what types of defenses can one present? Each of these issues will be explored at some length in the next two chapters.

Chapter Eleven

Prosecuting Criminals

Introduction

The question of whether one can be a prosecutor, witness or informant are, in their core, a single question—does Jewish law permit, prohibit, or mandate that a person inform governmental authorities of the fact that a Jew is violating one aspect or another of secular law. If one can inform the government, then it seems quite clear that one may prosecute, and the reverse as well. In discussing contemporary practice, this chapter will focus on the application of the classical rules of informing (*mesirah*) to modern day America, with its (procedurally) just system of government.[1]

---

1 The problems associated with informing are not unique to Jewish law. Every legal system confronts cases in which individuals use other legal systems improperly to resolve disputes. Consider the case of *Eastman Kodak v. Kavlin*, 978 F.Supp 1078 (S.D. Florida, 1997), which is a most fascinating example of the tort of informing in American law. The matter involves the Kavlin company, which was the sole licensee of Kodak products in Bolivia. Kodak sought to terminate this relationship in 1995, and Kavlin responded by filling a criminal complaint against Kodak's representative in Bolivia placing him in prison *prior to conviction* by the local Bolivian judge. (Kavlin's attorney was both the godfather of and the brother to the mother of the Bolivian judge's illegitimate child.) Kodak alleged that Kavlin brought the Bolivian criminal charges in order to extort an advantageous financial arrangement with Kodak, which in fact settled the claim against Kavlin on excellent terms in order to extract its employee from the local prison in Bolivia. The United States District Court Judge observed that the prison where Kodak's representative was incarcerated for eight days (the infamous La Paz prison) is "a place barely fit for the rats it houses." Here Kodak's representative was:

> sharing a filthy cell with murderers, drug dealers, and AIDS patients. Left without food, a blanket, or protection from the inmates, he was forced to bribe his way to survival. Prisoners ran the prison, and murdered each other....

Besides this introduction, this chapter is divided into two main sections. The first briefly explains the central principles related to informing and summarizes the *halakhah* as found in the *Shulhan Arukh* and decisors (*poskim*). The second section explores the various positions taken by modern decisors in regard to the prohibition to inform when society and government are just. A brief conclusion follows.

"Informing" is itself not a sufficiently precise translation of the Hebrew term[2] that is the concern of this chapter. Jewish law discusses three different problems: informing a bandit that a person has money or some other item of value, informing an abusive government of the same, and informing the government that someone has violated its laws. As is obvious to anyone with even a vague familiarity with the flow of Jewish history, Jews have generally lived in situations where government was unjust (or unjust towards Jews) or where bandits formed the basis for government. Thus, telling the abusive government that a Jew had money or that a Jew had broken the law was a dangerous act. Indeed, this conduct clearly, readily, and directly caused people to have their money taken; themselves beaten or tortured; and sometimes simply murdered. The Talmudic Sages had no choice but to enact rabbinic decrees prohibiting such informing.[3] This chapter confronts the modern variation thereof—how do these classical rules impact on a lawyer working for a just government, where government only acts to punish law-breakers.

As will become clear throughout this work,[4] this chapter is *not* discussing the proper response to violent criminals or people whose conduct endangers other people or the community as a whole.[5] Even in unjust soci-

---

Kodak and its representative sued Kavlin in Federal District Court in Florida alleging that Kavlin improperly informed upon Kodak's representative to the Bolivian authorities who tortured this employee, and are thus tortiously liable for the damage to Kodak and its representative. The matter was settled out of court after the district court judge allowed the lawsuit to proceed. For a discussion of the balancing problems involved in informing from a modern American law perspective, see Jack Weinstein, "The Informer: Hero or Villain?—Ethical and Legal Problems," *New York Law Journal* (Nov. 8, 1982) 1, col. 3.

2 The exact Hebrew term that is generally used is *mesirah*, although sometimes the word *malshin* is used.

3 See *Bava Kamma* 115b–117b.

4 See text accompanying notes 23 to 24, and *Shakh, Hoshen Mishpat* 388:20, and *Pithei Hoshen* 5:4, section 6.

5 Endangering the community is not limited to cases of communal punishment or immediate short term danger. Rabbi Yitzchak Adlerstein notes the following incident

eties, it was clear that one must bring such people to the attention of the secular authorities, if that was the only way to get them to cease their violent ways. Thus there is no issue in serving as a witness, prosecutor, or informant in such cases.[6] This chapter is discussing the problems of serving as a prosecutor, witness, or informant as it relates to violators of non-dangerous law or non-violent or regulatory laws, from cat-burglars and tax cheaters to zoning violators and prescription drug abusers. This chapter is *not* discussing serial killers, armed robbers, sexual predators, or muggers. They must all be informed upon if that is needed to protect society from them.[7]

---

recounted to him by Rabbi Mordecai Kaminetsky, in the name of Rabbi Ya'akov Kaminetsky.

There was a period in the 1970's when a group of rogues were smuggling valuables in *tefillin* (phylacteries) and other religious articles that would usually evade inspection; thus the thieves assumed their scheme would be successful. Often they would send these religious articles with unsuspecting pious Jews and asked to deliver them to certain locations near their final destinations. When United States customs officials got wind of this scheme they asked a few observant agents to help crack the ring. In addition to preserving the sanctity of the religious items, the customs authority felt that Jewish religious agents would best be able to mete out knowing accomplices from unsuspecting participants who had been duped into thinking they were actually performing a *mitzvah*.

The Jewish custom agent in charge of the operation decided to confer with my grandfather, Rabbi Ya'akov Kaminetsky on this matter. Though his advice on how to break the ring remains confidential, he told me how he explained how the severity of the crime was compounded by its use of religious items.

"Smuggling diamonds in *tefillin*," he explained, "is equivalent to raising a white flag, approaching the enemy lines as if to surrender and then lobbing a grenade. That soldier has not only perpetrated a fraud on his battalion and the enemy; he has betrayed a symbol of civilization. With one devious act, he has destroyed a trusted symbol for eternity—forever endangering the lives of countless soldiers for years to come. These thieves, by taking a sacrosanct symbol and using it as a vehicle for a crime have destroyed the eternal sanctity and symbolism of a sacred object. Their evil actions may cause irreparable damage to countless honest religious people. Those rogues must be stopped, by any means possible," he exclaimed.

6   According to many, but not all decisors, it would be better that there be a functioning Jewish court that would address these matters indigenously consistent with Jewish law; however this is unavailable in many historical eras, including our own. See, R. Yitzhak bar Sheshet Profiat (*Rivash*) 387 (page 115, column 3), Raphael Alnaqua (*Pa'amonei Zahav*), *Hoshen Mishpat* 26, 388 and *Pithei Hoshen*, 5:4 (n18).

7   This chapter is not really even discussing the question of whether one may inform on another whose conduct recklessly endangers people without malicious intent, such as a person with uncontrolled epilepsy who hides that fact from the government when

Classical Jewish Law and Informing: An Overview

Even though Jewish law expects people to observe the law of the land, and even imposes that obligation as a religious duty,[8] the Talmud recounts—in a number of places—that it is prohibited to inform on Jews to the secular government. While there are a number of exceptions to this prohibition (which are explained further in this section), the essential *halakhah* was that Jewish law prohibits such informing absent specific circumstances. Even if secular government were to incorporate substantive Jewish law into secular law and punish violations of what is, in effect, Jewish law, Jews would still be prohibited from cooperating with such a system.[9] Indeed, classical Jewish law treats a person who repeatedly informs on others as a pursuer (*rodef*) who may be killed even without a formal court ruling so as to prevent him from informing.

The prohibition of informing derives from three different talmudic incidents,[10] whose central theme is that informing on a Jew so that others take the property of the one informed upon is both prohibited and tortious. One of the talmudic incidents[11] clarifies that the act of informing causes one to be classified in the formal status of a pursuer (*rodef*), whose life may be taken to prevent the act of informing from occurring.

The reason for the rabbinic decree positing that an informer (*moser*) is a life-threatening pursuer (*rodef*) is simply stated by Rabbenu Asher (*Rosh*):

> One who runs to inform so that Jewish money is given to a bandit (*anas*)[12] is analogized by the rabbis to one who is running after a

---

seeking a driver's license; see e.g., R. Moshe Sternbuch, *Teshuvot ve-Hanhagot* 1:850 (the authorities may be apprised of one who drives recklessly or without a license).

8 See *Shulhan Arukh*, *Hoshen Mishpat* 369:8.

9 Consider a secular government that makes it a violation of secular law for a person to cut down fruit trees for no purpose (which is also a violation of Jewish law); Jewish law would prohibit informing the secular government of such a violation.

10 See Mishnah, *Bava Kamma* 116b, *Gittin* 7a and *Bava Kamma* 117a-b.

11 *Bava Kamma* 117a, where a talmudic Sage actually killed one who was going off to inform on another.

12 Precisely translating the word *anas* is important but hard. The word denotes an illicit oppressor. Thus, a rapist is an *anas*, as is an armed robber. A cat burglar would not be called an *anas*.

person to kill him. This is seen from the verse (Isaiah 51:20) "your children lie in a swoon at the corner of every street, like an antelope caught in a net." Just like when an antelope is caught in a net, the hunter has no mercy towards it, so too the money of a Jew, once it falls into the hands of bandits, the bandits have no mercy on the Jew. *They take some money today, and tomorrow all of it, and in the end they capture and kill him, since perhaps he has more money. Thus, an informer is like a pursuer to kill someone, and the victim may be saved at the cost of the life of the pursued.*[13]

According to Rabbenu Asher, informing can be worse than any other act which improperly damages another Jew because the resulting harm—often deadly—is not appropriate for the initial transgression—often only a small money matter. Once one is enmeshed with these types of people, one never can tell what will happen and even death can result. Thus one who informs is like a pursuer (*rodef*) who may cause the death of others.

Mordecai states the matter differently. He writes:

Even though as a general matter we do not push into a pit [to kill] any tort-feasor, even a thief or an armed robber, *the reason an informer is different is that the pagans gain and the Jews lose through this conduct; this is disgusting, and one who regularly trains himself to engage in such informing to pagans—his status is worse than other tort-feasors.*[14]

According to Mordecai, informing is different from any other act which damages another because the Rabbis decreed that a person who regularly involves himself in ensuring that Jews lose and gentiles improperly gain is engaging in an evil activity and forfeits his normal rights as a Jew.

A complete review of the rules related to informing is both complex and beyond the scope of this paper,[15] but a simple understanding of the

---

13 *Teshuvot ha-Rosh* 17:1 (Emphasis Added).

14 *Mordecai, Bava Kamma, ha-Gozel* §117 (Emphasis Added).

15 For a more complete review, see *Pithei Hoshen*, Volume 5, Chapter 4 and R. Ezra Batzri, *Dinei Mamonot 4:5*.

The question that is worthy of pondering is the relationship between the obligation to redeem captives (found in *Shulhan Arukh, Yoreh Deah* 253) and the prohibition to inform. In cases where there is no prohibition to inform (as informing is permitted,

nuanced rules is needed to understand why a just government might be different.

Eight different sets of rules can be given that outline the general approach *halakhah* takes.

1. It is prohibited to inform on a fellow Jew to a gentile, whether the act of informing is about monetary matters or physical security.[16] One may not inform on a Jew, even if the Jew is a sinful and bad person.[17]

2. One who informs is liable to pay damages if his act of informing damages another.[18] As a general rule one is not liable for torts done to another by a third party; informing is an exception to this rule.[19]

---

see *Darkei Teshuvah* 157:53) a logical case can be made that there is no *mitzvah* to redeem captives (as they are in prison properly) when there is nothing wrong with informing. This exact observation is made in the name of Rabbi Shlomo Zalman Auerbach in *Ve'aleihu lo Yibol*, volume 2:113–114, which recounts in the name of Rabbi Yehuda Goldreicht:

> I asked Rabbi Auerbach about a particular Jew who stole a large sum of money and he was caught by the police in America. He was sentenced to a number of years in prison in America. Was it proper to assist in the collection of money for him [we were speaking about a large sum of $200,000] in order to fulfill the *mitzvah* of redeeming captives to have him released from prison?
>
> When Rabbi Auerbach heard this he stated "Redeeming captives?! What is the *mitzvah* of redeeming captives here? The *mitzvah* of redeeming captives is only when the gentiles are grabbing Jews, irrationally, for no proper reason, and placing them in prison. According to what I [Rabbi Auerbach] know, in America they do not irrationally grab Jews in order to squeeze money from them. The Torah says 'do not steal' and he stole money— on the contrary, it is good that he serve a prison sentence, so that he learns not to steal!"

16 *Shulhan Arukh, Hoshen Mishpat* 388:9 (one who informs is denied a place in the world to come).

17 *Shulhan Arukh, Hoshen Mishpat* 388:9.

18 *Shulhan Arukh, Hoshen Mishpat* 388:2, *Sema* 388:5 and R. Shabtai ben Meir HaKohen, *Siftei Kohen (Shakh)*, 388:13.

19 This is derived from the talmudic incident recounted in *Bava Kamma* 116b and the comments of *Rashi, ad locum* s.v. *de-ahve ahvi* who notes that the informing is without any direct act of the informer, but yet the informer is still liable. Even in cases where the informer is not generally liable (such as when the informer is coerced) if

3. Even without the order of a Jewish law court, one may kill a person who has certainly set out to inform on another, prior to their act of informing, as informing poses a danger to the one who is informed upon.[20] Once a person informs, one may not kill the informer as punishment for the sin, and one may not steal from an informer (unless taking his property will stop him from informing).[21] One who regularly informs may be killed without warning.[22]

4. One who troubles the community through misconduct may be informed upon; so too one who engages in conduct that endangers members of the community may be informed upon.[23] One who hits other people, or otherwise engages in acts of violence against people, may be informed upon.[24]

5. When a Jew owes money to a gentile, the Jew is seeking to improperly avoid payment of the money to the gentile, and another Jew informs the gentile of this fact who then collects the money rightfully owed to him, that is not called informing, as the Jew who is informed upon only has to pay that which he ought to pay anyway.[25] Payment of taxes to the government is exactly such a debt.[26] Some say such informing is frowned on when it gratuitously benefits a pagan, and others say such conduct is proper.[27]

---

the informer actually takes the goods with his own hands from the Jew, the informer is generally liable; *Shulhan Arukh, Hoshen Mishpat* 388:2.

20 *Shulhan Arukh, Hoshen Mishpat* 388:10.

21 *Shulhan Arukh, Hoshen Mishpat* 388:11, 13.

22 *Shulhan Arukh, Hoshen Mishpat* 388:14. There is a dispute between various decisors about whether such a person may be killed directly or indirectly. Compare *Shulhan Arukh* with *Rema* on *ibid*.

23 *Shulhan Arukh, Hoshen Mishpat* 388:12 (troubles the community). Even a person who drives recklessly may be informed upon as such conduct endangers members of the community. See note 70.

24 *Rema, Shulhan Arukh, Hoshen Mishpat* 388:7, and R. Shabtai ben Meir HaKohen, *Siftei Kohen* (*Shakh*), 388:45.

25 *Rema, Shulhan Arukh, Hoshen Mishpat* 388:12.

26 R. Shabtai ben Meir HaKohen, *Siftei Kohen* (*Shakh*), *Hoshen Mishpat* 388:20 and *Pithei Hoshen* 5:4:15 (n44).

27 Compare *Ba'er ha-Golah, Hoshen Mishpat* 388:(*ayin*) (proper to report) with *Rema, Shulhan Arukh, Hoshen Mishpat* 388:12 (improper to report). This is because—even

All agree that when such conduct leads to a desecration of God's name, it is prohibited to decline to report such a person.[28]

6. A Jew who is threatened with physical harm unless he informs on another is not called an informer if he delivers information, and he is not liable for the damage causes.[29] There is a dispute as to whether such conduct is proper or simply immune from liability.[30]

7. There is a dispute about whether a Jew who is threatened with economic harm unless he illicitly informs on another is called an informer or not and whether such conduct is permitted or not.[31]

8. Many authorities rule that no liability is present if one informs on another to save one's own property without any gratuitous intent to hurt the other person.[32]

---

when there is no sin in helping a gentile, *halakhah* nonetheless directs that one should not involve oneself in matters where one need not be involved when a Jew loses and a bad gentile (pagan) or an apostatized Jew benefits. Thus, when one finds the lost object of a pagan, one should not return it to him, unless one is in a situation where either that is one's job, or one derives some other benefit, or doing such is a sanctification of the Creator's name, or not doing such is a desecration of the Almighty. For more on this, see Michael Broyde and Michael Hecht, "The Gentile and Returning Lost Property According to Jewish Law: A Theory of Reciprocity" *Jewish Law Annual* XIII 31–45 (2000).

28 *Bava Kamma* 113b, immediately following the passage which imposes no duty of restoration of the gentile's lost property, quotes the statement of R. Pinhas b. Yair: "Whenever the danger of causing a desecration of God's name exists, even the retaining of a lost article (of the gentile) is forbidden." Both Rambam and *Shulhan Arukh* incorporate this statement into the Jewish law as limiting the general rule, and requiring one to return such property. Rambam, *Gezelah V'Avedah* 11:3; *Shulhan Arukh, Hoshen Mishpat* 266:1. Moreover, *Shulhan Arukh* states that the return of a gentile's lost property where such an act would be likely to result in sanctification of God's name reflecting credit upon the Jew and his faith, merits the highest religious praise.

29 *Shulhan Arukh, Hoshen Mishpat* 388:2–3.

30 Compare *Sema, Hoshen Mishpat* 388:13 (such conduct is prohibited, but generates no liability) with *Taz, Hoshen Mishpat* 388:3 (*s.v. harei ze patur*) (such conduct is completely proper and without sin).

31 Compare *Rema, Hoshen Mishpat* 388:3 (liable) with R. Shabtai ben Meir HaKohen, *Siftei Kohen* (*Shakh*), 388:22 (exempt).

32 See *Rema, Shulhan Arukh, Hoshen Mishpat* 388:5; Responsa of Rema 88 endorses the view that informing, when done to save one's own property is not considered informing. See also Responsa of Maharshal 19.

Taken at face value, these rules would prohibit a person from calling the governmental authorities when he is aware of illicit activity by a Jew unless the informer is himself under duress to inform, the criminal is violent or threatening of the community, or according to some decisors, the informer does so to protect his own property.[33] (In cases of desecration of God's name, informing is also sometimes permitted.) These rules, by their simple direct application, would prevent a person from informing on his neighbor who is cheating on his taxes (since the government imprisons such people, and does not merely retake the money owed), violating a non-safety related zoning law, stealing cable television from the cable company, and a host of other violations of American law. Informing on a serial killer, mugger, assaulter, child abuser, or any other violent criminal would be permitted.[34]

These rules also would generally discourage a person from acting as a lawyer or a witness in all cases where informing was prohibited.

The next section considers whether according to Jewish law the application of the laws of informing are different for just governments.

Informing on People When Government is Committed to Procedural Justice: Five Opinions of Contemporary Decisors

How do the halakhic rules of informing apply to a just government of laws—with non-discriminatory laws properly enforced by police who obey the laws, and who punish people in accordance with its laws—is the question this section will address. This section is predicated on the following assumptions about the nature and operation of American law, its society, and its government.

---

33 For general sources to the above statements, see the rules above. For specific sources see, *Shulhan Arukh, Hoshen Mishpat* 388:2–3 (when an informer is himself under physical duress to inform and does so inform, no liability follows); *Shulhan Arukh, Hoshen Mishpat* 388:12 and R. Shabtai ben Meir HaKohen, *Siftei Kohen* (*Shakh*), 388:45 (permitting informing when the criminal is violent or threatening of the community); *Rema, Shulhan Arukh* 388:5 (according to some decisors, when one informs to protect his own property that is not informing).

34 See note 6 for a discussion of whether using a Jewish court, if available, is better.

(1) The government of the United States of America and of the various states and other governmental units are just and proper governments that do not, as a general matter, punish people beyond the dictates of the secular law.[35] They are not corrupt governments.[36]

(2) Governmental actions in America are not generally motivated by anti-Semitism, and the conduct of governmental officials is not anti-Semitic.[37]

(3) As a matter of American law, people cannot be compelled to go to a Jewish law court (a *bet din*) to resolve claims against them if they do not wish to submit to the authority of *bet din*.

(4) As a matter of American law, *batei din* are unable to adjudicate matters that require physical punishment, incarceration or restraint of people, and cannot respond in emergency situations when force is needed.

As will be shown throughout this section, disagreeing with any one of these four factual points will frequently lead to significant changes in the applicable Jewish law of informing.

---

35 However, it is important to add that while secular law punishes people without any anti-Semitic overtones, still the punishments meted out are not—typically—the punishments directed by Jewish law.

36 Measuring corruption is a complex matter, and beyond the scope of this author's expertise. There is a well respected international organization that has examined this issue for the last ten years named "The Center for the Study of Corruption" run by Transparency International <www.transparency.org> which annually publishes a measure of the corruption in all major countries. Ninety-one countries are ranked. Corruption is defined as "the abuse of public office for private gain," which is similar to the definition used by the *Arukh ha-Shulhan*. The survey used in compiling the corruption index asks questions "in line with the misuse of public power for private benefits, with a focus, for example, on the bribing of public officials or giving and taking of kickbacks in public procurement." The top 25 counties are generally viewed as without corruption. They are (in alphabetical order): Australia, Austria, Belgium, Canada, Chile, Denmark, Finland, France, Germany, Hong Kong, Iceland, Ireland, Israel, Japan, Luxembourg, Netherlands, New Zealand, Norway, Portugal, Singapore, Spain, Sweden, Switzerland, United Kingdom, USA.

37 Of course, one should not misunderstand assumptions one and two to posit that the secular government never makes mistakes or never acts corruptly or has no employees whose conduct is anti-Semitic. Rather, one cannot assume that to be true. Indeed, one can assume to the contrary, as this chapter posits.

As a general proposition, members of our secular society are not obligated, according to American criminal or tort law, to report violators of American law.[38] In modern American law, unlike Jewish law, if one did not cause the violation or have some other special relationship either to the victim or the criminal, one bears absolutely no legal obligation to intervene to stop a crime or even call the police.[39] In American law one need not report one's neighbor for tax fraud, or call the police when one witnesses a crime, or rescue a drowning person from a river. Thus, even in circumstances where Jewish law mandates that one not inform on a person, the person who has knowledge of criminal activity by another, and does not report it, is not violating American law at all. However, once one is summoned to testify, or even questioned by a government official, it is a crime to lie to a governmental official about a relevant matter.[40]

No less than five different halakhic answers have been presented with regard to whether the prohibition against informing applies in a just society. These five views can be summarized as follows:

---

38 See for example *In re The Liverpool Household Stores Ass'n*, 59 Law. Rep. 616, 617 (England, 1890) ("A misfeasance does not include a nonfeasance, and ... no complaint can be made ... of a sin of omission, as distinguished from one of commission...."); see also Restatement (Second) of Torts § 314 (1965) ("The fact that the actor realizes or should realize that action on his part is necessary for another's aid or protection does not of itself impose upon him a duty to take such action."). As one well known police officer stated "there is no law requiring citizens to report a crime ... or to stop a crime." quoted in Jennifer Bagby, "Justifications For State Bystander Intervention Statutes: Why Crime Witnesses Should Be Required to Call For Help," *Indiana Law Review* 33:571 at 572 (2000).

39 See Jessica R. Givelber, "Imposing Duties on Witnesses to Child Sexual Abuse: a Futile Response to Bystander Indifference," *Fordham Law Review* 67:3169–3205 (1999).

40 See for example 18 United States Code §1001 which states:

(a) Except as otherwise provided in this section, whoever, in any matter within the jurisdiction of the executive, legislative, or judicial branch of the Government of the United States, knowingly and willfully—

(1) falsifies, conceals, or covers up by any trick, scheme, or device a material fact;

(2) makes any materially false, fictitious, or fraudulent statement or representation; or

(3) makes or uses any false writing or document knowing the same to contain any materially false, fictitious, or fraudulent statement or entry;

shall be fined under this title or imprisoned not more than 5 years, or both.

(1) The rules of informing have not changed at all, as they are independent of the status of the government as just or unjust. Informing is thus only permitted in cases of harm to others, or any one of the exceptions permitting informing mentioned above.

(2) An informer is not a pursuer anymore, but informing is still a tort no different in nature than damaging a person's property with a baseball bat. One who informs on another without cause is liable for the damages caused.[41]

(3) Even a just government behaves improperly sometimes, or operates jails that are improper places, and the presence of even occasional improper behavior by government or its agents or in its prisons justifies the prohibition of informing. Thus, the rules of informing have not changed.

(4) There is no prohibition of informing to the secular government when the secular government is enforcing a law that Jewish law deems valid under "the law of the land is the law" or according to the obligation of gentiles to create a proper system of law (*dinim*).

(5) There is no prohibition of informing when government conduct is governed by law and order generally. The talmudic Sages prohibited informing to bandits and unjust governments only.

As has been made clear throughout this work—these five views are *not* discussing serial killers, armed robbers, sexual predators, muggers, or other similar violent criminals. They must all be prosecuted and it is proper to serve as a witness or informant in such matters.

The View of the Rabbi Eliezer Yehuda Waldenberg: No Prohibition to Inform when Government is Just

The view that the prohibition of informing does not apply to a government that protects property rights and is generally governed by law and order is first articulated in the writings of Rabbi Yehiel Mikhel Epstein in his restatement of Jewish law, the *Arukh ha-Shulhan*. He states:

---

41 In a lesser form, one could even state that "recounting information is governed by the rules of *lashon hara* (idle gossip) and is no longer even a tort, but it still might be a sin in certain circumstances."

Note: As is widely known, in times of old in places far away, no person had any assurance in the safety of his life or money because of the pirates and bandits, even if they took upon themselves the form of government. It is known that this is true nowadays in some places in Africa where the government itself is grounded in theft and robbery. One should remind people of the kingdoms in Europe and particularly our ruler the Czar and his predecessors, and the kings of England, who spread their influence over many lands in order that people should have confidence in the security of their body and money. The wealthy do not have to hide themselves so that others will not loot or kill them. *On all of this [the presence of looting and killing] hinges the rules of informing [moser] and slandering [malshin] in the Talmud and later authorities, as I will explain infra: These rules apply only to one who informs on another to bandits and so endangers that person's money and life, as these bandits chase after the person's body and money, and thus one may use deadly force to save oneself.*[42]

The question of whether the writer of the *Arukh ha-Shulhan* really meant what he wrote or he wrote it for the sake of the censor is still a matter in dispute.[43] However, Rabbi Eliezer Waldenberg adopts the view of the

---

42 R. Yehiel Mikhel Epstein, *Arukh ha-Shulhan*, *Hoshen Mishpat* 388:7 (Emphasis Added). Perhaps a similar such statement can be found in the *Ba'er ha-Golah*, *Hoshen Mishpat* 388: (*ayin*), who writes:

> It has been already well accepted as a custom and decree that the leaders of the community, charged with a fiduciary duty, do not lie or commit fraud to the secular community, and they publicize and give permission to publicize and reveal to the secular community those individuals who buy on credit without expecting to pay, or borrow money without expecting to repay it.

43 This matter is extensively discussed by Justice Menachem Elon in "Extradition in Jewish Law" *Tehumin* 8:263–286, 304–309 (1988), Rabbi J. David Bleich, "Extradition," *Tehumin* 8:297–303 (1988), and Rabbi Shaul Yisraeli, "Extradition," *Tehumin* 8:287–296 (1988). While one can dismiss the words of the *Arukh ha-Shulhan* as put in for the censor, there are at least three logical reasons why one might conclude that the words in the text actually reflect the normative Jewish law view of the *Arukh ha-Shulhan*. They are:

(1) All apologetic remarks for the benefit of the censor in *Hoshen Mishpat* in the *Arukh ha-Shulhan* are found in star footnotes in italics at the bottom of the page. This passage is found in the text and not in italics.

Arukh ha-Shulhan explicitly. In the course of discussing whether one may inform on a teacher who is molesting children, Rabbi Waldenberg states:

> Even in the understanding of the secular court system it appears that there is a difference between primitive and enlightened governments as is noted by the *Arukh ha-Shulhan* in *Hoshen Mishpat* 388:7 where it states that "every issue related to informing found in the Talmud and *poskim* deals with those far away places where no one was secure in his money or body because of the bandits and pirates, even those who had authority, as we know nowadays in places like Africa" such is not the case in Europe, as the *Arukh ha-Shulhan* notes . . . *"I write this as a notation of general importance in the matter of the laws of informing."*[44]

The halakhic predicate for this view is that the repeated use of the term bandit (*anas*) throughout the many halakhic texts dealing with informing is to be limited to its simple meaning—it is only prohibited to inform on people to bandits. The many different rules restricting when one may inform on a Jew are limited to cases where the people to whom you are informing are unethical and unjust individuals or an unethical and unjust government.

Tur's language supports this. He states:

> *One who delivers another's money into the hands of a bandit, whether the bandit is Jew or Gentile*, must pay damages that he caused, since he caused a loss of money. . . .[45]

---

(2) His mention of the British government is unexplainable if directed to the censor. Britain and the Czar were not allies at this time, and he is clearly referring to the British democratic tradition.

(3) The *Arukh ha-Shulhan* gives a logical and halakhic explanation for his view, which he never does when speaking to the censor.

Indeed, this writer notes that one could almost state that if there is a hand of the censor, it is not in terms of the principle that informing does not apply to just governments, but to the *Arukh ha-Shulhan*'s remark that the Czar is such!

44 *Tzitz Eliezer* 19:52 (Emphasis Added). The genuineness of the view of the *Arukh ha-Shulhan* is also noted by Rabbi Gedaliah Dov Schwartz in "The Abused Child—Halakhic Insights," *Ten Da'at*, Spring 1988 at page 12. One could claim that the view of the *Bah*, as cited in the *Darkei Teshuvah* 157:53, is identical to that of the *Arukh ha-Shulhan*.

45 *Tur, Hoshen Mishpat* 388:2 (Emphasis Added).

A close examination of Rabbenu Asher's words quoted above[46] does indeed indicate that it is the fear of improper murder or torture of the victim that caused this rabbinic decree.

Rabbi Yosef Shalom Elyashiv explicitly adopts this logic in response to the following query:

> The office of Religious Affairs in our location has been robbed of collected money on more than one occasion. All of the indications point to one of the workers, but all of our efforts have not led this person to confess. We are asking if it is proper to call the police, who after investigation, if successful, will bring the suspect to secular court. The matter could be serious, as we suspect that the person is the father of a large family, and this person is connected to Torah activities; it is possible that there will be a desecration of God's name, Heaven forbid. On the other hand, public money is missing, and who knows what else is gone.

Rabbi Elyashiv replied:

> See *Responsa Panim Me'irot* 2:155 dealing with our matter of one who found an open chest, and much was stolen from it. There are reasonable grounds to believe that one of his workers did this act of theft. Is it permissible to inform on this worker to the secular authorities? He proves from *Bava Batra* 117 and *Bava Metzia* 25 that there is a religious duty on the judge of this matter to hit and punish based on the knowledge that he has, when his knowledge is correct. He then quotes from the incident with Rabbi Heshel and the view of the *Shakh* but he concludes "nonetheless I [the author of the *Panim Me'irot*] say that is it improper to report him to secular authorities, as our Talmud sages recount 'they treat him like a caught animal' and one must be afraid that they will kill him." From this it is clear that such is not applicable in our [Rabbi Elyashiv's] times. *By the* halakhah *it would be proper to report him to the police.* But, you ponder the possibility that this will lead to a desecration of God's name, and it is not in my ability to evaluate this, since I do not know the facts.[47]

---

46 See text accompanying note 13 for the Rosh.

47 Rabbi Sinai Adler, *Devar Sinai* 45–46 (Jerusalem, 5760). See also the view of Rabbi Shlomo Zalman Auerbach, quoted in note 15, which concludes "According to what

This view posits that when fear of death or torture that comes as a result of informing is functionally gone, the rabbinic decree prohibiting informing does not apply.[48] This is true according to these authorities even when the government has no right (according to Jewish law) to enforce this particular law on its Jewish citizens or is punishing them in a manner far beyond that permitted by Jewish law, and even applies when the government is arresting an apparently innocent person, as the system as a whole is just and fair. Even non-violent criminals or people who violate regulatory directives (such as zoning laws) may be informed upon, in this view.

This approach posits that informing—even when the government does (as a matter of after-the-fact truth) use the information provided by the informer to produce an improper result—is not a classical tort at all in the eyes of Jewish law, but was a special rabbinic decree prohibiting conduct that was not intrinsically tortious, and that rabbinic decree prohibiting informing was limited to situations of banditry.[49] Thus in situations where

---

> I [Rabbi Auerbach] know, in America they do not irrationally grab Jews in order to squeeze money from the. The Torah says "do not steal" and he stole money— on the contrary, it is good that he serve a prison sentence, so that he learns not to steal!" This approach must be predicated on the view of either Rabbi Waldenberg or Rabbi Wozner, infra, p. 101.

48 Measuring this type of a phenomenon is difficult and complex. Perhaps, by analogy, one can compare this to any other obligation to examine whether one need be fearful of the presence of an item or activity through statistical sampling. Consider, for example, a very simple matter: Must one check vegetables for insects? *Halakhah* divides the obligation to check into three categories: (1) Cases where most of the vegetables have insect infestation; (2) Cases where a statistically significant (but less than 50%) of the vegetables have insect infestation (*mi'ut hamatzuy*); (3) Cases where insect infestation is statistically very very unlikely (*mi'ut she'eino matzuy*). In cases one and two one must check for infestation, and in case three one need not; See *Shulhan Arukh*, *Yoreh Deah* 39:1 and *Be'ur ha-Gra*, *Yoreh Deah* 39:2. See *Mishkenot Ya'akov*, *Yoreh Deah* 16 for a discussion of what are the exact statistical ranges for each category. Although logic would indicate that "physical danger is more severe than sin," nonetheless, in cases where danger is so remote, these rules would apply. This chapter posits that the United States of America is in a case three situation (danger very unlikely) when it comes to physical danger prior to conviction.

49 Rabbi J. David Bleich writes:

> Jewish law also posits severe strictures against delivering either the person or property of a Jew to a gentile. Thus, *Shulhan Arukh* declares that the person and property of even a "wicked person" and a "transgressor" remain inviolate even if that individual is a source of "trouble" or "pain" to others. There is,

there is no prohibition to inform, there is no violation of Jewish law to inform. Any damage that is caused is not attributable to the informer but to the one who does the damage.

Of course, being a prosecutor or a witness would certainly be permissible. Since the conduct by the government is proper, being a prosecutor is proper, too.

The View of Rabbi Ezra Batzri: There Are No Just Legal Systems and No Just Prisons

Rabbi Ezra Batzri, in his modern multi-volume treatise on Jewish commercial law, *Dinei Mamonot*, responds to the view discussed in the *Arukh ha-Shulhan* above. After stating the view that informing is prohibited, he notes the following:

> Do not be surprised by the rules in this chapter, and think that they are inapplicable nowadays since governments are enlightened and democratic, a beacon for people to travel. This should be thought true of only by the very naïve, as even in democracies, in truth when there is a matter that involves the government, the matter is treated as out of the normal protocol as happens when matters relate to security of the state. *All rules of informing are applicable even currently.* Anyone who knows and understands and sees not only what is externally visible, and what previously was, will see that only the external appearance has changed—the outside has changed—but the central characteristic [of government] has not changed. *Even if they bring all matters to court, it is clear that, through interrogation and the police, government can destroy people and in many places they do, in fact, destroy people.*[50]

---

however, an inherent ambiguity in this proscription. There may be reason to assume that the prohibition is limited to turning over a person or his property to the custody of an "oppressor" who inflicts bodily or financial harm in a manner that is malevolent or entirely extralegal. Indeed, the terminology employed by the *Tur Shulhan Arukh* ("*Tur*") in codifying this provision of Jewish law lends credence to such a restrictive interpretation since *Tur* incorporates the term "*anas*" or "oppressor" in recording the prohibition.

Rabbi J. David Bleich, "Jewish Law and the State's Authority to Punish Crime," *Cardozo L.R.* 12:829, 830 (1991).

50 Rabbi Ezra Batzri, *Dinei Mamonot* 4:2:5n.1 on page 86 (Emphasis Added).

Rabbi Batzri posits that even when the external justice system seems to work, nonetheless the executive and judicial systems are so deeply fraught with exceptions, extra-judicial misconduct, and coerced confessions, that one must assume injustice will occur. Thus, informing on a fellow Jew remains generally prohibited, as always.[51]

Rabbi Ya'akov Yeshaya Blau, author of the multi-volume *Pithei Hoshen*, raises a related point as a possibility. Even if the justice system works up until the point of incarceration:

> nonetheless the punishment of imprisonment is analogous to endangering a person's life by informing on them in a way that endangers their life, *since imprisonment poses a possibility of life threatening conditions.*[52]

Rabbi Blau proposes the possibility that even if a justice system works only to incarcerate people who are deserving of incarceration, jail is a most unpleasant place to be, with physical duress exactly of the type the Talmud imagined, and thus informing on a person on a matter that might result in a prison sentence is prohibited.[53] Being a prosecutor would also be problematic.

Evaluating this type of claim is very difficult, but Rabbi Blau's observation has a certain amount of merit in this matter. One well known commentator on prisons in America observed:

> Prisons, never safe places, are growing increasingly dangerous to inmates. The most recent Department of Justice research shows that 14% of all prison inmates—and 20% of those under the age of 25 have been assaulted while in prison.[54]

---

51 This writer posits, but acknowledges that he cannot prove without a doubt, that this basic argument is factually incorrect in America.

52 *Pithei Hoshen* 7:4 in note 1, in the course of a lengthy discussion of this issue discussed above in note 44 (Emphasis Added).

53 Prison, thus, has the status of an indeterminate sentence (*mas she'ein lo kitzvah*, see *Rashba* 1:1105, and *Pithei Hoshen* Volume 5, Chapter 12, paragraph 5 in the notes) which is definitionally void according to Jewish law, in that in prison one is subject to random extra-judicial punishment by both the guards and fellow prisoners.

54 See John R. Williams, Representing Plaintiffs in Civil Rights Litigation Under Section 1983, 596 PLI/Lit 117, 160 (1998). See also Sharone Levy, "Balancing

According to Rabbi Blau, it is in prison where *halakhah* now fears that the *Rosh's* observations are correct—people are abused and tortured without any basis in law.

If the approach of either Rabbis Batzri or Blau is correct, one divides cases of informing into three types of categories. One category includes a person being informed upon who is a violent, or potentially violent individual who threatens violence, induces harm to others, or endangers the welfare of the community. Such a person may be informed upon, as Jewish law recognizes the need to remove these people from the community, even if these people might be harmed by the brutal prison system.[55] The second situation is that of the non-violent criminal (white collar crimes such as intentionally bouncing checks or recreational personal drug use). Because the incarceration presents a significant likelihood of brutality,[56] Jewish law rules that one may not inform on them to the police

---

Physical Abuse by the System against Abuse of the System: Defining "Imminent Danger" Within the Prison Litigation Reform act of 1995," 86 Iowa L. Rev. 361 (2000) which notes that:

> studies demonstrate that life in prison is becoming more dangerous, and prison violence is increasing. In 1996, the U.S. Department of Justice found that fourteen percent of all inmates were assaulted while serving prison sentences. Further, not all of these incidents occur between inmates. Guards often subject both male and female prisoners to rape and physical abuse.

55 See the text above accompanying notes 23 and 24.

56 Assuming that these numbers are correct, a very strong case can be made that abuse in prison is a statistically noticeable event and must be considered an event of some real possibility (a *mi'ut hamatzuy*) with all of the ramifications associated with that. See note 48 for more on this statistically. Consider how one would respond if a judge explicitly sentenced a non-violent felon to "three years in prison where he might be raped by fellow prisoners as part of his sentence." We would all recognize that such a sentence is wrong and improper and ought to be defied, even if that meant no punishment for such a person, as this was the only sentence government can actually provide. Rabbi Blau is arguing that such is exactly the reality of a prison sentence for a non-violent prisoner sent to a prison with violent inmates (as is the norm outside of the Federal prison system). See for example *Rape in Prison*, The New York Times, April 22, 2001, Section 4; Page 16; Column 1 which states:

> Because convicted criminals enjoy little public sympathy, *prison guards and wardens routinely turn a blind eye as prisoners in their custody commit vicious sexual assaults on their fellow inmates.* Out of sight and out of mind for most Americans, rampant sexual abuse behind prison walls scars its victims for life, transmits H.I.V. and mocks the constitutional prohibition against cruel and unusual punishment.

because the punishment imposed is unacceptable according to Jewish law. Other areas of informing, such as parking violations, building code violations, unintentional environmental damage, and the like, where arrest and detention is not a possibility, would not be prohibited by this rationale.

In this writer's opinion, this observation—that prisons are (sadly enough and to the shame of our society) treacherous places with tortious conditions incapable of punishing people justly—has a powerful practical logic to it and seems factually persuasive. If American society cannot run a criminal justice system that punishes non-violent criminals properly, Jewish law should not be an accomplice to a criminal justice system that in fact brutally punishes people for non-violent offenses. If this approach is correct, this certainly would impact on the actions of a lawyer who functions as a prosecutor and would seem to impose clear halakhic limits on his role.

The View of Rabbi Yitzchak Shmelkes: Informing as a Tort in a Just Government

Rabbi Yitzchak Shmelkes advances a novel answer to the question of informing in a just society. He states:

> As you wrote on the central matter of one who informs about monetary matters nowadays, *such a person does not have the status of a pursuer (*rodef*), as there is no fear, nowadays that such informing will lead to danger to life*, and certainly such a person is not ineligible to serve as a witness according to Torah law. . . .[57]

A disturbing new report by Human Rights Watch *documents how rape in America's prisons has become commonplace* ... An academic study of inmates in men's prisons in four Midwestern states found that as many as one in five prisoners reported at least one instance of forced sexual contact since being incarcerated. . . .

America's two million prison inmates have been lawfully deprived of their liberty, but they have not been sentenced to physical and psychological abuse. Yet Human Rights Watch found that prison authorities rarely investigate complaints of rape, and prison rapists rarely face criminal charges. *Most prisons make little effort to prevent sexual assaults and provide minimal attention for victims* (Emphasis Added).

57 *Beit Yitzhak, Yoreh Deah* 49(12) (Emphasis Added).

According to Rabbi Shmelkes, one must make a factual determination as to whether informing can lead to life threatening conditions. If it can, then informing leads to one being classified as a pursuer; otherwise, such conduct is a generic tort and while damages have to be paid, one is not considered a pursuer (*rodef*) because of such conduct. One might not even be deemed a "sinner" but merely a tort-feasor.

A similar such view is seemingly endorsed by Rabbi Ya'akov Yeshaya Blau, writing in the *Pithei Hoshen*, who states:

> In the writings of many decisors we have seen that they found some merit (*lamdu zekhut*) on the kings and governments of their time that the rules of informing did not apply. But it is widely known that in these kinds of works the hand of the censor is present. In circumstances they wrote (or left out) matters out of fear of the censor or the government, or at the least because of hatred of the Jews (*eivah*), and it is thus hard to learn from these sources. *Nonetheless, in my humble opinion, there is an acceptable aspect of this view [that informing does not apply in just society] since the essence of the prohibition to inform even on monetary matters is 'lest they come to kill you.'* It is clear that in a country where the government is just, even though informing is clearly prohibited, nonetheless there is no fear that they will kill you. Thus an informer is no different from any other damager of the property of another, and none of the strictures concerning informing which can result in physical duress apply. . . .[58]

To understand this view, one must accept that there are really at least two distinctly different components to the rules of informing: the tort component of damaging another, and the sin of endangering the life of another through informing. In a society where, in fact, there is no danger of life and limb through informing to the governmental authorities, the informer loses his status as a pursuer, according to the view of Rabbi Shmelkes.

Indeed—although Rabbi Shmelkes does not state so explicitly—when only the tort prohibition is present, the only reason informing is prohibited is because one is *improperly* damaging the property of another. Absent the danger—both economic and physical—informing becomes

---

58 *Pithei Hoshen* Volume 5, Chapter Four, note 1 (Emphasis Added).

merely a tort. While it is an unusual tort according to Jewish law in that the causation is indirect, tort law would be the essence of the remaining rabbinic decree—that informing on another improperly creates liability according to Jewish law.[59] Once informing is treated like any other form of damages, the *halakhah* becomes much more complex in that it becomes permissible to engage in informing any time damaging another is permissible.[60] Thus, for example, consider the case of one who was improperly disposing of waste oil into another's backyard. If this person's misconduct did halakhically recognizable harm to another, and that person needed to abate the harm being done him, he could call the relevant governmental organizations, which would issue the suitable regulatory remedy. However, according to the rationale of Rabbi Shmelkes, if one simply called the relevant authorities in a case in which there was no harm to oneself, such action would be prohibited according to Jewish law, as it would be causing damage without any right to do so according to Jewish law.[61] One would then be liable for the full damages caused, including lawyer's fees and the like.

This view would, I suspect, leave a prosecutor with a considerable amount of halakhic leeway in continuing to act as a prosecutor, since (as we have noted elsewhere in chapter 7) in cases where if one lawyer does not act, another certainly will to accomplish the same goal, Jewish law permits the lawyer to act—even if the underlining litigation is improper.

---

59 As opposed to most forms of gossip, which do not ever lead to liability. See *Pithei Hoshen* Volume 5, Chapter 4, paragraphs 21–29.

60 Or where the tort causes no damage, such as when one informs on a person for a debt that they are liable to pay according to Jewish law.

61 The statement in *Shulhan Arukh*, *Hoshen Mishpat* 388:10 that "it is permitted to kill an informer in any place, even nowadays . . ." would, according to Rabbi Shmelkes not be applicable when informing will never lead to harm. Indeed, the *Shulhan Arukh* neatly divides these sets of rules into two components, and a fairly clear result is that only the rules found in *Hoshen Mishpat* 388:9–14 are a result of the sinful conduct of the informer.

The View of Rabbi Shmuel Wozner: Informing is Permitted when Jewish Law Recognizes Secular Law as Valid

Another view relates the prohibition of informing to the legality (from the perspective of Jewish law) of the secular government's actions. In this view, informing is prohibited only when the government seeks to enforce secular law that Jewish law does not consider obligatory upon Jews under Jewish law.

Consider, for example, Rabbi Shmuel Wozner's discussion of whether one may work as a tax auditor for the government.

> In the matter of one who works in the tax offices, and when he sees one who defrauds the government he has to report him to the courts. That person wants to know if he is in the status of an informer or "the law of the land is the law" [and is thus proper].
>
> It is clear that according to the *halakhah*, taxes—without dispute or controversy—are covered by the obligation to obey the law of the land....
>
> On the question of informing to the government, it is clear from the incident discussed in *Bava Metzia* 83b with Rabbi Eleazar who informed upon a person to the government, that this conduct was permitted because of loyalty to the government; even though they said to him "how long will you hand over God's nation to be killed?" that is because this matter relates to the danger to the life of a Jew. So too, that which Elijah recounts to Rabbi Yishmael [that he should cease informing] is applicable, but the technical *halakhah* appears that this matter has a benefit to the government....[62]

See also *Rema* [*Hoshen Mishpat*] 388:11 who notes that if one wishes to flee to avoid paying a gentile what he actually owes him, and another reveals this information, the latter person lacks the status of an informer. Even though that *Rema* concludes

---

62 Rabbi Wozner states:

> In the *Ba'er ha-Golah*, *Hoshen Mishpat* 388: (*ayin*) it states "it is already well established by decree and custom that the leaders of the community guard not to lie or cheat gentiles, and they inform on and give permission to reveal those who take improperly . . ."

"nonetheless, bad was done, as it is analogous to returning the lost object to a pagan," that is limited to returning the lost object to an individual pagan. However, *that which is relevant to the government and its designee, there is no sin* [either of informing or returning lost objects improperly]. Nonetheless, *ab initio* it is better not to accept an appointment to engage in such activity, since it entails informing on one even in a permissible way, which is not the conduct of the righteous, as is noted in the Jerusalem Talmud *Terumah* 8:4.... Furthermore this case is not analogous to other cases as those cases involve danger to life when the gentiles are informed; this case is different because punishment imposed on the violator nowadays never involves mortal danger.[63]

In this view, informing is a violation of *halakhah* only when Jewish law does not recognize the inherent validity of the right of the secular government to enforce its actions through the law of the land. Whether the conduct one is reporting violates autonomous Jewish law (absent secular law) is completely irrelevant to this mode of analysis. Whether the person is punished in a matter consistent with Jewish law is also irrelevant, because Jewish law only prohibits informing when secular law is invalid in the eyes of Jewish law.[64]

---

63 *Shevet ha-Levi*, *Yoreh Deah* 58. Rabbi Wozner also refers to Maharam Alshekh 66 who notes that one cannot be deemed an informer (*moser*) when the activity one is informing on violates "the law of the land." That view is also hinted at in *Darkei Teshuvah*, *Yoreh Deah* 157:53.

64 See *Niddah* 61a which states:

> It was rumored about certain Galileans that they killed a person. They came to Rabbi Tarfon and said to him, "hide us." Rabbi Tarfon replied, "What shall I do? If I do not hide you, you will be seen. Should I hide you? The Sages have said that rumors, even though they may not be accepted, nevertheless, should not be dismissed. Go and hide yourselves."

> The reason Rabbi Tarfon declined to aid is in dispute, and this dispute is undoubtedly related to this issue. *Rashi* states that the reason Rabbi Tarfon would not help these people was because if they were guilty, helping them would be prohibited. This would imply that Jewish law prohibits aiding defendants who might be guilty. *Tosafot* and Rabbenu Asher (*Rosh*) disagree and argue that the reason Rabbi Tarfon would not help them was because he was afraid that the government would punish him for helping criminals escape, but that helping them is halakhically permitted; *Tosafot*, *Niddah* 61a (s.v. *atmarinkhu*) and Rabbenu Asher, *Tosafot ha-Rosh* on *Niddah* 61a, both quoting R. Aha mi-Shabha, *She'iltot*, Numbers 129.

In this writer's opinion, this approach is broadly predicated on the conceptual analysis of Rabbi Shlomo Yitzhaki (*Rashi*), commenting on the Talmud, who seems to accept that Jewish law recognizes that the secular government may properly enforce any law validly promulgated under the rule "the law of the land is the law" (*dina de-malkhuta dina*)—even against Jews—as a function of the obligation imposed on gentiles to create a system of law (*dinim*).[65] Maintaining law and order is unquestionably one such function, as is collecting taxes. Indeed, once one accepts that gentiles are empowered by Noahide law (through the commandment of *dinim*) to make and enforce laws, it is not a far leap of logic to observe that such criminal laws, once made, are binding upon Jews to the extent that Jewish law does not mandate a different result. If that is so, the Jewish community may assist in the enforcement of Noahide law without stepping afoul of the rabbinic prohibition of informing (*mesirah*).[66]

As noted by Rabbi Wozner, this approach can be found explicitly in a number of talmudic incidents, and the commentaries of various *rishonim* on them. One of these sources states:

> Rabbi Eleazar son of Rabbi Simeon met a police officer. Rabbi Eleazar said to him, "How can you detect the thieves...? Perhaps you take the innocent and leave behind the guilty." The officer replied "And what shall I do? It is the king's command." [Rabbi Eleazar then advised this policeman how to determine who was a thief and who was not]... A report was heard in the royal court. They said, "Let the reader of the letter become the messenger." Rabbi Eleazar son of Rabbi Simeon was brought to the court and he proceeded to apprehend thieves. Rabbi Joshua son of Korhah, sent word to him, "Vinegar, son of wine! [i.e., inferior son of a

---

65 See e.g., *Rashi*, commenting on *Gittin* 9b ("*Hutz me-gitei Nashim*") who explicitly relates secular law to the *mitzvah* of dinim, and Rashi, commenting on *Niddah* 61a ("*mihush leih miba'ei*") who, at least as understood by *Rosh* (*Tosafot ha-Rosh* on *Niddah* 61a) adopts the view that if one kills and flees from the government, Jewish law prohibits one from assisting in avoiding the punishment of secular law, as secular law is proper in punishing in that case.

66 For a more complete analysis of this issue see Nahum Rakover, "Jewish Law and the Noahide Obligation to Preserve Social Order," *Cardozo L.R.* 12:1073, 1098–1118, and App. I & II (1991).

superior father] How long will you deliver the people of our God for slaughter?" Rabbi Eleazar sent the reply, "I eradicate thorns from the vineyard." Rabbi Joshua responded, "Let the owner of the vineyard [God] come and eradicate his thorns"... A similar incident befell Rabbi Yishmael the son of Rabbi Yossi. The prophet Elijah appeared to him and rebuked him.... "What can I do—it is the royal decree," responded Rabbi Yishmael. Elijah retorted, "Your father fled to Assia, you flee to Laodica [i.e., you should flee and not obey]."[67]

Thus, the Talmud records that two sages, Rabbi Eleazar and Rabbi Yishmael, were rebuked for assisting the government in the prosecution of criminals, indicating either that this conduct is not proper, or the subject of a dispute between Rabbi Eleazar and Rabbi Joshua (in which case it is not universally condoned). A number of commentaries advance an explanation which changes the focus of this reprimand. Rabbi Yom Tov Ishbili (*Ritva*)[68] states that even Rabbi Joshua—who rebuked Rabbi Eleazar for working as a police officer—admits that it is only scholars and rabbis of the caliber of Rabbi Eleazar and Rabbi Yishmael who should not assist the government as prosecutors or police officers. Even for these individuals such conduct was not prohibited, but only frowned upon.[69] Many authorities agree with this explanation.[70] According to this analysis, it is only the pious who should not engage in this type of work as it is undignified for

---

[67] *Bava Metzia* 83b–84a. For an excellent analysis of the issues raised by secular enforcement of criminal law, see Rabbi J. David Bleich, "Jewish Law and the State's Authority to Punish Crime," *Cardozo L.R.* 12:829–857 (1991); see also R. J. David Bleich, "Hasgarat Poshea Yehudi she-Barah le-Eretz Yisrael," *Or ha-Mizrah* 35:247–269 (1987).

[68] *Ritva* commenting on *Bava Metzia* 83b, as quoted in R. Betzalel Ashkenazi, *Shittah Mekubetzet* on ibid.

[69] This understanding might be based on an inference from the Jerusalem Talmud, *Terumot* 8:4 which indicates that this conduct is only prohibited to the pious.

[70] See *Ran*, commenting on *Sanhedrin* 46a; R. Solomon ben Adret, *Teshuvot Rashba* 3:29; R. Yosef Karo, *Beit Yosef, Hoshen Mishpat* 388; *Taz, Yoreh Deah* 157:7–8; R. Tzvi Hirsch Shapira, *Darkei Teshuvah*, commenting on *Yoreh Deah* 157:1; R. Meir Simhah of Dvinsk, *Or Sameah, Melakhim* 3:10; and R. Moshe Schick, *Teshuvot Maharam Schick, Yoreh Deah* No. 50.

scholars to act as government agents in these circumstances—but all others may.⁷¹ While it might not be a reflection of good character to inform on another, there is not a technical prohibition to inform in such cases.

If Rabbi Wozner's conceptual observation is correct, the scope of the prohibition to inform is inversely related to the scope of the obligation to obey the law of the land, about which there are three theories. While a full survey of the reach of the obligation to obey secular law is well beyond the breadth of this chapter, a brief review of the relevant theories is worthwhile and explains when informing is permitted, according to this theory. There are three principal perspectives regarding "the law of the land is the law":

(1) Rabbi Joseph Karo rules that secular law is binding under Jewish law only to the extent that it directly affects the government's financial interests. Thus, secular laws imposing taxes or tolls would be valid under Jewish law.⁷²

(2) Rabbi Moshe Isserles (*Rema*) agrees that secular laws directly affecting the government's financial interests are binding, but adds that secular laws that are enacted for the benefit of the people of the community as a whole are also, as a general matter, effective under Jewish law.⁷³

(3) Rabbi Shabtai HaKohen (*Shakh*) disagrees with Rabbi Isserles in one respect. He believes that even if secular laws are enacted for the benefit of the community, they are not valid under Jewish law if they are specifically contrary to indigenous Jewish law obligations.⁷⁴

---

71 The *hashavat aveidat akum behinam* problem is not significant because the Jew is being paid to work; he is not working for free. In general, this problem is not significant when the Jew derives significant benefit from the activity of informing, and is only relevant when the informing is gratuitous. So too, in cases of desecration of God's name these factors disappear, as explicitly noted in *Shulhan Arukh, Hoshen Mishpat* 266:1. See also note 27 for a long discussion of this issue.

72 *Shulhan Arukh, Hoshen Mishpat* 369:6,11.

73 *Shulhan Arukh, Hoshen Mishpat* 369:11.

74 R. Shabtai ben Meir HaKohen, *Siftei Kohen (Shakh), Hoshen Mishpat* 73:39.

While there is substantial debate among Jewish law authorities as to which approach to follow,[75] nevertheless, it seems that most modern authorities agree that, at least outside of the State of Israel, Rabbi Isserles' view should be applied, and such is the view of all four of the deans of Jewish law in America in the previous generation: Rabbis Moses Feinstein[76] Joseph Henkin,[77] Joseph Soloveitchik,[78] and Yoel Teitelbaum.[79] In this view, almost all applications of secular law are valid under Jewish law.[80]

---

75 Shmuel Shilo, *Dina de-Malkhuta Dina*, at pp. 145–160 who lists authorities adopting either the approach of *Shakh* or Karo.

76 *Iggerot Moshe*, *Hoshen Mishpat* 2:62.

77 *Teshuvot Ibra* in *Kol Kitvei ha-Rav Henkin* 2:176.

78 This is indicated in *Nefesh ha-Rav* 267–269, and has been confirmed by many other sources as well.

79 *Divrei Yoel* 1:147.

80 See also Shmuel Shilo, *Dina de-Malkhuta Dina*, at p. 157, who asserts that most Jewish law authorities adopt *Rema*'s view and lists many of these authorities.

A contemporary, Rabbi Menasheh Klein, questions whether *dina de-malkhuta dina* applies in the United States. He states:

> [The applicability of the principle of] *dina de-malkhuta dina* in our times, when there is no king but rather what is called democracy needs further clarification. As I already explained the position cited in the name of *Rivash* quoting *Rashba*, one does not accept *dina de-malkhuta dina* except where the law originates with the king. But in a case where the law originates in courts, and the judges have discretion to rule as they think proper, or to invent new laws as they see proper, there is no *dina de-malkhuta dina*, as there is no law of the king ... This is even more true since we have here [in the United States] an institution called a "jury" where the government takes drunks from the market who have never studied law and who establish the law based on a majority vote. Indeed, even the government sometimes creates law and the Supreme Court contradicts it. Certainly in such a system there is no *dina de-malkhuta dina* according to *Rivash* and *Rashba*.

R. Menasheh Klein, *Mishneh Halakhot* 6:277. (Needless to say, Rabbi Klein, *Mishneh Halakhot* 7:285 also prohibits informing, although his factual predicate is so contrary to that found in this chapter that no response is needed.)

Despite R. Klein's views, it is important to note that most authorities have held that *dina de-malkhuta dina* does not apply only to laws issued by a king. Moreover, a number of preeminent Jewish law authorities have specifically held that *dina de-malkhuta dina* applies within the United States and have not found any problems caused by the democratic form of government, the judiciary, the jury system or the possibility of judicial review. See references to Rabbis Moshe Feinstein and Joseph Henkin, above.

Based on this approach—informing is only prohibited where Jewish law rules that one need not obey secular law—one could argue cogently that informing is actually permitted in any situation in which the person on whom one is informing has actually violated secular law that Jewish law deems valid, and the person who is informing on the person gains financially from governmental enforcement, or from the abatement of the tort.[81] So too, in a situation where silence would lead to a desecration of

> Indeed, once one acknowledges that *dina de-malkhuta dina* applies to non-monarchical governments, it is unclear why these other factors would, as a general matter, be problematic as a matter of Jewish law. For example, juries (and sometimes judges) perform fact-finding roles that are a necessary element in the application of law. A Noahide system of law could surely invest juries (and judges) with this responsibility without impairing the legitimacy of *dina de-malkhuta dina*.
>
> Nor is there any apparent Jewish law deficiency in the secular system for interpreting the law. Even if a king were to promulgate written laws, he would undoubtedly delegate the daily responsibility of judging cases to others, and such judges would have to interpret the law. An argument might be made that in the American system, a jury is sometimes required not only to find facts but to make decisions regarding "mixed questions of law and fact." Although a comprehensive analysis of the jury function is beyond the scope of this work, the question of jury interpretation is insignificant as a matter of Jewish law. A secular system must delegate the interpretative function to someone and it is not fatal under Jewish law even if the secular system were to delegate some aspect of this function to juries. Although Rabbi Klein obviously questions the jurors' ability to make any reasonable decisions, he has not demonstrated that this criticism is significant under Jewish law.
>
> In any event, even if there were some irregularity in the secular procedure for applying the law, and even if this would deny Jewish law validity to the *outcome* of a secular case, it would not prevent *dina de-malkhuta dina* from rendering the substantive rules of secular law valid as a matter of Jewish law. For example, disputes between Jews, even when *dina de-malkhuta dina* applies, are supposed to be litigated in Jewish courts who would decide the dispute in accordance with secular law rules. In such instances, the Jewish courts themselves would serve as the fact-finders.
>
> Judges are also required to determine whether legislative acts are consistent with legally superseding documents—such as treaties, constitutions or even certain other legislative acts. There seems to be no reason why a secular legal system division of power between legislative and judicial branches should impair *dina de-malkhuta dina*.
>
> (The above material and the three paragraph's preceding it are quoted nearly verbatim from Michael Broyde & Steven Resnicoff "The Corporate Paradigm and Jewish Law," *Wayne State Law Journal* 43:1685–1818 (1997).)

81 Thus avoiding the problem of *meshiv avedat akum behinam*, which can also be avoided based on *hillul ha-Shem* factors as noted explicitly by *Shulhan Arukh* 266:1.

Based upon this mode of analysis, Rabbi Hershel Schachter posits:

God's name and informing would lead to a sanctification, informing would be permitted.[82]

In this writer's view, this understanding of Jewish law—that the prohibition of informing does not apply when the secular government is acting consistent with its rights under Jewish law, and Jews are duty bound under Jewish law to obey such laws—has a powerful theoretical logic to it and seems halakhically persuasive.[83] If Jews are obligated to obey any particular secular law, and Jewish law recognizes as valid any particular penalty that the secular government imposes for a violation of that secular law, it makes no halakhic sense to rule that assisting the government in enforcing that law is a violation of the rules of informing and a tort. It ought not be tortious to help enforce a secular law that Jewish law rules one obligated to obey. Certainly, serving as a witness or a prosecutor would be without any problem.

The View of Rabbis Feinstein and Breisch: The Prohibition is Unchanged by a Just Government

The view of Rabbi Breisch (explicitly) and Rabbi Moshe Feinstein (implicitly) is that the rules relating to informing are unrelated to the status of the government as just or unjust, proper or improper. In three distinctly different responsa, Rabbi Feinstein appears to posit that the prohibition of informing remains identical in a just society.[84] In 1961 Rabbi Feinstein answered a question concerning whether the communal

---

> One critical point should however be added: there is no problem of *"mesirah"* [informing] in informing the government of a Jewish criminal, even if they penalize the criminal with a punishment more severely than the Torah requires, because even a non-Jewish government is authorized to punish and penalize above and beyond the [Jewish] law . . . for the purpose of maintaining law and order. However, this only applies in the situation where the Jewish offender or criminal has at least violated some Torah law.
>
> R. Hershel Schachter, *"Dina Di'Malchusa Dina*: Secular Law as a Religious Obligation," *J. Halacha & Contemporary Society* 1:103, 118 (1981). In contrast with this, see the statements of Rabbi Feinstein, text accompanying notes 84 to 99.

82 As *meshiv avedat akum* issues disappear in situations of *kiddush ha-Shem* or *hillul ha-Shem*. See *Shulhan Arukh, Hoshen Mishpat* 266:1.

83 Assuming just prisons, but see the section on Rabbi Ezra Batzri's position.

84 There is no doubt from the many different responsa that Rabbi Feinstein wrote that he considered the government of the United States of America to be a proper government, to which full fidelity to the law of the land is expected. Besides his repeated

rabbinate may report to the police a person who had been selling non-kosher food as kosher, if this person, instead, is willing to consent to a *din Torah* by the rabbis themselves. Rabbi Feinstein writes:

> I received your letter with regard to an evil doer who came into a kosher factory and forged the kosher symbol, placed it on non-kosher items, which he sold to Jews as kosher. The question is can one inform on him to the secular authorities who will judge him severely with either a fine or prison, or must the rabbis judge him according to Jewish law? In my opinion, even though his sin is great, and he shows no repentance, nonetheless so long as we cannot say that the Jewish judges cannot judge him, one may not turn the matter over to the secular authorities. . . . *In addition, since it is certain that the secular authorities will adjudicate the matter through incarceration or a fine inconsistent with Jewish law, one must be fearful of the prohibition of informing, as it is prohibited to inform on a Jew to the secular authorities, whether through danger to his body or his money, even if he be a sinner.*[85]

No mention is made of the fact that the secular authorities (in this case, the state of Maryland) will adjudicate the matter fairly (i.e., consistent with its laws) or that prison was the proper penalty according to secular

---

invocation of the principle of the law of the land is the law, consider the following statement:

> *because of the fact that the government is a pious one*, whose whole purpose is to benefit all of the inhabitants of the land, the government has created a number of programs to benefit students ....

Iggerot Moshe, Hoshen Mishpat 2:29 (emphasis added).

85 *Iggerot Moshe, Hoshen Mishpat* 1:8 (Emphasis Added). See also *People v. Drelich*, 506 N.Y.S.2d 746, 124 A.D.2d 441 (2d App. Div 1986). In this case, a person appealed his murder conviction on the grounds that his confession of the "brutal stabbing murder of his 23-year-old pregnant wife" to his communal rabbi, Rabbi Dr. Moses Tendler, a *rosh yeshiva* and professor at Yeshiva University (as well as Rabbi Feinstein's son-in-law), ought not to have been admitted at trial. Rabbi Tendler testified against the defendant and recounted the confession, which resulted in his conviction. The court determined that no rabbi-penitent privilege attached as "the defendant's communications to R. Tendler were made for the secular purpose of seeking assistance in the retention of counsel, and in negotiating with the prosecutor's office and securing other assistance in connection with the preparation of his defense to the charges." Rabbi Menasheh Klein appears to prohibit this type of conduct; see R. Menasheh Klein, *Mishneh Halakhot* 7:285. For a response, see R. Samuel Turk, *Peri Malka* 76:2.

law. Rather, Rabbi Feinstein adopts the view that unless one of the exceptions permitting informing is present, it is prohibited to inform on a person according to Jewish law as the punishments imposed by secular law violate Jewish law, and thus may not be imposed on a person lest one violate the prohibition of informing.[86]

This view of Rabbi Feinstein is repeated again in Rabbi Feinstein's discussion of whether one can be a tax auditor for the government. Rabbi Feinstein states:

> In the matter of one who wants to be an auditor for the government such that on occasion one will encounter the tax returns of one who has cheated, and he will detect the fraud, [and will thus report it to his superiors] and will be like one who informs the government, and they will punish this person more than he is liable according to Jewish law. *It seems logical to me that since anyone who examines tax returns will encounter fraud, and even if this person declines the job, others will take the job and discover the fraud, one sees from this that the one who commits the fraud suffers no loss whether this person takes the job or not and another is there, and thus the one who cheats loses nothing whether or not this person takes the job and without a loss there is no prohibition.*[87]

Again, Rabbi Feinstein posits that there is no justification to inform on a person given the just American government. Rather he provides a narrow "tech-

---

86 Of course, Rabbi Feinstein accepts that if the person will not consent to attend a *bet din* or will not listen to the directive of that *bet din* after the fact, such a person may be informed upon as this conduct falls under the category of troubling the community; *Shulhan Arukh, Hoshen Mishpat* 388:12.

87 *Iggerot Moshe, Hoshen Mishpat* 1:92 (Emphasis Added). It is incorrect to maintain that Rabbi Feinstein refers to a tax auditor who can only recommend civil and not criminal penalties, as no such position exists. Rabbi Feinstein's rationale hinges on the legitimacy of the government's collection of taxes and the fact that others will collect the taxes anyway, and not on the penalties available to the government.

The reader should note that throughout chapters eleven and twelve the term "criminal law" is used to denote those areas of secular law where the government seeks to physically punish (through jail or other corporeal punishment) violators of the law; see R. David ben Samuel Halevi, *Turei Zahav (Taz) Yoreh Deah* 157:8. When the government uses the criminal justice system to seek only monetary fines (even punitive damages), Jewish law does not classify that as criminal litigation; that is more properly categorized as civil litigation and subject to the rules discussed in chapters five through eight.

nical" explanation for why this particular activity of informing while working for the IRS is not prohibited to this particular person. Rabbi Feinstein would rule that in a case where if any particular person did not inform, then the cheater would *not* be caught, then it would be prohibited to inform.

Indeed, in a responsum entitled "May One Inform on a Thief to the Courts of the Land" Rabbi Feinstein states:

> It is prohibited for us to inform on a person for a matter *where the punishment is unfounded in Jewish law*. In Jewish law, theft is resolved through restitution as measured by an expert, and secular law punishes through imprisonment, unfounded in Jewish law.[88]

Although Rabbi Feinstein provides no explicit discussion of whether a just government is of any relevance, Rabbi Feinstein repeatedly focuses on the fact that the punishment imposed by the secular government is contrary to Jewish law in its magnitude or scope, and thus when one Jew causes another to be punished in excess of the punishment directed by Jewish law, that is a prohibited form of damage grounded in the tort of informing, as the punishment is unjust by definition because Jewish law has a different punishment. Thus, in all of these responsa Rabbi Feinstein posits that the punishment authorized by the secular statute is greater than that permitted by Jewish law, and thus the conduct of informing is prohibited. In cases where the punishment is not greater than that directed by Jewish law, it would appear logical to posit that Rabbi Feinstein would not prohibit informing as (in Rabbi Feinstein's own words) "there would be no damages and when there are no damages, there is no prohibition."[89]

A different rationale is explicitly stated by Rabbi Ya'akov Breisch, who notes that the rules which prohibit informing cover even cases where there is no threat to bodily harm. Rabbi Breisch was asked:

> Is the prohibition of informing specifically when they are chasing after Jews, and thus if one informs on one's friend they punish him because he is a Jew, but if a gentile did this they would not punish him, then one is called an informer (*moser*), or it is even nowadays, when they are not pursuing Jews through law, and if a gentile had violated the law they would punish him as what he did is a crime, is that too called informing as defined in *Shulhan Arukh, Hoshen Mishpat* 388?

---

88 *Iggerot Moshe, Orah Hayyim* 5:9(11) (Emphasis Added).
89 *Iggerot Moshe, Hoshen Mishpat* 2:92.

Rabbi Breisch answers:

> One who looks in *Shulhan Arukh* and other decisors will see explicitly that there is no difference, and even when one who uses secular courts to reclaim his own, the matter is in dispute in *Hoshen Mishpat* 388:5 and the *Shakh* views such a person as an informer. A similar view is taken in *Berakhot* 58a concerning ... [a person who slandered government] and such a person became a pursuer [to destroy the government] and he was killed. Even though it is certain that if a gentile had done the same thing and called the government bitter they would have punished him, still Rav Shelai considered him an informer (*moser*) and killed him; while it is true that this case is different in that Rav Shelai was certain that they would be punished for mocking the government. ... Even the money of a Jew, once it falls into the hands of a gentile, they show no mercy on it, as is quoted in *Shulhan Arukh* and other decisors, and as a matter of normative *halakhah* this matter does not change. ... [90] That which we have seen in recent times [the Holocaust] provides proof to this.[91]

Rabbi Breisch is stating that even when there is no illicit harming of one's body, money is taken contrary to Jewish law, and that alone validates the rabbinic prohibition against informing.

---

90 In the ellipses, Rabbi Breisch invokes the phrase *vehesed leumim hatat* ("sin is a reproach to all people"), found in Proverbs 14:34. See also *Bava Batra* 10b in a discourse between Rabbi Yohanan and his students. Rabbi Breisch is undoubtedly referring to the Midrash that even when gentiles engage in what appears to be righteous activity, one should assume an ulterior motive and discount fear of heaven as a possibility. *Rashi* gives as an example stealing from one to give charity to another. See also Midrash Zuta on Shir Hashirim (Buber edition) 1:15, Responsa of the *Maharil ha-hadashot* 123, *Beit Yosef*, *Yoreh Deah* 247 and other sources. The invocation of this phrase in this context is hard to explain as a legal device in the context of the prohibition of informing, as this rabbinic phrase notes only that one can assume that divine reward will not be forthcoming in such cases, rather than (as Rabbi Breisch implies) such activities by gentiles ought not be encouraged or counted as significant in the eyes of Jewish law to determine whether it is a tort. See for example, *Responsa Ateret Paz*, *Even ha-Ezer* 4 where such a conclusion is reached. (It is worth noting that there is an alternative understanding of the verse which posits that righteous deeds by gentiles serves instead of the sacrificial rite of a *hatat*, and thus grants atonement to gentiles for their sins; see Ibn Ezra on Proverbs 14:34.)

91 *Helkat Yaakov*, *Hoshen Mishpat* 5 (new edition), 3:96 (old edition).

Both of these approaches find considerable halakhic justification in the alternative approach developed by the *rishonim* to explain the conduct of Rabbi Eleazar and Rabbi Joshua in *Bava Metzia* 83b–84a.[92] This approach rejects the opinion of Rabbi Eleazar that one may serve as a police officer and informant, and states that Rabbi Joshua, who rebuked Rabbi Eleazar, represents the normative opinion which prohibits this conduct.[93] If Rabbi Joshua's opinion is normative, then the only time it would be permitted to assist the secular government in criminal prosecutions is when the person poses a threat to others through his conduct[94] or where the criminal poses a threat to the community through his conduct.[95] Both of these situations are based upon the rules of a pursuer (*rodef*). Indeed, in Jewish law, one who poses a threat to the life of others must be prevented from accomplishing the intended harm; force—even deadly force—may be used in such a case without the need for a court hearing. This threat need not be limited to the possibility that the criminal will actually harm another, but includes such factors as the possibility that in response to a Jew being apprehended for committing a crime, other Jews will be injured or anti-Semitism will be promoted.[96]

If the approach of either Rabbis Feinstein or Breisch is correct, one divides cases of informing into two types of categories, no different in a procedurally just society than in an unjust society. One situation occurs when the person being informed upon is an individual who is violent, threatens violence, induces harm to others, or endangers the welfare of the community. Such a person may be informed upon, as Jewish law recognizes the need to remove these people from the community, as such conduct is not prohibited, given the lack of authority the *bet din* has in the

---

92 Discussed above in text accompanying note 67.

93 Such an approach can be inferred from Rambam, *Rotzeah* 2:4; *Tosafot*, *Sanhedrin* 20b; R. Moshe Schreiber, *Hatam Sofer, Likkutim* 14; and Rabbi J. David Bleich, "Jewish Law and the State's Authority to Punish Crime," *Cardozo L.R.* 12:840–844 (1991).

94 See e.g., R. Shmuel di-Medina, *Maharshdam, Hoshen Mishpat* 55:6; R. Moshe Sternbuch, *Teshuvot ve-Hanhagot* 1:850 (the authorities may be apprised of one who drives recklessly or without a license).

95 See R. Shimon Duran, *Tashbetz* 3:168, and R. Isserles (*Rema*), *Hoshen Mishpat* 388:12, both of whom address communal dangers.

96 See *Rema* commenting on *Shulhan Arukh, Hoshen Mishpat* 388:12 (discussing one who counterfeits coins), 425:1. For a complete analysis of the various permutations of this rule, see R. Yaakov Blau, *Pithei Hoshen* 5:ch. 4.

community currently.⁹⁷ Of course, in such a case one may act as a prosecutor and witness also.

In all other cases, informing is prohibited, and is subject to the rules of informing, as explained in the second section of this chapter.⁹⁸ In cases where the outcome is identical in secular law and Jewish law, Rabbi Feinstein would aver that there is no problem of informing, as there is no damage.⁹⁹ Being a voluntary witness in such a case would presumably be prohibited, although one could argue that being a prosecutor is less directly prohibited as the prosecutor (as explained above) could be considered as just doing the bidding of the government, which will seek a different prosecutor if this one declines to act.

Conclusion

This chapter has sought to elaborate on and explain the Jewish law prohibition of informing, with a particular focus on how the prohibition applies to a democracy with a just system of government that grants freedom to its many different citizens. One group of decisors posits that just governments are exempt from the prohibition of informing, either because the whole prohibition did not apply when government was just, or because governments that operate within the confines of the Jewish law obligations of the "law of the land is the law" are exempt. To this group, being a prosecutor is a perfectly proper activity, fully consistent with Jewish law.

Another group of decisors posits that the prohibition of informing fully applies even to just governments, as the rabbis did not want Jews assisting in the punishing of Jews in a manner inconsistent with Jewish law—even if the government itself can engage in this conduct, Jews should not help it. According to this school of thought, being a witness or

---

97 *Shulhan Arukh, Hoshen Mishpat* 388:12.

98 Indeed, one authority has argued that on a functional level there is no difference between the various approaches because disobedience of the law generally will surely lead to anarchy and crime, and thus all significant violations of the law can be punished under the pursuer rationale. R. Zvi Hirsch Chajes (*Maharatz Chayes*), *Torat Nevi'im* Ch. 7.

99 See *Iggerot Moshe, Hoshen Mishpat* 1:92 which states "there would be no damages and when there are no damages, there is no prohibition."

informant is prohibited, and being a prosecutor is, at the very least, not conduct of the pious.

A third group of decisors posits that the system—even as it appears just—is not, and thus informing is prohibited. This group would argue that acting as a prosecutor is a significant error when the individuals being prosecuted are unworthy of serious punishment.[100]

---

100 For a general survey of the issues raised in this chapter within the context of the extradition of a Jewish defendant from Israel to France, see *Aloni v. Nakash*, Israel High Court of Justice (Supreme Court) 852/86, 869/86, where Justice Menachem Elon discusses at great length Jewish law's apppproach to assisting in the criminal prosecution of Jews. He states:

> [S]ome scholars saw in an unfavorable light Jewish assistance in the discovery and extradition to the secular authorities of Jewish criminals, as they felt it preferable that "the owner of the vineyard—the Lord—should come and destroy the thorns from the vineyard" rather than deliver these "thorns" to the judicial authority of rulers who have no mercy for the people and property of Jews. Other Sages disagreed and gave assistance, both in theory and in practice, to the secular authorities in order "to remove the thorns from the vineyard" . . . One should, however, take care not to act in this way from the outset for it is not "the teaching of the pious."
>
> In time, even those who had reservations agreed that one should hand over *ab initio* Jewish transgressors whose acts could endanger the [Jewish] public since these people were considered pursuers. . . . Other Sages considered the extradition of Jewish criminals to the general authorities as a necessity in order to uphold order and public welfare based upon the validity of the "law of the land is law" which could not be condemned.

For two detailed criticisms of Justice Elon's opinion in *Nakash*, both of which assert that Elon is relying on Jewish law material inserted for the benefit of the censor, and is not indigenous to Jewish law, see R. J. David Bleich, "Extradition," *Tehumin* 8:297 (1988), and R. Shaul Yisraeli, "Extradition," *Tehumin* 8:827 (1988).

Chapter Twelve

Defending One Accused of a Crime

Introduction

Having addressed the question of when it is permissible to assist the prosecution of criminals, it is now necessary to determine if one can aid accused criminals in their defense, and if so, what type of help is permitted.[1] Within the American adversarial system of justice, while a lawyer may not lie on behalf of his client, he must defend his client zealously, even if he knows the case against his client is factually correct.[2] This is even more so true, and of constitutional magnitude, in a criminal case, because the government bears the burden of proving guilt beyond a reasonable doubt in all such cases.

An initial question must be addressed. May a defendant, according to Jewish law, plead "not guilty" in secular court to a crime that he knows he has committed but which the government cannot prove, or must a Jew plead guilty when charged, if actually guilty? It would appear to this writer that one may plead not guilty even if one knows that he is factually guilty.

---

1 Certainly one may represent a defendant who wishes to plead guilty and only desires a reduced sentence. Such negotiations are the end result of more than 98 percent of the criminal indictments issued in the United States; see Donald Newman, "Reshape the Deal," *Trial* 9:11 (May/June 1973) ("The frequency of conviction by plea approaches 98% of all those charged.").

2 See for example, Washington D.C. Rules of Professional Conduct, Rule 1.3(a) ("A lawyer shall represent a client zealously and diligently within the bounds of the law") and Model Code of Professional Responsibility, Canon 7 ("represent a client zealously within the boundary of the law"); but see Model Rules of Professional Conduct, Rule 1.3, which does not mention the word "zeal" in any form.

According to Jewish law, a confession is not admitted in court, and in fact does not prove guilt.[3] Requiring a person to plead guilty if he actually is, and thus waive his right to a trial, is tantamount to requiring a person to confess to his crime. A Jew thus may plead not guilty so as to force the government to prove its case according to law.[4]

While it might appear to some that a defendant is lying when he pleads "not guilty" if he knows he is factually guilty, such is a misunderstanding of the secular law involved. A defendant need not plead to any offense in American law. In the absence of any plea, a plea of "not guilty" is entered (in harmony with the American rule of innocent until proven guilty). Thus, by entering a plea of "not guilty," a defendant does not assert that he is actually innocent—he can only do that through testimony—but only that he wishes to be tried in a court of law.[5]

So too, when the government has not proven its case, a defense lawyer may advise the jury to acquit his client simply because the evidence has not proven "beyond a reasonable doubt" that his client is guilty. This is true, in this author's opinion, even if the client has told the lawyer that he is factually and legally guilty. In the American legal system, as in Jewish law, the government bears the burden of proving each element of a criminal charge, and in any situation in which the government has not done so, the defendant is legally entitled to an acquittal. Any other rule is tantamount to requiring a Jew who is actually guilty of a crime to plead guilty, even if the government cannot prove its case. A Jew, like all other citizens, is entitled to a trial in which the government meets its burden of proving guilt.[6]

---

3 Maimonides, *Sanhedrin* 18:6; R. Norman Lamm, "Self Incrimination in Law and Psychology: The Fifth Amendment and the Halakhah," republished in R. Norman Lamm, *Faith and Doubt* (Ktav, 1986).

4 See R. Yaakov Emden, *She'elat Ya'avetz* 2:9; R. J. David Bleich, *Contemporary Halakhic Problems* II:349–357 (and note 19). Rabbi David Cohen (of *Gvul Yavetz*) notes in a letter dated 17 Av 5754/July 23, 1994 to this author, that it is obvious that a person need not plead guilty to a crime, even if he is guilty.

5 Proof to this can be derived from the American law rule that a person who testifies that he is innocent when he is not actually innocent, can be prosecuted for perjury, but merely pleading "not guilty" when one is actually guilty is not grounds for a perjury charge as no testimony has occurred.

6 That Rabbi Tarfon (see *Niddah* 61a quoted in text accompanying note 7) did not advise the Galileans who came to him that if they are guilty they should turn themselves in to the authorities, indicates that a defendant can plead innocent when charged, as both fleeing and pleading innocent are a form of resisting imprisonment.

Assisting the Guilty

Given the fact that a defendant may take steps to insure that he is given a fair trial, one might argue that a lawyer representing the defendant could take any action on his client's behalf. This is not so. The scope of a lawyer's role in aiding a criminal defendant is directly connected to a discussion in the Talmud which states:

> It was rumored about certain Galileans that they killed a person. They came to Rabbi Tarfon and said to him, "hide us." Rabbi Tarfon replied, "What shall I do? If I do not hide you, you will be seen. Should I hide you? The Sages have said that rumors, even though they may not be accepted, nevertheless, should not be dismissed. Go and hide yourselves."[7]

The reason Rabbi Tarfon declined to aid is in dispute, and this dispute is critical to understanding the status of criminal defense work according to Jewish law.

Rashi states that the reason Rabbi Tarfon would not help these people was because if they were guilty, helping them would be prohibited. This would imply that Jewish law prohibits aiding defendants who might be guilty. *Tosafot* and Rabbenu Asher (*Rosh*)[8] disagree and argue that the reason Rabbi Tarfon would not help them was because he was afraid that the government would punish him for helping criminals escape, but that helping them is halakhically permitted. Most early authorities accept the reasoning of *Tosafot* and Rabbenu Asher (*Rosh*).[9] According to their explanation, any help which the government allows one to provide would be permitted, since it poses no danger to the provider (e.g., being a defense attorney).

Rabbi Shlomo Luria argues that this ruling of *Tosafot* and Rabbenu Asher only applies in cases where, in the aider's mind, the guilt of the defendant is in doubt, as it was in the Talmud.[10] In the case of known guilt,

---

7 *Niddah* 61a.

8 *Tosafot, Niddah* 61a (s.v. *atmarinkhu*) and Rabbenu Asher, *Tosafot ha-Rosh* on *Niddah* 61a, both quoting R. Aha mi-Shabha, *She'iltot*, Numbers 129.

9 See e.g., Meiri on ibid (in the name of most authorities).

10 R. Shlomo Luria, *Hokhmat Shlomo*, commenting on *Niddah* 61a; this interpretation can also be found in the comments of R. Akiva Eiger on *Niddah* 61a.

no help is permitted. Basing his opinion on this ruling, Rabbi Hershel Schachter states:

> If a lawyer *knows* that his client has committed a crime, it is forbidden for him to help the criminal escape the consequences of his act, by relying on some technical legal points or other devices. The lawyer, just as any Jew, is directed by the Torah to "eradicate the evil from our midst," and may not actively assist someone to avoid his punishment.[11]

Thus, according to Rabbi Schachter a lawyer may not advance "technical legal points or other devices" when the client is known to be actually guilty. On the other hand, it is apparent that the defendant must be presumed innocent by the lawyer.[12]

In addition, it is also important to distinguish between those situations in which the lawyer advances a defense of "technical legal points" for a client he knows to be guilty, and those situations in which the lawyer advances defenses that are true, that mitigate the seriousness of the crime, or that cast doubts on the validity of the government's case. For example, under Rabbi Schachter's ruling, it would seem that while a lawyer cannot advance at trial a defense of "my client did not commit the crime" when the client has informed his lawyer to the contrary,[13] a lawyer may advance numerous defenses which indicate that a guilty verdict is inappropriate. Thus, he may advance an insanity defense, or a defense of necessity, duress, or inadvertence, providing that the client has told him that these mitigating factors are present, or that the lawyer reasonably believes them

---

11 R. Hershel Schachter, "*Dina Di'Malchusa:* Secular Law as a Religious Obligation", at 121–122.

12 See *Kitzur Piskei ha-Rosh*, *Niddah* 9:5. One could argue that all defendants who have not told their lawyers that they are factually guilty, have the status of "in doubt" until conviction at trial. The overwhelming majority of defendants are in this category. It is clear that this type of reasoning does have some outer limit. For example, Rabbi Oshry concludes that Jewish law would prevent a Jewish lawyer from defending a Nazi war criminal, and discusses his response in a case when a lawyer wished to do so; see R. Ephraim Oshry, *Responsa from the Holocaust* 104.

13 This also violates many professional ethics rules; see chapter three. Obviously a lawyer may not use techniques at trial whose sole purpose is to confuse the finder of fact or to produce error and a reversal on appeal. Both of these tactics are unethical in American law.

to be present. So too, any rule of evidence or law whose goal is one of "truth-seeking," and whose violation by the prosecution casts doubt on the credibility of the evidence, may be invoked by a lawyer to the benefit of a client, since such rules promote justice by the court. Thus, for example, both hearsay evidence and a confession given after torture may be suppressed as the evidence's validity may be reasonably doubted.

The status of the prophylactic rules occasionally promulgated by the Supreme Court in the field of criminal procedure could be debated.[14] While these rules were not authorized in order to insure justice in a particular case, they are part of the government's program to reduce violations of law by governmental officials and to promote justice in society at large. While the efficacy of such a policy could, and is, debated by lawyers, there is little doubt that the goals these policies seek to advance are ones which Jewish law respects, and also are a fulfillment of the obligation to eradicate injustice from society.

In the more typical case where the client does not tell the lawyer he is guilty and instead protests his innocence (notwithstanding the evidence to the contrary), it would seem that a complete defense would be permitted according to Rabbenu Asher and *Tosafot*. In such a case, a lawyer may advance all defenses which are tenable and which the client represents as correct.

Obviously a lawyer may also advance a defense that the facts, as stated by the government, do not constitute a crime under the relevant statute, and thus the client ought to be acquitted. For example, in a prosecution for criminal tax fraud, the defense frequently argues that not only was no crime committed, but that the tax return of the defendant was properly filed, and the IRS is misinterpreting the relevant tax law.[15]

---

14 E.g., *Mapp* v. *Ohio*, 367 US. 643 (1961). A "prophylactic rule" corresponds to the rabbinic concept of a "fence around the torah" (*seyag latorah*) and refers to those rules designed to remove the temptation to violate the law. *Mapp*, for example, ruled that illegally seized evidence will not be admitted into court. This rule created a "fence" around the Fourth Amendment's prohibition of illegal searches and seizures by reducing the incentives on a police officer to violate the law, as the products of such searches may not be used in court.

15 It is permissible under Jewish law to challenge the IRS's understanding (called Regulations) of the Internal Revenue code, as the executive branch of the federal government is not constitutionally given the power to interpret laws in a manner that binds citizen. That task is left to the judiciary, whose interpretation binds the other two branches, as well as the citizenry. Thus, in America, *dina de-malkhuta dina* only applies to laws that the judiciary sanctions as valid.; see also note 13 of chapter eight.

Assisting the Guilty: A Second Approach

An understanding of Rabbi Tarfon's dilemma, different from that advocated by Rabbi Luria, is possible and better explains the position of *She'iltot*, *Tosafot*, and *Rosh*. The *She'iltot*, *Tosafot*, and *Rosh*, might in fact make no distinction between known guilt and mere rumors of guilt. Rather Rabbi Tarfon might have hesitated to act solely out of fear of violating the secular law (and being punished for that violation). Under this explanation, the sole limitation upon aiding a person accused of a crime would be the danger to the aider. All aid permitted by the government, (and hence without any danger to the provider) would thus be permitted. Rabbi Yaakov Ettlinger advances exactly such an explanatipn. He denies that there is any intrinsic halakhic obstacle to aiding criminals who seek help—and he asserts this as *Rashi*'s opinion as well as that of *Tosafot* and Rabbenu Asher (*Rosh*). He states:

> In my opinion one could state that *Rashi* does not disagree with *She'iltot*. When *Rashi* states that it is prohibited to save the murderers, he does not mean that it is prohibited according to Jewish law to save them, *but rather that secular law prohibits that conduct*. Once secular law prohibits this conduct, Jewish law does also, since saving these individuals would involve great risk to the savior.[16]

If this approach is correct, and it certainly best reflects the formulation of *Tosafot* and Rabbenu Asher (*Rosh*), any form of aid legally permitted by the secular society (e.g., being a defense attorney) would be halakhically permitted, as it is only because of the danger that one may not help a criminal.[17] According to Rabbi Ettlinger, the only type of aid prohibited is that which the secular government does not allow.[18]

---

16 R. Yaakov Ettlinger, *Arukh la-Ner*, commenting on *Niddah* 61a (emphasis added). For others who appear to adopt this approach see R. Yaakov Emden, *She'elat Ya'avetz* 2:9; R. Moshe Schreiber, *Hatam Sofer* 6:14; and R Yaakov Breish, *Helkat Yaakov* 4:23. See also *Asefat Zekenim*, *Niddah* 61a and R. Yosef Shapira, *Hiddushei Mahari Shapira*, *Niddah* 61a, for other authorities who explain *Niddah* 61a in this manner.

17 *Rashi* could be arguing that secular law can halakhically prohibit this activity; see *Rashi*, commenting on *Gittin* 9b ("*dinim*"). *Tosafot* and *Rosh* reject this rule; see generally, R. Bleich, "State's Authority to Punish," at 852–857.

18 On a practical level, there is nearly no distinction between the positions taken by Rabbi Luria (*Hokhmat Shlomo*) and Rabbi Yaakov Ettlinger (*Arukh la-Ner*). The sole

Particularly in light of American law, Rabbi Ettlinger's position appears logical. Since the secular government not only allows, but actually requires that a criminal be represented by a competent lawyer at trial (a conviction is invalid without this representation), a lawyer's participation as a defense attorney simply insures that society fulfills its obligation to remove evil from its midst—but only in the manner that society has designated as just.[19]

According to both approaches, a lawyer may not assist a client in the creation of a false defense—i.e., allow his client or any other witness to commit what the lawyer knows to be perjury. Needless to say, such conduct is prohibited under relevant American law as well.[20]

Numerous individuals, whose guilt was never doubted when their trial began, have shown themselves through able defenses, to have been factually innocent of the charges leveled. Regrettably enough, history is also full of innocent people who were punished because of unavailable or incompetent defense attorneys. That is not to say that all defense strategies are permissible—many are not—but rather, the zealous advocacy of truthful defenses enhances, rather than detracts from justice in society. To the extent a lawyer helps his client to benefit from legal rules designed to ensure justice, such conduct is permitted, and perhaps even mandated, according to Jewish law.

One final note is needed. It is important to distinguish between the role of a lawyer in defending a particular client, and the role of a lawyer, as an informed citizen, in shaping public policy. Merely because Jewish law permits—in the opinion of some authorities—one to offer a full zealous defense for a specific client that a lawyer has agreed to defend in a criminal case, does not mean that lawyers should not seek reform of the criminal justice system even if that reform reduces either the rights of

---

point in contention would be whether a lawyer could advance defenses at trial not on the issue of the person's guilt but on procedural issues for a person who has acknowledged to the lawyer his factual guilt.

19 Such a conclusion is agreed to (albeit with somewhat different reasons) by Rabbi David Cohen (of *Gvul Yavetz*) in a letter to this author dated 17 Av 5754/July 23, 1994.

20 See Harry Subin, "The Criminal Lawyer's 'Different Mission': Reflections on the 'Right' to Present a False Case," *Georgetown Journal of Legal Ethics* 1:125 (1987) (stating that false defenses are improper and ethical lawyers do not use them); and *Nix v. Whiteside*, 475 U.S. 157 (1986) (lawyer may, and most states require that he must, inform the court of perjury by his client).

those accused of crimes or the role of attorneys in trials. However, these broader public policy issues are of no relevance when a lawyer defends a specific person charged of a specific crime. The lawyer's goal in such a case should be to provide the best defense of that client permitted by Jewish and American law.

Family Law Issues

Chapters thirteen and fourteen discuss family law issues. The first chapter discusses wills, living wills, and the halakhic problems associated with their use. Chapter fourteen focuses on the issues related to ending a marriage, including divorce and child custody.

Chapter Thirteen

Wills and Inheritance

Wills that Bequeath

This chapter will not focus on the permissibility of using a standard secular will to transfer one's estate according to Jewish law,[1] but rather only on the permissibility of a Jewish lawyer writing such a will as a service to a client.

Indeed, two distinctly different issues are involved when considering secular wills. The first is the appropriateness of bequeathing one's assets to people who are not the proper heirs according to Jewish law. There are numerous opinions on how much of one's estate may be left to individuals other than the proper heirs—these opinions range from the majority to only *de minimis* amounts.[2] Since there are a broad variety of halakhically proper opinions advanced, it seems to this writer that a lawyer may write

---

1 For an overview of the issues involved in using secular wills, see R. Ezra Batzri, *Dinei Mamonot* 3:140–198 with particular focus on the analysis found in pages 192–196 and particularly n. 2. For an English discussion of these issues, see R. Judah Dick, "Jewish Law and the Conventional Last Will and Testament," *J. Halacha & Contemporary Society* 2:5 (1982), and Arthur Silver, "May One Disinherit Family in Favor of Charity?" *Tradition* 28(3):79 (1994).

2 See R. Judah Dick, "Last Will and Testament," at 5–7; R. Dov Baer Weidenfeld, *Dovevei Mesharim* 1:97; and *Maharam Schick, Hoshen Mishpat* 42, for examples of the relevance of this issue. *Rishonim* took a number of approaches to charitable gifts. R. Yitzhak ben Aba Mari, *Sefer Ha-Ittur* (*shekhiv mera* 40:109), ruled that one need only leave a token amount to family and this is agreed to by R. Shimon Duran, *Tashbetz* 147. *Rambam* (*Nahalot* 6:11) disagrees and prohibits any deviation from the Torah priorities of inheritance. R. Menahem ben Meir, *Meiri, Bava Batra* 133b and *Ketubot* 50a, permits only a third to be given to charity. R. Weiss, *Minhat Yitzhak* 1:233, and R. Feinstein, *Iggerot Moshe, Hoshen Mishpat* 2:50, both appear to permit

such a will for a client so long as at least a *de minimis* amount is left to the proper heirs.

The second issue is whether Jewish law recognizes a secular will as a valid means of transferring assets after death—i.e., is the property bequeathed through a secular will actually owned by the legatee or by the heirs mandated by Jewish law. This is the fundamental issue from the perspective of a lawyer, because if the transfer is not valid, the lawyer is assisting in a theft. Rabbi Feinstein states that such a method of transfer is valid (perhaps only if the language in the will is that of a gift).[3] Although many authorities disagree with him,[4] it is certainly not inappropriate for a lawyer to rely on Rabbi Feinstein's opinion as to the validity of the transfer if the client desires such a will, since most authorities agree that this will, once used, does in fact validly transfer title.[5]

Since there are halakhic authorities who recognize a secular will as a *post-facto* valid means of transferring one's assets,[6] it is likely that a lawyer can aid in the creation of such a document—even if the lawyer himself is of the opinion that such a document is not halakhically acceptable, since it is not the lawyer who is using the will. In this context, the lawyer is at most forbidden only to assist a person in a violation of Jewish law, since the client could certainly write the will himself or go to another

---

the giving of all of one's estate except for nominal amounts to a charity (see also *Iggerot Moshe, Hoshen Mishpat* 2:49).

3 See R. Moshe Feinstein, *Iggerot Moshe, Even ha-Ezer* 1:104, 105. (Any will written by an attorney invariably begins with the language of "I give and bequeath," thus fulfilling Rabbi Feinstein's implied condition.)

4 See R. Aryeh Grossnass, *Lev Aryeh* 1:53; R. Isadore Grunfeld, *The Jewish Law of Inheritance* (London, 1973); and R. Feivel Cohen, *Kuntres Midor L'dor: Laws of the Torah Relating to the Writing of a Will and the Distribution of One's Estate* (Targum, 1982).

5 See R. Shalom Mordecai Shwadron, *Maharsham* 224; R. Yaakov Ettlinger, *Binyan Tziyyon* app. 24; R. Ezekiel Ledvalla, *Sefer Ikkarei ha-Dat, Orah Hayyim* 21; and R. Aaron Parchi, *Perah Mateh Aharon* 1:60. Even R. Hayyim Ozer Grodzinski states that a *beit din* would enforce such a will, although he thinks the will is halakhically improper; see *Iggerot Ahiezer* 1:25. R. Yitzhak Isaac Herzog also maintains that these wills are at least post fact valid; see R. Isaac Herzog, *Tehukah le-Yisrael al pi ha-Torah* 2 ch. 5 (1989).

6 R. Judah Dick, "Last Will and Testament," at 13–15, and sources cited in note 5 of this chapter.

lawyer.⁷ This is certainly true if the client accepts Rabbi Feinstein's opinion that any will which uses the form of transfer of a gift (rather than the form of a bequest) validly transfers the property.⁸ Even if the lawyer does not accept as correct those authorities who permit a secular will (many authorities do not accept such a will as valid), the fact that the client does is sufficient. From the perspective of the lawyer, the prohibition of aiding another in a violation of Jewish law (*lifnei ivver*) would not apply since the sinner thinks his conduct is proper, and has competent halakhic authorities on which to rely. Furthermore, others will aid him if an observant lawyer does not.⁹

It could also be argued that according to all authorities there is no problem for anyone to write or witness a will; the sole problem occurs after death when the executor seeks to probate the will without the consent of the Jewish law heirs. A will could be written solely to inform the heirs mandated by Jewish law of the wishes of the deceased. In many situations, the Jewish heirs would consent to such a will since it is proper to fulfill the wishes of the deceased (*mitzvah lekayyem divrei ha-met*). When the Jewish law heirs consent, all problems in regard to Jewish law would cease. Under this reasoning, no difficulties attach to preparing a will. The sole problem occurs at probate when the heirs according to Jewish law claim the property. This is a classic example of a lawyer "providing assistance for the purpose of a legitimate endeavor" (the *mitzvah* of fulfilling the wishes of the deceased) which is later "misappropriated for a proscribed use." As Rabbi Bleich notes, that action by a lawyer "does not constitute a violation of" the rules prohibiting assisting one in a violation of Jewish law (the *lifnei ivver* rules).¹⁰

---

7   See chapter seven.

8   This author is inclined to believe that a lawyer may assume reliance by the client on R. Feinstein's opinion, even if the client is completely unaware of Jewish law.

9   This is because one may, without violating the *lifnei ivver* prohibition of assisting in a violation of Jewish law, assist a person in an action that some authorities consider permissible if the principal himself accepts this opinion, even if the aider does not. See R. Moshe Feinstein, *Iggerot Moshe, Even ha-Ezer* 4:61; R. Shlomo Zalman Auerbach, *Minhat Shlomo* 44; and "Enabling Sin" at 16, 31–32.

10 R. J. David Bleich "A Letter to a Student," ch. 5 at note 18.

The prohibition of devising one's estate to heirs other than those directed by Jewish law is subject to great dispute, and its severity is limited by the Talmud's statement that one who does so acts only without the spirit of the Sages.[11] This seems on its face not to apply to one who assists in creating such a document.[12] Of course, when a will considered valid and proper by all Jewish decisors would be drafted if the client knew about the various opinions, it is unquestionably preferable to encourage the client to request such a document. Indeed, in almost all cases a will conforming to the mandates of Jewish law can be written which merely changes the formulaic process of inheritance, and does not require any change in the distribution under the will.[13]

Living Wills

One final type of will is now commonly being written: a living will, which addresses the client's medical needs should the client be incapacitated. These wills themselves fall into two types. The first, called a "durable power of attorney" makes no specific decisions about the treatment of the patient, but instead simply designates who shall make those decisions if the client is not capable of making them. It would appear to this author that there are no halakhic problems associated with writing such a document even if the person named might not (or will not) make decisions in accordance with Jewish law. Essentially, the lawyer in this circumstance is assisting in the appointment of an agent, who might,[14] at some point in the future, not behave in a manner consistent with the dictates of Jewish law. As noted above[15] in a situation where the one being assisted merely might

---

11 *Bava Batra* 133b; Maimonides, *Nahalot* 6:11; *Shulhan Arukh*, *Hoshen Mishpat* 282:1.

12 Thus it is only considered "preferable" not to be a witness for such a document; see Maimonides, *Nahalot* 6:11; and *Shulhan Arukh*, *Hoshen Mishpat* 282:1.

13 For a detailed description of how to write such a will, see R. Feivel Cohen, *Kuntres Midor L'dor: Laws of the Torah Relating to the Writing of a Will and the Distribution of One's Estate* (Targum, 1982). In a situation where an estate tax will be assessed (because of the size of the estate), and thus a will that reduces tax liability is needed, a claim can be made that both wills should be used, with one clearly noted as valid only in a Jewish court.

14 It is important to realize that many contingencies could occur that would cause the agency to be irrelevant, such as the sudden (rather than drawn out) death of the client.

15 See authorities found in note 4 of chapter nine.

violate Jewish law, there is no problem to assist that person. This is even more so true when the one being assisted merely might appoint someone who *may* violate Jewish law.

The second type of living will instructs the hospital or doctor about details of the client's end of life treatment. Many of these directives would certainly violate Jewish law, and others are in dispute as to their acceptability according to Jewish law.[16] Writing a living will for a person where the person's orders are currently in dispute within Jewish law would not seem to be problematic. As noted above, there would seem to be no significant halakhic problem to aiding a person whose conduct is approved of by some halakhic authorities.[17] Writing a living will, which contains within it directives that directly contravene the undisputed mandates of Jewish law, places the lawyer in the same situation as he would be in when he represents a plaintiff in a lawsuit against a Jew that should be heard in Jewish court (*beit din*). In a situation where the client will go to another lawyer if this lawyer declines to write the living will and the client is sufficiently distant from rabbinic Judaism that rebuke would be either ineffective or is inapplicable, there are many authorities who would permit the lawyer to write this document.[18]

Conclusion

Thus, it is very likely that no significant problems are associated with writing a will for a client, even if there can be difficulties associated with a person using a classical secular will as a way to transfer all or most of his estate. The lawyer's role in will-writing is not one of being a principal, but only that of an aider—in a document that some (but not all) authorities maintain will not be efficacious without consent in the future of the heirs mandated by Jewish law.[19] Many of these leniencies apply with even

---

16 For a discussion of these various issues, see R. Abraham S. Abraham, *Nishmat Avraham*, throughout volume four. For a discussion of time of death issues, see R. J. David Bleich, *Time of Death in Jewish Law* (Z. Berhman, New York, 1991).

17 See authorities cited in note 9 of this chapter.

18 See text accompanying notes 25 to 39 in chapter four on admonishment and rebuke.

19 Whether a lawyer could seek to probate a will that will be contested by the Jewish law heirs is a question addressed in chapter seven, in the text accompanying note 39. Indeed, one who would write such a will is, at most, only in a secondary way (*lifnei de-lifnei*, see note 10 of chapter seven) assisting in a violation of Jewish law, as these decisions are made by the executor, and not the lawyer.

greater force to the writing of a living will, in that the living will might (but need not ever[20]) be used. The violation of Jewish law occurs when the document is used (to force a violation of Jewish law) and not in the writing of it.

---

20 See note 14.

Chapter Fourteen

Family Law and Child Custody

General Problems in Family Law

The interaction between Jewish and secular law is of the most difficulty in the field of family law (i.e., marriage, divorce, and child custody). It is in this area that many of the values that are at the core of Jewish law have been rejected by normative Western society. When an attorney who practices family law deals with a dispute involving a Jewish couple, an intermarried couple, or a couple seeking to become married, it is very important to analyze carefully the implications of the legal advice given according to Jewish law.

In addition, unlike Jewish law, where marriage and divorce are essentially private contracts, common law requires family arrangements (including child custody) to be sanctioned by the government—in the case of divorce and custody, by the courts.[1] Thus, lawyers are frequently called upon to mediate disputes between spouses who are seeking a divorce and disputing custody of the children.

A number of basic issues need to be addressed. As an initial matter, a lawyer may not advise a client, for financial or social reasons, to stay married to someone whom Jewish law prohibits one from marrying.[2] Thus, when a lawyer is involved in giving legal advice in an intermarriage, it is

---

1 I have addressed some of these issues elsewhere; see Michael Broyde, "The Establishment of Maternity and Paternity in Jewish and American Law," *National Jewish L.R.* 3:117 (1988).

2 Such as one's brother's wife after their divorce. This was first pointed out in a slightly different context by Rabbi Yosef while discussing the role of a therapist; see Rabbi Ovadia Yosef, *Yabia Omer* 3:21, where he discusses numerous issues that relate to

incumbent upon the lawyer either to give no advice as to how to salvage the marriage or to counsel the client not to try to save the marriage. Giving advice to continue a prohibited relationship is most likely a biblical violation of the rules related to assisting a violation of Jewish law (*lifnei ivver*)—as it is classically "bad advice."[3]

Similarly, it would seem proper for an attorney who is aiding a Jewish couple seeking a divorce to advise the couple that they must also seek a divorce which is proper according to Jewish law (a *get*). While a lawyer may continue to represent a client who has indicated that he or she will seek only a secular divorce,[4] the experience of many in this field has indicated that even many non-observant couples will in fact seek a proper divorce according to Jewish law once the obligation to do so, and the consequences according to Jewish law of not doing so, are presented to them.

So too, it is prohibited for a lawyer to encourage a Jew who is seeking to use the requirement that a couple be properly divorced according to Jewish law (i.e., that a *get* be given) in order to demand money from a spouse lest he or she be left incapable of remarrying in a situation where Jewish law mandates that a Jewish divorce be given.[5] Aiding or encouraging a person to extort money as payment for a *get* would undoubtedly violate both the "bad advice" and "aiding a sinner" aspect of the *lifnei ivver* prohibition governing assisting in a violation of Jewish law. Once the marriage is functionally over, and each side genuinely seeks to dissolve the marital bonds, the withholding of a *get* is improper. As Rabbi Joseph Henkin states:

> One who withholds a Jewish divorce because he desires money for no just cause is a thief. Indeed, he is worse than a thief as his conduct violates a sub-prohibition related to taking a human life.[6]

---

    counseling. See also Rabbi Moshe Sternbuch, *Teshuvot ve-Hanhagot* 1:730. Rabbi Yehudah Amital notes, in *Rebuking a Jew*, at 130, that such is the practice of the rabbinical courts in Israel on a daily basis. In this author's opinion a clear distinction can be found in these two works between a prohibited marriage and a marriage where the couple does not observe Jewish law, but are permitted to marry each other and remain together. Encouraging the former is prohibited and the latter is permitted.

3 See "Enabling Sin," at 6–9.

4 For reasons explained in chapters seven and eight.

5 For an excellent discussion of the various proposed solutions to the *agunah* problem, see Irving Breitowitz, *Between Civil and Religious Law: The Plight of the Agunah in American Society* (Greenwood, 1994).

6 Rabbi Yosef Eliyahu Henkin, *Edut le-Yisrael* 143–144; reprinted in *Kol Kitvei ha-Rav Henkin* 1:115a–b. The term "sub-prohibition" is a translation of the Hebrew term

Indeed, unlike most of the situations involving civil litigation,[7] in the context of providing assistance in withholding a *get* the observant lawyer is most properly categorized as "two sides of the river"—vital service—since in reality religiously-observant attorneys can best provide this kind of assistance.[8]

Child Custody

Involvement in child custody arrangements in a civil court can also lead to problems. Courts in the United States will not allow the binding arbitration of child custody disputes in any forum other than the secular court. Thus, while a Jewish court (*beit din*) can decide such matters, its decision very likely will be challenged in court by a dissatisfied parent. Unlike monetary disputes, which most states enforce without reviewing the merits of a *beit din*'s determination, courts in custody disputes will review all arrangements *de novo*.[9] Thus, notwithstanding Jewish law's rules for determining the appropriate parent (or other) to receive custody in the ease of divorce or separation, there is no guarantee that the court will accept the *beit din*'s judgment.

A certain familiarity with the substantive rules used by Jewish law in the area of child custody is needed to appreciate the problems confronted

---

"*abizrayu*." In the previous paragraph, Rabbi Henkin stated that "if a husband and wife separate and he no longer desires to remain married to her and she desires to be divorced, in this case divorce is a *mitzvah* [obligation] and commanded by Jewish law." Even in response to adultery most authorities rule that it is improper to withhold a *get*; see R. Eliezer Waldenberg, *Tzitz Eliezer* 19:58.

7   These are typically cases where the lawyer's assistance is only "one side of the river," and thus frequently permitted; see chapters five, six, and seven.

8   See Rabbi Judah Rosanes, *Mishneh le-Melekh, Malveh ve-Loveh* 4:2, who rules that in situations where only Jews can provide the prohibited assistance, a biblical prohibition is violated when one Jew assists, even if others will. For more on this, see note 14 of chapter seven.

9   Melissa Philbrick, "Agreements to Arbitrate Post-Divorce Custody Disputes," *Columbia Journal of Law and Social Problems* 18:419, 459 (1985) ("While [the courts] strictly enforce non-custody arbitration clauses, courts in custody cases retain the power of *de novo* review in the name of *parens patriae*. This stance accentuates procedural problems of delay and uncertainty, thereby destabilizing the divorced family..."

by a lawyer representing a client in the area of child custody.[10] The Talmud[11] seems to lay down three rules that govern child custody disputes between parents:

(1) Custody of all children under the age of six is to be given to the mother;

(2) Custody of boys over the age of six is to be given to the father;

(3) Custody of girls over the age of six is to be given to the mother.[12]

The Talmud[13] also indicates that these ideal rules of child custody presuppose that both the mother and the father desire custody of the children, are financially capable of custody, and are at least minimally competent parents. Jewish law, however, rules as a matter of law that mothers (at least upon termination of the marriage) are under no legal obligation to support and maintain their children, whereas fathers are.[14] Indeed, these rules are

---

10 I have addressed the issue of child custody at some length elsewhere. See "Child Custody: A Pure Law. Analysis," *Jewish Law Association Studies VII: The Paris Conference Volumes* 1–20 (1994).

11 *Eruvin* 82a, *Ketubot* 65b, 122b-123a.

12 *Shulhan Arukh, Even ha-Ezer* 82:7 seems to indicate that the mother may keep custody of the children in all circumstauces if she is willing to forgo the father's financial support. Thus, according to *Shulhan Arukh*'s way of understanding the rule, children are placed according to these presumptive rules, and parents are obligated to support them in these circumstances. Should one parent wish to keep custody beyond the time in which it is in the children's own best interest to stay with that parent, the other parent would cease being obligated to pay for their support; R. Moshe Alshekh, *Responsa* 38. As has been noted by R. Yom Tov ben Moshe Zahalon, *Maharit Zahalon* 1:16, 2:232, and others, most authorities reject this rule and state that the mother may not keep custody of the children beyond the time in which it would be in the children's own best interest, even if she were willing to do so without child support payments from the father. This appears to be the majority opinion; for more on this issue, see "Custody in Jewish Law," at 2–3 (1994).

13 *Ketubot* 59b.

14 *Rambam, Ishut* 21:17–18; *Even ha-Ezer* 82:6,8. This presupposes that others can and will raise and support the children if the mother does not. However, in a situation in which a child is so attached to a particular parent that if this parent does not care for the child, the child will die, Jewish law compels one to take care of the child, not because of a special legal obligation between a parent and a child, but because of the

codified in Maimonides' Code and *Shulhan Arukh* and are the basis of much of the discussion found among the later authorities.

These rules, read in a vacuum, appear to provide no measure of flexibility at all and mandate the mechanical placement of children into the appropriate category. However, Jewish law never understood these rules as cast in stone; all decisors accepted that there are circumstances where the interest of the child overwhelmed the obligation to follow the rules.[15]

It is apparent, however, that this interpretation of the talmudic precepts, which turns these rules into mere presumptions which may be disregarded, is understood by the various authorities in different ways. Two issues need to be addressed. First, in what circumstances may one reject the talmudic presumption—need the presumptive custodial parent be "unfit" or is it enough that others are "more fit"? Second, in cases in which the talmudic presumption has been rejected, who should then be assigned custody? Is that determination based purely on the "best interest of the child", or must custody be granted to the other parent as a matter of law, assuming that the parent is "fit."?

Indeed, there is a significant dispute within Jewish law as to the very nature of the right of parents to custody of their children, with a number of authorities arguing that Jewish law really only considers the best interest of the child as relevant, whereas many other authorities focus on both the best interest of the child and—equally significantly—parental duties (and the resulting right to custody). This issue remains in dispute to this day, with various Jewish courts (*batei din*) ruling in conflicting directions).[16] Compounding this problem is the fact that the children, whose custody is being determined, cannot consent to the use of legal rules other

---

general obligation to rescue Jews in life-threatening situations. This situation arises when a woman has been nursing her child and does not wish to continue to do so; if the child will not nurse from another and thus will die without the mother's nursing, Jewish law compels the mother to care for and nurse the child as part of the general obligation of not standing by while one's neighbor's blood is shed, see e.g., *Tur, Even ha-Ezer* 82:6,8.

15 For more on the exact nature of this, see "Child Custody," at 5–9.

16 For more on this, see Eliav Shochatman,"The Essence of the Principles Used in Child Custody in Jewish Law," *Shenaton la-Mishpat ha-Ivri* 5:285 (1978) (best interest of the child is the normative *halakhah*); R. Hayyim David Gulevsky, "Question on the Custody of Children," *Sefer Kevod Harav: Essays in Honor of Rabbi Joseph B. Soloieitchik* 104 (New York, 1984) (paternal rights a significant factor); Ronald Warburg, "Child Custody: A Comparative Analysis," *Israel Law Review* 14:480–503 (1978) (best interest is the rule); and Israel Tzvi Gilat, "Is the Best Interest of the

than those mandated by Jewish law; thus, arbitration (or compromise) also appears to have no place in child custody matters.[17] In short, custody matters nearly always must be determined by a *beit din*.[18]

It would be a violation of Jewish law for a lawyer to advise a client to refuse to go to a *beit din* to arrange child custody matters or to ignore the ruling of *beit din* once its judgment is given. The use of the secular courts, which place considerably less emphasis on the proper religious training of children, can (without a prior agreement between the parents) result in custodial arrangements contrary to the dictates of Jewish law and perhaps the best interests of the child on a religious level. These considerations are even more significant when one of the parents is not fit to be a parent according to Jewish law, but yet is considered qualified according to secular law.

Representing a parent unfit according to Jewish law in a custody dispute with a qualified parent is most likely a violation of Jewish law, since the lawyer cannot argue that the client should be entitled to custody.[19] This is analogous to presenting a false defense in a civil action, which is prohibited.

In cases where none of the participants would consider going to *beit din* under any circumstances, the role of a lawyer in child custody matters would appear to be no different than in civil matters generally and thus is permissible in the circumstances discussed in chapters six through eight.

Child a Major Factor When Parents Conflict on Custody of a Child," *Bar Ilan Law Studies* 8:297–349 (1980) (parental rights is a major factor). Much of this is summarized in "Child Custody," at 3–15.

17 This has not been stated explicitly by any authority, but flows logically from the requirement that one cannot be forced to consent to arbitration or compromise. Free consent must be given; see chapter seventeen. A minor cannot provide that consent, and thus may not agree to a compromise. Even if one claims that the minor's guardian can provide that consent (see *Hoshen Mishpat* 290:13), it is difficult to maintain that this consent can be used to determine who is the child's guardian.

18 In addition, all of the rules contained in chapter seven apply equally to family law issues. Obviously, it would be permitted to litigate in secular court custody issues in any situation where a proper *beit din* can not be convened or *beit din* gives permission to litigate in secular court. On the question of whether a *beit din* can convene and hear cases through a televideo conference, see Rabbi Howard Jachter, "The Use of a Video Teleconference for a *Get* Procedure," *J. Halacha & Contemporary Society* 28:5–47 (1994).

19 See text accompanying note 8 of this chapter.

Where the fit parent has already initiated proceedings in a Jewish court, which the other parent who is proceeding in secular court is defying or ignoring, it is prohibited to aid the latter for the reasons explained at the end of chapter seven.[20]

In summary, child custody arrangements ordered by a Jewish court (*beit din*) will not automatically be honored by the secular courts in the United States. It is a violation of Jewish law for a lawyer to assist a secular court in declining to follow the order of Jewish court or to assist a litigant in having such a matter heard in secular court when one of the litigants wishes to have the matter adjudicated by *beit din*.

Support Payments

It seems that litigating child support payments (as opposed to child custody arrangements) in secular court poses (only) the problems that litigating any financial transaction in secular court poses, and thus in many situations a lawyer can engage in that litigation, provided that the conditions specified in chapter eight are satisfied.

The status of alimony payments ordered by a secular court as part of a separation or divorce is no different from the status of any other secular financial obligation not based on Jewish law, but rather on the fact that it is a common practice and the law of the land. As explained in chapter six, the authorities have adopted different approaches to determine how and when secular law is incorporated (either by "the law of the land" or by consent of the parties) into private commercial dealings.[21]

---

20 Thus, the situation that lawyers should exercise the most caution before undertaking to represent, involves the case of two "fit" parents, only one of whom is religiously fit. It is extremely problematic to represent the "fit," but unobservant parent in that case, particularly since the "fit" observant parent would almost certainly prefer to go to *beit din*.

21 Few responsa can be found that even address this issue. For a very similar case which rules, in the alternative, that secular law provides a woman with financial rights against her husband (or his estate); see R. Yehuda Leib Grauburt, *Havalim ba-Neimim*, *Even ha-Ezer* 55. R. Joseph Trani, *Mabit* 1:309, is yet another such responsum. For a similar type of claim, see R. Yitzhak Isaac Liebes, *Beit Avi* 4:169. Similar reasoning can be inferred from R. Moshe Feinstein's ruling (*Iggerot Moshe, Even ha-Ezer* 1:137) that the wife's waiver of past due support payments mandated by secular law, in return for the husband's issuing a *get*, is a form of permissible coercion which does not

invalidate the *get* (create a *get me'useh* situation). This waiver of a financial claim is valid coercion only in a case where the woman's claim to the money is halakhically valid, as the wife is entitled to these payments through *dina de-malkhuta*.This issue is addressed at some length in the appendix to this book, which discusses the 1992 New York *Get* Law.

Business Law and the Law Business

This section discusses the many halakhic issues raised when a lawyer assists in a business deal. Chapter fifteen contains a detailed discussion of the issues raised when a lawyer participates in a financial transaction that involves interest payments, which is a very common event. The next two chapters focus on Jewish law issues involved in negotiations and arbitration. The final chapter deals with lawyers' billing by the hour.

Chapter Fifteen

Usury

Interest Charging: An Introduction

The topic of charging interest on loans is an enormously complicated one, and the tension between Jewish law and common secular commercial practice is very great. Jewish law forbids charging interest on loans between two Jews except in certain circumstances, the most common being by use of a *heter iska*, a document which reclassifies the loan as a partnership (of sorts) according to Jewish law.[1] This book will assume that the typical lawyer will not be able to routinely convince clients to use a *heter iska*, and it does not address the ramifications of using a *heter iska*.[2]

More likely than not, it is this area, and not the prohibition of litigating in a secular court, that poses the greatest challenge to one's ability to

---

1 For a general overview of usury issues in Jewish law in English, see R. Joseph Stern, "Ribis: A Halachic Anthology," *J. Halacha & Contemporary Society* 4:46 (1982), and R. Yechiel Grunhaus, "The Laws of Usury and Their Significance in Our Times," *J. Halacha & Contemporary Society* 21:48 (1992). For a more historical approach to the problems of interest charging, see Haym Soloveitchik, *Pawn Broking: A Study in the Interrelationship between Halakhah, Economic Activity and Communal Self-Image* (Magnes, 1985). This book will not discuss interest charging by lawyers as part of their billing process.

2 For more on *heter iska*s see text accompanying note 20 of chapter four. For a detailed explanation of how a *heter iska* works, see R. J. David Bleich, *Contemporary Halakhic Problems* II:376 (1983). For an excellent analysis of the effect a *heter iska* has on transactions according to American law, as well as a brief discussion of other issues relating to charging interest, see Steven Resnicoff, "A Commercial Conundrum: Does Prudence Permit the Jewish 'Permissible Venture [*Heter Iska*]'?" *Seton Hall L.R.* 20:77 (1989).

function as a lawyer according to Jewish law. Moreover, these difficulties are not limited to the practice of law, but are present in all areas of commercial transactions, from real estate to banking to retail sales. In fact, the violations committed by a lawyer assisting in these transactions are of a considerably lower degree than those of the person actually engaging in such transactions. The primary obligation not to charge interest falls on the one engaging in the prohibited transactions, and not on the lawyer assisting.

Limitations

Two initial substantive limitations exist on the scope of the prohibition to charge interest. The most significant restriction on the prohibition of charging or paying interest is that it is permissible to charge or pay interest on loans to or from gentiles, businesses owned by gentiles, or a corporation controlled by or primarily owned by gentiles.[3] In the diaspora virtually all banks fit into this category.

The second limitation relates to Jewish-owned corporations. As has been ruled by a number of authorities, including Rabbi Feinstein,[4] any time the borrower does not personally obligate himself to repay the loan, but only accepts the limited liability of a corporation, no violation of the laws of taking or paying interest occur. If one accepts these authorities' view, since the underlying interest-bearing transaction is permitted, a lawyer may assist in the arrangement in any situation where the borrower is borrowing as a corporate entity and not as an individual.[5] Even those

---

3 Aaron Kirschenbaum, "Legal Persons" *Encyclopedia Judaica* 10:1569–70; *Shulhan Arukh, Yoreh Deah* 159:1; R. Moshe Sternbuch, *Ta'am Ribbit* 1:1–4; R. Yaakov Blau, *Berit Yehudah* 30:16. Although this book is not the place to address this issue in detail, most authorities permit one to lend money with interest to an apostate (*mumar*), although not to borrow money from him; see *Shulhan Arukh, Yoreh Deah* 159:2. The distinction between an apostate and one brought up in a gentile society without knowledge of Judaism (literally, *tinok shenishbah*, a baby who has been captured) in our current society, however, is difficult to define; see *Ta'am Ribbit* 1:4; *Berit Yehudah* 30:8–15.

4 R. Moshe Feinstein, *Iggerot Moshe, Yoreh Deah* 2:62, 63; R. Shimon Greenfeld, *Maharshag, Yoreh Deah* 5; R. Joseph Rozin, *Tsofnat Paneah* 184.

5 In a situation where the owner of the corporation must also sign a personal liability note, this permissive ruling does not apply. On the other hand, a limited (and perhaps even a regular) partnership that borrows on a "non-recourse" basis most likely is a corporation for the purpose of this ruling.

who argue with Rabbi Feinstein's approach (and many do), maintaining that according to Jewish law a corporation is treated no differently from a partnership, concede that a corporation's paying interest is only prohibited according to rabbinic, and not biblical, law[6]—a factor whose significance will be explained later in this chapter.

Most commercial interest-bearing transactions fit into either this exception or involve one party who is not Jewish. Virtually all transactions which require the assistance of a lawyer (except for a seller's mortgage) involve lending money either to a corporation, from a gentile bank or, more typically, both.

Rabbinically Prohibited Interest

From the perspective of a lawyer, one other significant rule has to be explained. Many common forms of interest charging are only forbidden according to rabbinic decree rather than biblical law. In any situation in which only a rabbinic prohibition of interest-charging is violated, the prohibition for a lawyer to aid in the prohibited transactions is one not of lending with interest, but of aiding in the commission of a sin. This is not true if the prohibited type of interest involves a biblical violation, since the Talmud considers that all who facilitate the prohibited lending with interest violate the biblical prohibition of lending with interest as well as the prohibition governing assisting in a violation of Jewish law (*lifnei ivver*).[7] However, it is accepted that the prohibition to lend with interest does not apply to the facilitator (lawyer, scribe, witness) when the underlying prohibition is only rabbinic in nature.[8] In short, a person who assists in an interest-bearing transaction which is only rabbinically prohibited, is confronting only an assisting in a violation of Jewish law (*lifnei ivver*) problem and not the substantive prohibition of lending with interest.

---

6 See R. Yaakov Blau, *Berit Yehudah* 7:24 (quoting numerous authorities who argue with Rabbi Feinstein); and n. 66 (stating that only a rabbinic prohibition is involved).

7 *Bava Metzia* 75b. For the biblical verses, see Exodus 22:24 and Leviticus 25:36–37.

8 See *Shulhan Arukh, Yoreh Deah* 160:1 and particularly the commentary of R. Yaakov Lorberbaum, *Havat Daat*, 160:1, and *Sedei Hemed*, at 6:26(3) (stating that most authorities agree with R. Yaakov Lorberbaum). For a complete discussion of this issue, as well a discussion of whether other authorities disagree, see R. Sternbuch, *Ta'am Ribbit* 160:1, n. 3–4.

A careful study of the laws of usury leads one to conclude that in nearly all transactions in which the lender loans the money through the issuing of a check, rather than directly in cash or commodities, the lender only violates the rabbinic prohibition of charging interest, even if the loan was of a type that is normally biblically prohibited.[9]

Before this is explained halakhically, it is important to understand what a check is, and how it works according to American law. While one might view money on deposit in a bank as a form of bailment, this is incorrect. Rather,

> [s]uch funds become the property of the bank, which can commingle and use them as it sees fit....The depositor acquires, in return for the deposit, a claim on the bank as its general, unsecured creditor, and in some accounts, authority to write a check, payment order, or draft against that claim in favor of another person.[10]

In essence, money deposited in a bank is a debt owed by the bank to the depositor. A check issued against an account with a positive balance is simply a direction to the bank to repay the debt owed to the depositor to a third-party. This understanding of a check has a significant impact on Jewish law, and has been widely-recognized by a number of authorities. For example, many authorities do not treat the sale of a check at a discount as a form of prohibited interest payment since all that is actually occurring is the purchase of a debt.[11]

---

9 As was explained, this is of great significance to a lawyer.

10 Peter Smedresman & Andreas Lowenfeld, "Eurodollars, Multinational Banks, and National Laws," *N.Y.U. Law Rev.* 64:733 (1989) paraphrasing Michie on Banks & Banking, 5A §(A)4(b) (1983). A bank is a bailee on a safe deposit box, since it does not have the right to use the valuables in the box.

11 This assumes that there is money in the account to cover the check and the check is not post-dated. See e.g., R. Joseph Hazan, *Hikrei Lev, Hoshen Mishpat* 2:155; R. Yaakov Blau, *Berit Yehudah* 15:16–18 (n. 37–39); R. Ezra Batzri, *Dinei Mamonot* 5:5 (n. 4–5); R. Moshe Hershler & R. Eliyahu Hershrik, *Torat Ribbit* 18:18–19 (n. 34; but see notes 35–56); R. Shmuel Shor, *Minhat Shai, Yoreh Deah* 173 (2d ed); and R. Sternbuch, *Ta'am Ribbit*, at 9:1–4. This position can also be found in authorities from previous generations; see R. Yitzhak Weiss, *Minhat Yitzhak* 7:64; R. Moshe Schick, *Maharam Schick, Yoreh Deah* 161; and R. Yaakov Emden, *She'elat Ya'avetz* 1:39; but see R. Shlomo Englander, *Kelala de-Ribbita* Introduction, n. 7. For a review of this area, see Rabbi Tzvi Yehuda Ben-Yakov, "Checks: Their Essence and Legal Status,"

Once the mechanism by which a check works is understood, it can be argued that no biblical violation of the laws of lending with interest is possible whenever the funds lent are transferred by check (providing that the bank used by the lender is owned by a gentile). In any situation in which one Jew desires (in violation of Jewish law) to lend money (with interest) to another Jew, but instead of lending the money in cash, directs that the money loaned be paid through a check, no biblical violation of the laws of lending with interest will have occurred. This is so because the lender is actually only directing a gentile (the bank) to transfer money the gentile owes the lender (the money on deposit in the bank) and to convey the debt to a new (and Jewish) borrower. When the borrower deposits the check, money previously owed by the bank (to the lender) is now owed by the Jewish borrower to the lender. A debt owed to a Jew (and the obligation to pay interest on that debt) was transferred from a gentile borrower to a Jewish borrower.

Although it is true that the net effect of this transaction is that one Jew owes money and interest to another Jew, the fact that the money was not directly transferred from one Jew to another, but rather was passed through a gentile "middle-man," is of enormous halakhic significance. While the status of using a gentile as a straw man for an otherwise prohibited interest-bearing transaction is a topic of much controversy within Jewish law, and was a topic of significant dispute among the early authorities (*Rishonim*), it is now well-accepted that the prohibition involved in authorizing an interest bearing loan through a gentile "middle-man" is at most a rabbinic one.[12]

Tehumin 13:422–470 (1993). The sale of a post-dated check at a discount is generally thought to be permissible also, as all understand that there might not be money in the account in the future to cover this check; see R. Yaakov Blau, *Berit Yehudah* 15:17.

Rabbi J. David Bleich, in a recent article has argued that a check should not be classified as a note of indebtedness according to American law since the issuer of the check has the legal right to stop the check at any time after issuing it; the check does not by itself create any obligation to the payee and is not a promissory note; see Uniform Commercial Code §3–408. Thus a check should not be halakhically classified as a "note for indebtedness" (*shtar hov*); see R. J. David Bleich, "Survey of Recent Halakhic Literature: Checks," *Tradition* 24:74 (1989).

12 See R. Moshe Isserles, (*Rema*) *Yoreh Deah* 168–9:3,9; and R. Yaakov Blau, *Berit Yehudah* 33:1–6; and the notes accompanying paragraph 6. A number of authorities maintain that this transaction is permitted; most maintain that this transaction is rabbinically prohibited. Maimonides maintains it is a biblical prohibition.

A second reason can also be advanced for labeling virtually all interest-bearing commercial transactions as only violating a rabbinic prohibition. While the prohibition to lend with interest is violated whether cash or commodities are lent and repaid, it is also accepted by most authorities, though not all, that the biblical prohibition is not violated when one lends with interest a note of indebtedness (*shtar hov*) and is repaid with a note of indebtedness as well. (For example, "A" lends "B" a $1,000 AT&T bond for a year on the condition that "B" returns to "A" a $1,500 AT&T bond at the year's end.) Such a transaction violates only the rabbinic usury prohibition.[13] Since "checks have the status of notes of indebtedness" for the purposes of the laws of prohibited interest,[14] no violation of the biblical prohibition of lending with interest can occur when both the loan and the repayment are by check. Jewish law would view the two checks as identical to the two AT&T bonds in the above example. Only a rabbinic violation of the laws of lending with interest has occurred since notes of indebtedness are used by the parties to transfer funds.

Indeed, the claim that no biblical violation of the usury rules occurs when a check from a gentile bank is issued to provide the loan is even

---

The basis for ruling that no biblical violation can occur whenever a gentile "middleman" is used, is that Jewish law accepts that according to biblical law, a gentile cannot be an agent for a Jew to create legal culpability for the one directing the agent. Since there would be no agency according to biblical law, there can be no biblical violation.

The fact that the money actually originates from the Jew is what would create the rabbinic prohibition. Additionally, according to Jewish law, the illicit transfer of an interest-bearing debt from one party to another seems only to be a rabbinic prohibition in almost all circumstances; see *Berit Yehudah*, 6:1–9.

Even if the bank is owned by Jews, some authorities still maintain that the lender has not violated any biblical violation, since there never is any agency for a prohibited act ("*ein shaliah li-devar averah*"). It would be the Jewish bank that transgresses biblical law—the Jewish lender has only violated rabbinic law; see *Rema* commenting on *Shulhhan Arukh*, *Yoreh Deah* 160:16, and comments of R. Shabtai Meir ha-Kohen (*Shakh*) on ibid. Many authorities reject this rule; see *Berit Yehudah* 6:12 and R. David Tzvi Hoffmann, *Melammed le-Ho'il* 2:59.

13 See text accompanying notes 11 to 12 and note 15. The reasons for this ruling are beyond the scope of this book. For a complete explanation, see *Tosafot*, *Bava Metzia* 61a s.v. *im eyno*; *Tur*, *Yoreh Deah* 161; *Shakh*, *Yoreh Deah* 161:1; R. Yaakov Lorberbaurn (*Me-Lisa*) *Havat Daat* 161:1; and R. Yaakov Blau, *Berit Yehudah* 2:7 (particularly notes 17, 18, and 19).

14 R. Yaakov Blau, *Berit Yehudah* 2:7 (n. 19). The reason this is so is explained in the text above.

stronger than the medieval case of the gentile straw man. The bank—modern gentile middle man—is a *bona fide* debtor who is actually transferring a debt that was not created as a mere sham to avoid the Jewish law restrictions on interest-charging. Nearly all decisors agree that no biblical violation is possible when the middle man is genuine and is actually transferring his own money. This is correct no matter how payment through a check is classified in Jewish law.[15]

Accordingly, virtually all modern-day commercial transactions involving a Jewish borrower and lender only concern rabbinic prohibitions, since almost all such transactions are done through a bank or involve checks rather than cash. Any time a transaction is arranged such that the lender does not give the money directly to the borrower (and vice-versa upon repayment of the loan), no biblical violation of the interest-charging prohibition has occurred.[16] As has been stated above, any time the prohibition to lend is only rabbinic, the prohibition to assist the borrower or lender is only governed by the rules related to assisting an illegal transaction —*lifnei ivver*.

Usury and the Lawyer

Once the prohibition the lawyer is transgressing is properly categorized as assisting another in a violation of Jewish law (*lifnei ivver*) and not the principle prohibition itself, the scope of the lawyer's conduct permitted by

---

15 If a check is a mere directive to pay most authorities view this transaction as violative only of rabbinic law; see *Tosafot, bava Metzia* 71b s.v. *matzo yisrael*. *Havat Da'at* 168:2; *Berit Yehudah* 33:6(n.15 and 16); *Teshuvot Rivash* 276; *Kitzot Ha-Hoshen* 126:15; and *Torat Ribbit* 22:3 (second approach). Neither *Shakh* (*Yoreh Deah* 168:16) nor *Beit Yosef* (*Yoreh Deah* 168) disagree, as one is merely explaining *Bach* who is explaining *Tur* and the other retracts his ruling in *Shulhan Arukh, Yoreh Deah* 168:4–5, However, some do rule this a biblical violation; see *Torat Ribbit* 22:3 (first opinion) and the strained arguments provided by Asher Meir, "Money and Means of Payment in Halakha," *Alei Etzion* 4:119, 127–139 (1995). If checks are the sale of a debt, it is clear that no violation of biblical law occurs; see *Torat Ribbit* 23:1–3. Rabbi Moshe Feinstein, *Iggerot Moshe Hoshen Mishpat* 2:15 (s.v. *hem*) and R. Tzvi Ben-Yaakov, "Checks" *Tehumin* 13:422–470 (1993) both adopt this approach. If checks are a note of indebtedness, the leniency of a Gentile middleman discussed in note 12 applies, and no biblical violation is possible.

16 *Shulhan Arukh, Yoreh Deah* 160:1–6; R. Yaakov Blau, *Berit Yehudah* 6:1–8.

Jewish law greatly increases. As discussed previously[17] the parameters of the prohibition of *lifnei ivver* are subject to significant dispute, and in a situation where there are many lawyers who will do the work if the Jewish lawyer declines to, a lawyer who is willing to rely on the lenient opinions of *Tosafot, Rema, Shakh*, and Rabbi Landau (the author of the *Dagul me-Revavah*), may represent a client in a transaction involving the payment of interest. Thus, a lawyer who participates in the typical interest-bearing transaction should be aware of the various *lifnei ivver* issues involved in assisting another in a violation of Jewish law; however a lawyer can, according to many authorities, conduct himself with care, in a manner not in violation of Jewish law.[18]

The laws of charging interest are among the most complex in Jewish law, and have been in tension with the general commercial practices of the secular society that European Jews have lived in for over eight hundred years. Difficult as these issues are, solutions to many problems do exist, and one should hesitate to foreclose as halakhically impermissible any of the more common professions—law or any other—merely because interest-charging occurs.

---

17 See chapters seven to nine; see also "Enabling Sin," at 12–18.

18 Even in such a circumstance a lawyer may not actually encourage a client to enter into such a transaction, as that would be a form of "bad advice" classically prohibited by Jewish law. However, the lawyer may create contracts or other financial instruments that implement the client's wishes, even if they involve charging interest.

Chapter Sixteen

Negotiations

The Problem of Puffery

The issues raised by negotiations are, in reality, outside the scope of this work, as they are applicable only peripherally to a lawyer; they primarily fall on the principal carrying out the negotiations, and not his agent (the lawyer). Nonetheless, one very important point must be made in regard to the conduct of negotiations. Jewish law recognizes that within certain limitations, many of the non-specific assertions made in the context of negotiations, particularly about state of mind and price, are subjects of puffery and exaggeration. Since all the parties are aware of this, such statements are permitted. For example, the Talmud[1] rules that the reciprocal oaths taken by the buyer and the seller not to change their asking price for the product are not generally understood to be binding oaths, but mere hyperbole. (An example explains this phenomenon well. Such an oath occurs when the buyer states "I swear that I will not offer you more than $2 for your product," and the seller states that "I swear that I will not sell the product for less than $4.")[2]

---

1 *Nedarim* 21a-b.

2 There is, in fact, a dispute in such a case as to whether the oath-taker can still offer the product at the exact price ($2 or $4) or whether the bargaining must start at $2.01 and go as high as $3.99. *Rema* (*Yoreh Deah* 232:2) indicates that the oath-taker is precluded from accepting an offer at the precise price he foreswore, but can accept some very similar price. Many other authorities argue that the whole oath is void, as mere hyperbole, and the oath-taker can buy or sell the object at any price; see comments of *Shakh* (*Yoreh Deah*, 323:3) and *Bah* (on *Tur* 232:1). *Arukh ha-Shulhan*,

Thus, a lawyer who engages in negotiations on behalf of a client is entitled to engage in a certain amount of exaggeration. For example, a lawyer could indicate that the other party's offer is so low that his client would rather keep the property than sell at that price, even though the client has told the lawyer in confidence that even the initial price is acceptable.[3] Of course, specific assertions about the product—but not about the state of mind of the buyer—must always be true. Thus, the assertion that the real estate taxes on the property are a specific amount, that the plaintiff has never been sued before on this issue, or that the car has never been in an accident; must always be true.[4] On the other hand, the statement made in the context of negotiations by a lawyer that the defendant would not consider settling this suit for less than $100,000 need not be true, as everyone knows that such statements are mere hyperbole.

A Limitation and an Expansion

There is one crucial exception to this rule. A statement made in a context where it is clear that it could not be understood as hyperbole, but was made as a legally binding statement, is in fact binding[5] and must be accurate. Thus, for example, if there were a judicial conference designed to promote a settlement, and a judge asked a lawyer what his client thought of a proposed settlement of the claim for $50,000, and the client had previously stated to the lawyer that he would take that settlement—but the lawyer realized that if he replied that his client would settle for $60,000, such a settlement would be accepted—the lawyer may not misrepresent the word of the client in that setting. The reason for this is that a judicial

---

Yoreh Deah 232:2, indicates that the common practice is to accept that the whole oath was mere hyperbole and is void. (This is from the section of the *Arukh ha-Shulhan* that was recently published on the Laws of Oaths; *Arukh ha-Shulhan Hilkhot Nedarim* (Hoboken, 1991). It is not found in the standard editions of the *Arukh ha-Shulhan*).

3 For an explanation of these various issues in a broader context, see Aaron Levine, *Economics and Jewish Law* (Hoboken, 1987), at 51–54, and *Shulhan Arukh, Even ha-Ezer* 65:1–2.

4 For more on the details of this, see R. Aaron Levine, *Economics and Jewish Law*, at 43–73.

5 See *Arukh ha-Shulhan, Yoreh Deah* 232:3 and authorities cited therein.

conference is a formal setting analogous to a courtroom where it is understood by lawyers that hyperbole is unacceptable, and its use would be grounds for disciplinary action. The same rule is true for all similar situations in which no one expects exaggeration to be employed.

The reverse situation occasionally arises for a lawyer, as where the client is not seeking advice, but is merely seeking reassurance regarding a deal just concluded. Similar behavior is the subject of a dispute between Beit Hillel and Beit Shammai (*Ketubot* 17a), as the Talmud reports:

> It is taught: What does one sing to the bride? Beit Shammai states: one sings "The bride as she is" [one states the truth about the couple]. Beit Hillel states: "Beautiful and alluring bride." Beit Shammai replied to Beit Hillel, "If the bride was crippled or blind, should one still say "Beautiful and alluring bride"? Rather the Bible states "be distant from falsehood." Beit Hillel replied to Beit Shammai, "If you are correct, when a person makes a bad purchase in the market [and the purchase is irreversible], should one praise it or deprecate it? One should praise it."

The law is in accordance with Beit Hillel;[6] one should not reply candidly to a person's request for comments on an already completed and essentially irreversible action, such as the purchase of goods. For example, when a client comes to a lawyer asking him to comment on the terms of a now irreversible purchase agreement, the lawyer could reply with a generic "You did fine," even if, in fact, a better settlement is possible.[7]

---

6 *Even ha-Ezer* 65:1

7 There is an ongoing dispute as to whether one may actually lie in such a circumstance, or merely shade the truth (such as using very subjective words like "beautiful" or "fine"); compare comments of *Beit Shmuel* with *Helkat Mehokek* on *Even ha-Ezer* 65:1.

Chapter Seventeen

Arbitration and Compromise

As a general rule, Jewish law favors the use of compromise (in Hebrew, *pesharah*[1]) rather than law (*din*) to resolve legal disputes.[2] Thus, it is certainly appropriate for a Jewish lawyer to encourage the use of mediation or arbitration as a substitute for litigation between two Jewish clients who cannot privately settle their dispute and who will not go to a Jewish court. Ideally such mediation or arbitration would take place under the direction of a Jewish court (*beit din*) or even a panel of lay Jewish arbitrators, although both mediation and arbitration are certainly valid (i.e., not prohibited by the rules against Jews using secular tribunals) under the direction of secular arbitrators.[3]

---

1 What exactly is a *pesharah* remains a matter of some dispute. While the *Shulhan Arukh, Hoshen Mishpat* 13, seems to label it compromise, others view it as functioning closer to law; see R. Abraham Yitzhak Kook, *Orah Mishpat, Hoshen Mishpat* 1; and R. Hershel Schachter, *Nefesh ha-Rav, Hoshen Mishpat*, at 267–268 (in the name of Rabbi Joseph B. Soloveitchik).

2 See R. Dov Bressler, "Arbitration and the Courts in Jewish Law," *J. Halacha & Contemporary Society* 9:105, 107–12 (1985).

3 R. Akiva Eiger, *Hoshen Mishpat* 3; R. Eliezer Waldenberg, *Tzitz Eliezer* 11:93. See generally *Shakh, Hoshen Mishpat* 22:15 (allowing arbitration with gentile arbitrator); but see R. Yaakov Lorberbaum (*Me-Lisa*), *Netivot ha-Mishpat* 22:14 (prohibiting arbitration with gentile arbitrator). See also R. Yehiel Mikhel Epstein, *Arukh ha-Shulhan, Hoshen Mishpat* 22:8 (accepting opinion of *Shakh* as normative), and *Kovetz ha-Poskim*, at 2:22(2) (p. 136) (list of authorities who accept *Shakh*'s ruling as normative); but see *Halakhah Pesukah al Hoshen Mishpat* 22:2 (Makhon Harry Fischel, Jerusalem, 1988) (accepting *Netivot* as normative, but noting *Arukh ha-Shulhan*'s contrary rule).

The distinction between litigating in the "secular courts" which is normally prohibited, and the resort to "secular arbitration," which is permitted, seems to be that arbitrators are not bound by any legal system—Jewish law or otherwise—whereas secular courts accept an alien legal system. The fundamental prohibition violated by using an alternative legal system is the acknowledgement of primary fidelity—even for private disputes—to a system of law other than Jewish law. Arbitration, since it lacks a system of law, would thus be permitted, as no "legal system" is used.[4]

Mandatory Arbitration?

A frequently asked question is whether a Jew must consent to the use of secular binding arbitration (i.e., not from *beit din*) rather than use the secular courts in a case where the defendant will not go to a Jewish court (*beit din*). One example is where a Jewish plaintiff in a lawsuit is faced by a defendant who refuses to go to *beit din*, but indicates that he would consent to secular arbitration. Is such a defendant considered as one who "will not go to a Jewish court," thus permitting a Jew to summon him to secular court? Or must the Jew consent to secular arbitration to spare the defendant from having to litigate in secular court?

In this author's opinion, the plaintiff need not consent to secular arbitration, since according to Jewish law, arbitration—even in Jewish court—is not mandatory and can never be imposed without consent.[5] Therefore,

---

[4] See R. Abraham Isaiah Karelitz, *Hazon Ish, Hoshen Mishpat*, essay 16. It was based on this rationale that a number of authorities initially labeled the use of administrative law hearings to settle private disputes as permitted; see *Kovetz ha-Poskim*, at 207. These authorities felt that administrative law tribunals, since they were not bound by the law as the courts were, and could resort to equitable principles, were not considered "courts" according to Jewish law. Certainly this is no longer the case in the United States, as administrative courts are now fully integrated into the judicial structure of every state and the federal government. For a discussion of the situation in Israel, see R. Meir Issaacson, *Mevasser Tov* 1:85.

[5] See *Shulhan Arukh, Hoshen Mishpat* 12:1–3. Thus, even in the confines of *beit din*, a litigant has the right to insist on law rather than compromise; see generally *Piskei Din Rabani'im* 13:259–274 and R. Naphtali Bar Ilan, "Edut al Tenuat Derakhim be-Beit Mishpat," *Tehumin* 10:179–189. A contrary answer is given in R. Abraham Sherman, "Ma'amad Beit Din Penimin shel Tenuah al pe Halakhah," *Tehumin* 14:159–164

the plaintiff may compel the defendant either to use a Jewish court or the secular courts once the *beit din* gives him permission to do so. It is worth noting, however, that attending arbitration in such a case is doubly desirable: first, arbitration is generally preferred over litigation (*din*), and second, its use spares the defendant from violation of the prohibition of litigating in secular court.

(1994). Rabbi Sherman's point is that when there is an accepted communal practice to use an arbitration panel, Jewish law will compel that arbitration, even if one party wishes to use *beit din*. Such a custom is essentially non-existent in America, except in very local businesses.

Chapter Eighteen

Billing by the Hour

This book has avoided a discussion of the various issues related to the business side of the practice of law for three different reasons. First, these issues are conceptually unrelated to the other problems discussed in the book, all of which revolve in one way or another around the relationship between Jewish and secular law in the practice of law. Second, these issues are well addressed in the more general literature of "Jewish business ethics." To cover "Jewish legal business ethics" well would require a separate book covering topics unrelated to those addressed in the first seventeen chapters. Finally, the "business of law" is itself much more diverse than the "practice of law," and such a book would have to cover both the problems of being a solo practitioner and being a partner in a thousand lawyer firm—as well as all the cases in-between. Thus, the task of business ethics as applied to the practice of law will have to wait for separate treatment in its own volume. One Jewish law issue, however, seems to span many different legal practices and raises common questions, and is nearly unique to law as a business. These are the issues related to billing by the hour as the primary way of charging for services. Lawyers, unlike most other professionals, generally charge by the hour (or increment thereof).[1]

The Role of Custom in Billing Questions

Jewish law requires that a person who works by the hour (or any other time unit) insures that he charges only for those time units that it is

---

[1] See for example, The American Bar Association Standing Committee on Ethics and Professional Responsibility Formal Opinion 93–379 (Jan. 6, 1993).

customary to charge for;[2] any deviation from the customary norm must be agreed on prior to the commencement of the business relationship.[3] So too, a person who hires another to work by the hour, should expect to pay for all customary wages and rates, and any deviation must be agreed to in advance.[4] In this area of Jewish law, more than in most other areas,[5] the custom of the locale is incorporated as the norm of Jewish law.

This same rule governs expense reimbursement. If a lawyer's standard-fee agreement states that the client shall reimburse the lawyer for all "costs and expenses" related to a case, that limits the lawyer to seeking reimbursement for actual costs and expenses. A lawyer may not seek reimbursement at a rate that would provide the lawyer with a profit. Thus, if a hotel or a phone company provides a lawyer with a rebate for a particular activity, the lawyer must pass that along to the client. Of course, a lawyer may charge a client more, if he wishes; the rate, however, must be disclosed.[6]

A lawyer whose fee agreement with a client specifies that billings shall be by the hour is prohibited from using any other fee basis for determinations of amount due without agreement from the client. If "work product" created for one client is "recycled" to another, only the actual time spent preparing the work for the second client may be charged to that client; this is true even though the second client has received a windfall of

---

2 *Shulhan Arukh, Hoshen Mishpat* 331:1–2 and R. Yaakov Blau, *Pithei Hoshen, Sekhirut* 7:7.

3 *Shulhan Arukh* and comments of *Sema, Hoshen Mishpat* 331:2. Thus, a worker who is hired at an agreed-upon price to do a "good, but not excellent" job, cannot seek more money at the end of the job even if an "excellent" job is done; *Pithei Hoshen,* at n. 18. So too, whether a person is paid for time spent eating is dependent on local custom; *Shulhan Arukh, Hoshen Mishpat* 231:2.

4 *Shulhan Arukh, Yoreh Deah* 331:1.

5 For a discussion of why this is so in this area more than most areas of commercial law, see R. Yitzhak bar Sheshet Profiat, *Teshuvot Rivash* 475, and R. Tzvi Hirsch Ashkenazi, *Hakham Tzvi* 61.

6 The permutations of this problem make this a complex issue in certain cases. Thus, a lawyer whose billing plan for long distance calls includes a discount that grows in percentage depending on year-long volume has no way to determine true cost of that call, and no way to seek accurate reimbursement. The same can be said for many other rebate cases. It seems to this writer that the custom in America is that non-monetary incidental fringes (such as frequent flyer miles) are considered property of the one who flies, even if the ticket is paid for by another. Thus one would not have to discount the reimbursed cost of a ticket by the value of the frequent flier miles one receives.

some sorts.[7] For example, consider the lawyer who is asked by a client to write a legal brief on a topic. The lawyer wrote a similar brief for a previous client and at that time spent five hours writing that brief; however, the lawyer only needs two hours to modify the previous work for use by this client. Only two hours' time may be billed, even though it would have taken a different lawyer five hours to write the brief, and perhaps the client even recognizes that five hours is the appropriate amount of time for such work. Since only two hours were spent on the project, and time spent is the agreed on billing method, only two hours may be billed.

A similar case occurs when a lawyer spends two hours getting to and from court and four hours in court representing three different clients on the same day. He has only spent six hours *total* on all the matters and may only bill the three different clients a total of six hours, and may not bill each client more than their share of the common time.[8]

In the same vein, when a lawyer promises to work by the hour, the lawyer is under an obligation to insure that the hours billed represent reasonable working effort, such that the lawyer is capable of functioning in proper form. Thus, a lawyer, who is suffering from a serious cold and has medicated himself to the point at which he is no longer capable of functioning as a lawyer, must discount those hours from the full billing rate.[9] On the other hand, the common custom in America is that full hourly billing is proper, even in situations where the lawyer is not completely

---

[7] This conclusion results from the fact that the agreement provides that time spent is the only determination of the wage rate to be paid, and there is no customary exception in American legal practice for "value billing" unless there is a clear agreement between the lawyer and client for such billing; see Formal Opinion 93–379, and Patrick Tuite, "ABA Ethics Opinion Refines Standards on Fees and Billing," *Chicago Daily Law Bulletin* 140:24:6.

[8] The rule is very simple; absent any agreed upon modifications or a clear custom to the contrary, a lawyer who agrees to bill by the hour may not bill twelve hours time when only six hours were spent.

  It is worth noting that Jewish law prohibits a worker who is paid by the hour from working at two different jobs at the same time (without the consent of both of them); see *Shulhan Arukh, Hoshen Mishpat* 333:5, and this is true even if there is no obvious decrease in the quality of the product.

[9] *Shulhan Arukh, Hoshen Mishpat* 337:19; but see R. Shalom Mordecai Schwadron, *Teshuvot Maharsham* 2:215, where it is argued that there is a custom that is widely recognized that people come in to work sick, and so long as a person is not continuously ill, it is understood that this work counts as a full day's work. This argument is accepted by *Pithei Hoshen* at n. 27.

functional, so long as the lawyer is trying to work diligently.[10] Thus, a lawyer working with a temporary small disability—such as a headache—need not reduce his hourly rate.[11]

Billing Travel Time

The case of billable hours during travel time is more complex. The classical situation is as follows:

> A lawyer's fee agreement specifies that he is paid by the hour for travel time that is inter-city, even if no work is done. The client is aware of this. Thus, while on a six-hour plane ride, the lawyer could, if he wishes, sleep or read a book for six hours and still record those six hours as billable to the client. Instead of wasting this time, however, the lawyer works during those six hours on a different client's matter.

Can the lawyer now bill both clients for the time, or is it an obvious impropriety to allow for twelve billable hours in a six-hour period?

Recently the American Bar Association issued an opinion stating that this type of billing practice is not ethical,[12] and in those states that automatically incorporate the Association's ethical guidelines into its rules,[13] such conduct is thus prohibited, as these guidelines have the status of "local custom" according to Jewish law, and absent client consent, would be the normative rule that a lawyer would have to follow.[14]

---

10 However, once the lawyer leaves his work to recuperate for more than a very short period of time (a few minutes), that resting time may not be billed.

11 See sources cited in note 9 of this chapter.

12 Formal Opinion 93–379.

13 See for example, *In re Vrdolyak* 137 Ill.2d 407, 560 N.E.2d 840 (1990), making the Association opinions "mandatory, minimum rules to which attorneys are expected to conform."

14 It is important to understand that these rules are not incorporated into Jewish law because they are the "law of the land" (since for reasons explained in note 17 of chapter three, disciplinary rules can never be the "law of the land"), rather they are incorporated into Jewish law as they become the customary practice of the community, upon which all business deals are predicated, absent an agreement among the parties to the contrary. For more on this distinction, see *Pithei Hoshen*, at n. 17.

In a state that does not necessarily incorporate the Association's rules, and has no local custom prohibiting this type of billing arrangement, a strong case can be made that this double billing is completely permissible, even though it appears to allow for billings in excess of time actually spent. The reason for this is that Jewish law recognizes that the first client, in agreeing to pay for travel time even when no work is done, has released the lawyer temporarily from the status of an hourly worker, and that this permits the lawyer to work for another at the same time.[15] Thus, absent a rule in the jurisdiction, a custom of practice, or an agreement between a client, it would be permissible for a lawyer to bill one client for travel time while billing another for the work actually done during travel.[16]

---

15 For an example of this see R. Hayyim Halberstam, *Divrei Hayyim, Even ha-Ezer* 2:26, who discusses what other occupations a woman who is a wet nurse may pursue while paid to be a wet nurse.

16 This assumes that the travel itself is not so stressful that the client specifically needs the lawyer to rest while traveling so that the client can work with zeal once he arrives. In such a case the lawyer must rest, as that is the "job" the client wishes for him to do; for an example of this, see *Shulhan Arukh, Yoreh Deah* 245:17, which notes that a teacher is obligated to sleep at night to be fit to teach in the morning.

Chapter Nineteen

Conclusion

This work has attempted to systematically survey many of the halakhic issues raised by the practice of secular law, and proposes halakhic and practical solutions to these problems when such are obviously available. At times it is clear that the problems posed by a particular issue are not as serious from the perspective of Jewish law as one might suspect they are. In some circumstances, the propriety of a particular activity is dependent on how one resolves a fundamental dispute among the early authorities, while in others, the problems appear to be very serious indeed. Indeed, each situation, and each case, poses its own unique factual setting; at best, only general rules can be given.

The practice of law, like all fascinating professional journeys, is full of potential pitfalls; yet the Jewish lawyer can—with study and diligence—steer clear of these snares and engage in a religiously proper, economically, intellectually, and socially rewarding practice of law encompassing many areas of law within the common law's legal system. This is not to say that there are no limitations upon what a religious Jew may do; it is only that with care and study these obstacles can be overcome.

Indeed, one spiritual hazard from the practice of law has not been addressed and requires consideration before one embarks on a "life of law." Judaism recognizes that there is a danger from infatuation with secular legal systems. Rabbi Solomon ben Adret (*Rashba*), writing seven hundred years ago in response to a question of whether a particular issue is governed by Jewish law or secular law, concludes:

> And if you do not agree with my result [and limit secular law's impact] what will be the purpose of the holy works that were written by Rabbi Judah, and after him, Rav Ashi [i.e., Jewish law]. We

will just teach our children secular law and build houses of worship in law schools! Such should not be in the house of Israel.[1]

The study and practice of law is a fine profession. It cannot, however, be made into a substitute for a religiously fulfilling existence.

Thus, while this book argues that many of the common halakhic obstacles to the practice of law can be overcome or avoided, that does not mean that there are no problems present. Besides the possibility raised by Rabbi Solomon ben Adret above, vigilance is required to insure honesty in the practice of law. One problem many lawyers confront relates to the financial stresses encountered periodically in the legal profession. There is pressure to over- or double-bill a client, a practice that is surely a form of theft. So too, one is occasionally tempted to deceive others in order to avoid the repercussions of one's mistakes, or to blame others when the fault lies within oneself.

Law, more than most professions, leaves much to the good judgment and honesty of its practitioners, and some are occasionally enticed to violate these trusts for personal gain.

On the other hand, the legal profession affords lawyers many opportunities to sanctify the Lord's name publicly, by providing many occasions in which to fulfill the divine commandment of "justice, justice, you shall pursue."[2] Regrettably enough, the reverse is true as well: misconduct in the practice of law frequently raises the specter of public denigration of Judaism and the Almighty.

The practice of law, like many professions, can be an instrument for justice and morality—but only in the hands of just and moral attorneys.

---

1 R. Solomon ben Adret, *Responsa of Rashba* 6:244.

2 Deuteronomy 16:20.

Appendix

The 1992 New York Get Law: A Markedly Less Than Ideal Solution That Creates Many Halakhic Problems[1]

If a husband and wife separate and he no longer desires to remain married to her and she desires to be divorced from him, in such a case divorce is a mitzvah [obligation] and commanded by Jewish law....One who withholds a Jewish divorce because he desires money for no just cause is a thief. Indeed, he is worse than a thief as his conduct violates, a sub-prohibition related to taking a human life.[2]

—*Rabbi Joseph Elijah Henkin*

---

1 This appendix derives from a number of articles and exchanges I have had in *Tradition: A Journal of Orthodox Jewish Thought*. See "The New York State *Get* Law," *Tradition* 29:(4)3–14 (1995) and "The 1992 New York *Get* Law: An Exchange" *Tradition* 31:(3)23–41 (1997), as well as letters to the editor in *Tradition* 32:(1)99–100 (1997) and *Tradition* 32:(3)91–97 (1998).

2 R. Yosef Eliyahu Henkin, *Edut le-Yisrael* 143–144, reprinted in *Kol Kitvei ha-Rav Henkin* 1:115a–b. The term "sub-prohibition" is a translation of the Hebrew term "*abizrayu.*"

Introduction

The 1992 New York State *Get* Law directs the courts of New York to consider the withholding of a Jewish divorce as one of the many factors to be balanced by the courts when determining the equitable distribution of marital assets in the context of a divorce.[3] The purpose of this law was to economically pressure recalcitrant husbands who were withholding Jewish divorces (called in Hebrew a *get*) into issuing such documents and thus freeing their wives to remarry. This recent law is but one of the many potential "solutions" that have been proposed in modern times to the perennial problem of women unable to terminate their marriage in a way recognized as valid by Jewish law, commonly called the *agunah*[4] problem.

One of the issues beyond the scope of this appendix, but implicitly dealt with in it, is that Jewish law does not generally recognize the right of either spouse to a divorce without the consent of the other.[5] "No fault divorce" thus may only be by mutual agreement. Absent mutual agreement, a judicial determination by a Jewish court (*beit din*) of fault by one party to the marriage must be made before a divorce against the wishes of one of the parties will be permitted.[6] On the other hand, it is commonly

---

3   Domestic Relations Law §236B(5) formally states:

> In any decision made pursuant to this subdivision the court shall, where appropriate, consider the effect of a barrier to remarriage, as defined in subsection six of section two hundred and fifty three of this article, on the factors enumerated in paragraph (d) of this sub-division.

Section 253(6) limits "barriers to remarriage" to situations where a *get* is withheld.

4   "*Agunah*" is the popular term used to denote an estranged wife denied a divorce conforming to Jewish law (the issuing of a *get*) due to either a missing or recalcitrant husband; the term *agunah* literally refers to the chains that bind this woman to her marriage. In Talmudic times this term was used only to refer to cases where the husband had disappeared and thus could not effectuate a divorce, but has now taken on the more generic meaning of a case where a woman cannot terminate her marriage and is desirous of doing so. For a critical examination of the contemporary *agunah* problem as well as proposed solutions, see my *Marriage, Divorce and the Abandoned Wife in Jewish Law: A Conceptual Understanding of the Agunah Problems in America* (Ktav, 2001).

5   See e.g. Benzion Schareschevsky, *Dinei Mishpahah* 348–375 (3rd. ed., Jerusalem, 1983).

6   *Ibid.* This will be elaborated on in the next subsection.

recognized within the Jewish tradition that it is morally improper to "chain" one's spouse to a marriage that is, in fact, over and that one party in the marriage wishes to end.[7] Thus, various forms of pressure to end such marriages have always been applied to recalcitrant husbands.[8] However, great care has always been exercised in applying this pressure to insure that the persuasion applied does not rise to the level of actual duress, which can create a coerced *get* (in Hebrew, a *get me'useh*), as such a *get* is void according to Jewish law, and would not end the marriage even if issued.[9]

This law has been criticized by many Jewish law scholars, because it improperly diminishes the capacity of the husband and wife to offer and receive a *get* with free will, a requirement of Jewish law.[10] Simply put, the threat of economic penalty undermines the free will needed by Jewish law, and that this duress rises to the level of illicit coercion which could void the resulting *get*.[11] This criticism stands in contrast to the approval given to an earlier New York *Get* law, which merely withheld a civil divorce in certain circumstances until a religious divorce was granted.[12]

---

7 See for example the comments of Rabbi Henkin with which this appendix opened.

8 For example, see R. Moshe Isserless (*Rema*), *Even ha-Ezer* 154:21 who permits the community to impose a form of ostracism on a man who will not issue a *get* when his marriage is actually over, even though no judicial determination of fault was (or could be) found. This ruling is based on the earlier decision of Rabbenu Tam, found in his *Sefer ha-Yashar, Helek ha-Teshuvot* 24.

9 For more on the details of a *get me'useh*, see *Shulhan Arukh, Even ha-Ezer* 134 and 154.

10 For a review of this area, and of the various criticism of the law, see Irving Breitowitz, *Between Civil and Religious Law: The Plight of the Agunah in American Society* (Greenwood Press, 1993) at 209–238 as well as various articles and letters to the editor in the pages of *Tradition, supra* note 1.

11 The crucial words are "illicit coercion." Not all coercive pressure is illicit; R. Tzvi Hirsch Eisenstadt, *Pithei Teshuvah* on *Even ha-Ezer* 134 and many commentators, both before and after, devised many perfectly legal forms of coercion to encourage the giving of a *get*. This includes social ostracism, dismissal from one's job, denouncement, withholding of benefits, and many other actions. Even in circumstances where there is no halakhic reason to give a *get*, such coercion or persuasion is still permitted.

12 For more on this, see Breitowitz, *Between Civil and Religious Law*, at 179–209.

The Problems with the 1992 *Get* Law

In essence, Jewish law mandates that ideally a *get* be given with no coercion present. The 1992 *Get* law introduces a significant amount of economic coercion in some cases, since the wife can seek to use the penalty provisions of the *Get* law to impose financial pressure on a recalcitrant husband.

There are three distinct problems with the 1992 Get Law:

(1) The law permits economic coercion by the secular authorities to induce the issuing of a *get* in cases where Jewish law does not allow coercion.

(2) Even in cases where Jewish law directs that a *get* be issued, this law makes no distinction between the various categories of obligation to issue a *get*. In some cases of obligation, coercion is not allowed.

(3) The law does not require any participation of a Jewish court (*beit din*); thus even in cases where perhaps coercion should be ordered, no such order was ever issued by a *beit din*.[13]

Others have replied to these objections by noting that these allegations are correct, but that the law is still a basically good one because in a situation where illicit coercion exists the *beit din* will realize that it is present and decline to write the *get*.[14] In other situations, supporters of the *Get* law argue that the law can be an effective tool to curtail instances where a *get* is improperly withheld.[15]

However, even supporters of the general halakhic validity of this *Get* law must realize that using the instrument of secular law to solve some of

---

13 See Responsa of R. Yosef Shalom Elyashiv, 1 Elul 5752, and Breitowitz, *Between Civil and Religious Law*, at 230–236.

14 In addition there are those who argue that the law as written itself exempts from its application those cases where Jewish law would not allow an economic penalty. For more on this line of reasoning, and an extremely thorough reply, see Breitowitz, *Between Civil and Religious Law*, at 233–238.

15 R. Gedalia Dov Schwartz, "The 1992 New York *Get* Law" *J. Halacha & Contemporary Society* 27:26–34 (1994).

the *agunah* cases (when the secular law's halakhic validity and prudence are contested by significant numbers of Jewish law decisors[16]) creates a problematic precedent for the use of secular law to decide internal Jewish law disputes. Coercive secular regulation to enforce Jewish law, in a way that does not allow those who disagree with the secular law's understanding of Jewish law to opt out of it, should be sought to enforce only those Jewish law norms that are accepted by (nearly) all members of the halakhic community. This should be true for secular *kashrut* (dietary laws) enforcement laws[17] and secular Jewish autopsy laws as well as secular *Get* laws. For this reason alone, in this author's opinion, the 1992 *Get* Law is, at the very least, a bad idea (even if its intentions are laudable and its goals commendable).

It is not the role of the secular authorities to determine whether a particular form of governmental interference is permitted or prohibited according to Jewish law. Indeed, secular interference in the internal workings of Jewish law has been profoundly discouraged throughout Jewish history.[18]

Halakhic Considerations

Nevertheless the 1992 *Get* Law is currently the law in New York State, and similar laws have been passed in other countries and proposed in other states.[19] Repeal of the law in New York seems extremely unlikely, and retroactive repeal is not even under consideration. Couples are still divorcing and Jewish divorces are still being written. Divorced individuals are seeking to marry again. Thus an examination of the after-the-fact ramifications of the law is needed. This appendix will address whether Jewish

---

16 See, e.g., R. Yosef Shalom Elyashiv, as cited in Breitowitz, *Between Civil and Religious Law*, at 230–231.

17 See, e.g., *Ran-Dav's County Kosher, Inc., v. New Jersey*, 608 A.2d 1353 (N.J., 1992) (stating that New Jersey may not, as a matter of constitutional law, permit only one standard of kosher and prohibit other, tenably kosher, institutions that adhere to a lower standard to claim to be kosher).

18 See, e.g., Menachem Elon, *Jewish Law: History, Sources, Principles*, (Jewish Publication Society, 1994), at 50–51 and 1914–1917.

19 See Breitowitz, *Between Civil and Religious Law*, at 163–179.

divorces issued since 1992 are valid in jurisdictions with such law, and if so, under what circumstances.[20]

Ten different rationales (seven grounded in Jewish law, and three in the reality of America) can be advanced that incline one to rule that a typical *get* given in the shadow of the 1992 law is valid, even if the controlling secular statute is fundamentally unwise.

First, Rabbi Moshe Feinstein states that there is no issue of "coerced divorce" (*get me'useh*) where it is clear that the husband actually wishes to end the marriage and be divorced and is contesting only the fiscal details of the divorce.[21] Similar sentiments are expressed by Rabbi Abraham Isaiah Karelitz when he states that even when there is illicit coercion, if the husband really does want to give the *get* and be divorced, the *get* is still valid, since the true desire of the husband is to be divorced.[22] This point appears to be agreed to, in modified form, by Rabbi Yitzhak Isaac Herzog, who also states that coercion does not invalidate a *get* that is commanded even if it cannot be judicially compelled.[23]

---

20 Who should determine when and if an apparently valid *get* is actually invalid is answered simply: before one asserts that a validly written *get*, given by recognized *mesader* which comes with a strong presumption of validity, is not valid, one should investigate to determine what the facts were. The burden should be on those who question the *patur* of a recognized *beit din*, which attests to the validity of the *get*. As Rabbi Feinstein (*Iggerot Moshe, Even ha-Ezer* 1:137) states: "We should not contemplate that invalidity of a *get* arranged by a rabbi appointed for this process, and claim perhaps a *get* was written in violation of *halakhah*."

21 R. Moshe Feinstein, *Iggerot Moshe, Even ha-Ezer* 3:44. Rabbi Feinstein, however, is hesitant to rely on this rationale absent other lenient factors. The rationale for his ruling is very simple. He argues that the prohibition of a compelled *get* is limited to situations where the compulsion is used to divorce a couple who actually wish to remain married. Compulsion in a case where divorce is truly desired does not create a *get me'useh*.

22 R. Abraham Isaiah Karelitz, *Hazon Ish, Even ha-Ezer* 99:2.

23 R. Yitzhak Isaac Herzog, *Otzar ha-Poskim* 2:11–12 (appendix) and *Hekhal Yitzhak* 2. The ruling that coercion does not invalidate a *get* when divorce is genuinely desired can perhaps be also explained by combining the rulings of Rabbi Henkin and Herzog discussed above. First, one must realize that there is an obligation to have a Jewish divorce once there is an irreconcilable separation and that this is commanded by Jewish law, as Rabbi Henkin states above. Second, Rabbi Herzog rules that coercion does not invalidate a Jewish divorce that is an obligation (*mitzvah*) even if not judicially mandated (*kofin*). Thus, since all cases where the husband genuinely desires divorce are irreconcilable separations, one comes to the conclusion that once there is a desire to end the marriage, and the only disagreement concerns terms, coercion does not invalidate the *get*, since the *get* is obligatory.

A close examination of Rabbi Feinstein's responsum is in order. That responsum states:

> There is another reason to validate the *get* [in a case of courtordered coercion] even if there was coercion. You [the questioner] asked the husband if he would have divorced his wife anyway without the settlement after the secular divorce, and he answered that he would have, but he would have demanded certain arrangements concerning the children's education; we see from this that he really wanted to be divorced, and only did not ask for certain things for the children because of the settlement, and gave the *get* immediately. In such a case, even if the settlement is coerced, or even actual force is used to write the *get*, we see that there is no coercion on the giving of the *get*, but only to prevent the *get* from being used to extract other things from her.... Every person desires to [support his wife]; however, one who does not wish for this woman to be his wife, or he knows that she will not reside with him in a marital relationship, such a person really does want to be divorced, and it is merely because she desires a *get* that he wishes to extract from her certain things . . . It is not good for a person to be legally married when one lacks any of the marital virtues from one's wife.[24]

Rabbi Feinstein advances two very important insights. The first is that in a situation where the marriage is actually over, there is no halakhic problem with using what would otherwise be illicit coercion to compel the giving of a *get*, even if no money is paid to the husband. The second is that where payment is made by the wife to settle this matter and is combined with some coercion placed on the husband (but where the marriage is in fact over) that coercion does not violate Jewish law and void the *get*. In the eyes of Jewish law, the husband is issuing the *get* in return for the payment of money, since the marriage really is over and he derives no real benefit from continuing it.

The first insight, while by no means unique to Rabbi Feinstein, is found in only a small number of authorities.[25] However, the second insight

---

24 R. Moshe Feinstein, *Iggerot Moshe, Even ha-Ezer* 3:44.

25 See R. Tzvi Hirsch Brody, *Tiferet Tzvi, Even ha-Ezer* 102; R. Meir Eisenstadt, *Imrai Aish, Even ha-Ezer* 57; R. Meir Simha of Dvinsk, *Or Sameah* on *Rambam, Gerushin* 2:20; *Vayishal Shaul, Even ha-Ezer* 2:20; and R. Isaac ben Moshe, *Or Zarua, Teshuvah* 126.

is found in a large number of halakhic authorities of the last thousand years and is completely normative. Writing about a case where a husband received payment and was then coerced into writing the *get*, Rabbi Avraham Boorstein in his *Avnei Nezer* states:

> [Those who prohibit this type of coercion] are referring to a case where the husband wishes to live with this woman and represent her as his wife. In such a case *halakhah* never says because of the coercion and the money he divorced her [rather, the *get* is void because illicit force was used]. Certainly, even if one gave a man all the money in the world, he would not divorce his wife [with whom he is living]. But a man such as this who betrayed his wife, and abandoned her for many years, we certainly do say the coercion and the money persuaded him to sell the divorce to an even greater extent than it persuades one to sell a field, since this man desires his wife not at all, and only desires leverage over her so that she cannot marry another without his permission, and he can get money from her for this. Certainly in such a case we say because of the money he divorced her. This is very logical.[26]

Included in the list of Jewish law decisors who accept this rule that payment of money with some coercion, in a case where the marriage is over (and in the case of some of the authorities, even if it is not) and the husband does not desire to return to the marital abode, produces a valid *get* are the above-mentioned Rabbi Boorstein, Rabbi Samuel Ehrenfeld, R. Simeon bar Tzemah Duran Rabbi Abraham ibn Tawah, Rabbi Shlomo ben Shimon Duran Rabbi Yosef [Paimer] of Slutzk, Rabbi Moshe Zev Ya'avetz, Rabbi Shlomo Kluger, and Rabbi David Tavli Rubin, as well as perhaps Rabbi Raphael Yom Tov Lipman Halpern. Similar but not identical analyses can be found in the works of Rabbi Shlomo Zalman Lipshitz and Rabbi David Shlomo Eibeschutz and is mentioned in the writings of Rabbi Yitzhak Elhanan Spektor and Rabbi Tzvi Hirsch Orenstein.[27] One

---

26 R. Avraham Boorstein, *Avnei Nezer, Even ha-Ezer* 167.

27 R. Avraham Boorstein *Avnei Nezer, Even ha-Ezer* 167; R. Samuel Ehrenfeld, *Hatan Sofer* 59; R. Simeon bar Tzemah Duran, *Tashbetz* 1:1; R. Abraham ibn Tawah, *Tashbetz (Hut ha-Meshulash)* 4(iii):35; R. Shlomo ben Shimon Duran, Responsa of *Rashbash* 339 (argues with *Rema, Even ha-Ezer* 134:8); *Rabbenu Yosef* of *Slutzk* 79; R. Moshe Zev Ya'avetz, *Agudat Azov, Even ha-Ezer* 19(18); R. Shlomo Kluger, *Kuntres Tikun Olam, Tikun* 3, *Teshuvah* 1:1 and R. David Tavli Rubin, *Nahlat David*

can add to this list the above-mentioned decisors who accept an even broader rule.[28] Indeed, no less an authority than the *Beit Shmuel*[29] notes that there are many circumstances in which one can rely on this approach, even when only a small amount of money is given by the woman. Many other authorities could be cited to support this halakhic rule, and it appears to be accepted *ab initio* (*le-khathillah*) by many.

Rabbi Tzvi Gartner, in his recent work *Kefiyah Be-Get*, dealing with many aspects of coerced divorce, summarizes the matter by stating:

> It appears that it is difficult to rely on the approach of *Iggerot Moshe* and *Tiferet Tzvi* in a case where the only benefit which accrues to the husband is removal of the obligation to support his wife, since this is a matter in dispute between *Tosafot* and *Rashba*. Nonetheless, their analysis is persuasive at the minimum in the case where the husband does not desire a marital relationship and only desires to extract something from the woman in exchange for a *get*, and she gives him money for the divorce.[30]

Indeed, a plausible reading of Rabbi Feinstein's own words incline one to accept that his expressed hesitancy to rely on his "novel insight" applied only to the first of them, where there was no payment to the husband. The second insight is certainly accepted by many great authorities as normative Jewish law, and validates any *get* given in the process of a settlement where the wife gives anything of value to the husband to which he is not entitled. Nearly all contested secular divorces fit into this latter category.

Second, the *Get* Law is problematic only if it takes the husband's property away from him in order to induce him to issue a *get*. If Jewish law recognizes secular law's equitable distribution of marital assets as valid through the principle that the law of the land is the law (*dina de-malkhuta dina*), then there is no illicit coercion, since nothing is "taken" from the husband that he

---

34, as well as perhaps R. Raphael Yom Tov Lipman Halpern, *Shut Oneg Yom Tov* 168. Similar but not identical analyses can be found in R. Shlomo Zalman Lipshitz, *Hemdat Shlomo*, *Even ha-Ezer* 80(3) and R. David Shlomo Eibeschutz, *Naot Deshe* 144 and is mentioned in R. Yitzhak Elhanan Spektor, *Be'er Yitzhak*, *Even ha-Ezer* 10:1 and R. Tzvi Hirsch Orenstein, *Berkhat Retzeh* 118.

28 The first, more expansive insight of Rabbi Feinstein and others, *supra* notes 24 and 25.

29 R. Shmuel ben Uri, *Beit Shmuel*, *Even ha-Ezer* 134:14.

30 R. Tzvi Gartner, *Kefiyah Be-Get*, at 244.

owns; rather a "bonus" is withheld from him in order to induce his issuing of a *get*,[31] since secular law rules that equitable distribution assets belong individually to neither partners in the marriage. That withholding is completely permissible. Such an approach is adopted by Rabbi Yitzhak Isaac Leibes.[32] Additional support for the proposition that secular law's rules related to equitable distribution can be incorporated into Jewish law through the law of the land principle can be found in other authorities.[33]

The theory of equitable distribution is very simple and needs to be understood in this context. Unlike the classical common law, which ruled that the person in whom title resided kept the item on divorce, modern American equitable distribution law recognizes that marital property is held in the marital estate which is like a trusteeship, and upon divorce the court divides the property according to the statutory direction. (In communal property states, the division is always even.) One recent hornbook stated:

> In all states today statutes provide that upon divorce the property of the spouses shall, in one way or another, be divided between them, regardless of the state of the title.[34]

An article devoted exclusively to New York family law notes:

> Contrary to the title theory of property, equitable distribution is based upon the premise that marriage should be viewed as a form of economic partnership. This concept reflects the modern awareness that marriage is a union dependent upon a wide range of non-remunerated services to the partnership, such as homemaking, raising children, and providing emotional and moral support necessary to sustain the other spouse.[35]

---

31 For a full discussion of these issues, see R. J. David Bleich, *Contemporary Halakhic Problems* II:94–103 and *Piskai Din Rabaniyim* 10:300–308.

32 R. Yitzhak Isaac Leibes, *Beit Avi* 4:169.

33 See R. Yehuda Leib Grauburt, *Havalim be-Neimim*, *Even ha-Ezer* 55, which rules, in the alternative, that secular law provides a woman with financial rights against her husband (or his estate). Such can also be found in R. Joseph Trani (*Mabit*), *Responsa* 1:309.

34 Homer Clark and Carol Glowinsky, *Domestic Relations*, 5th ed. at 809.

35 David Kaufman, "The New York Equitable Distribution Statute," *Brook. L. Rev.* 53:845 (1987).

This theory is equally valid in secular law for both maintenance payments and marital asset division.[36]

The scope of the halakhic duty to follow the law of the land, or the ability of the Jewish community to incorporate the law of the land into Jewish financial dealings through common commercial custom (*minhag ha-soharim*), remains one of the fundamental issues in the discussion of the *Get* law. I believe that the custom of the Orthodox Jewish community, or vast portions of it, is to accept as part of the customary financial law the concept of alimony, post-divorce payments, and very likely equitable distribution. Indeed, a number of Jewish law authorities seem amenable to this practice,[37] and many divorces have occurred in the Orthodox community where alimony has been paid without the rabbinic community ruling such payment to be theft.

In truth, reliance on exogenous practices and customs in Jewish divorce settlements is a practical necessity in light of the decrees enacted by Rabbenu Gershom, the great leader of 10th century European Jewry, which fundamentally changed Jewish family law so that the marriage contract no longer forms the foundation document upon which the financial aspects of divorce are adjudicated. The reason this is so requires a further digression.

---

36 One commentator who sought to claim that any situation where the secular law recognizes that the parties "are free to reach any agreement they want" precludes an application of *dina de-malkhuta dina* misunderstands the relevant issue here. The question is "does the husband own the assets according to secular law," and the answer is that assets in the marital estate are owned by neither party, and can be distributed only by mutual consent or judicial declaration. This type of ownership can certainly be accepted by *halakhah* and is even more legitimate under a theory of common commercial practice (*minhag ha-soharim*) than under *dina de-malkhuta*.

37 See R. Yehuda Leib Grauburt, *Havalim ba-Neimim, Even ha-Ezer* 55, which rules, in the alternative, that secular law provides a woman with financial rights against her husband (or his estate); R. Joseph Trani, *Mabit* 1:309, is yet another such responsum. For a similar type of claim, see R. Yitzhak Isaac Liebes, *Beit Avi* 4:169. Similar reasoning can be inferred from R. Moshe Feinstein's ruling (*Iggerot Moshe, Even ha-Ezer* 1:137) that the wife's waiver of past-due support payments mandated by secular law, in return for the husband's issuing a *get*, is a form of permissible coercion which does not invalidate the *get*. This waiver of a financial claim is valid coercion only in a case where the woman's claim to the money is halakhically valid, since the wife is entitled to these payments through *dina de-malkhuta dina*. Indeed, Rabbi Feinstein implies that this is the more likely result in his analysis found in *Iggerot Moshe, Even ha-Ezer* 1:137; see also R. Tzvi Hirsch Eisenstadt, *Pithei Teshuvah, Even ha-Ezer* 134:9–10.

According to the Talmud's understanding of Biblical law, the right to divorce rested solely with the husband, absent hard fault on his part.[38] However, the Talmudic sages promulgated a required dower contract (*ketubah*) for all brides payable upon divorce or death of the husband as a precondition to all marriages. By imposing a clear contractual financial obligation on the husband to compensate his wife if he exercised his right to engage in unilateral divorce (absent judicially declared fault on her part), the *ketubah* served as an economic deterrent against rash conduct.

The enactments attributed to Rabbenu Gershom significantly altered this: In his view it was necessary to restrict the rights of the husband and prohibit unilateral no-fault divorce by either husband or wife. By his decrees, divorce became limited to cases of provable fault or mutual consent. (In addition, fault was vastly redefined to exclude cases of soft fault such as repugnancy, and in only a few cases could the husband be actually forced to divorce his wife or the reverse.[39]) Equally significant, they prohibited polygamy (also originally permitted by Biblical and Talmudic law, to strongly deter abandonment). Together, the decrees of Rabbenu Gershom not only reduced the instances in which divorce was likely, but also essentially vacated the economic provisions of the *ketubah* by prohibiting outright that which the Talmudic sages sought to discourage.

This point can hardly be emphasized enough: as the Talmudic rabbis instituted the *ketubah* payments so as to deter the husband from impetuously divorcing a wife, the basic value and purpose of the *ketubah* in cases of divorce is limited to cases where the husband can divorce his wife without her consent, and yet has to pay the *ketubah*. *However, in cases where the husband cannot divorce his wife without her consent, there is no need or purpose to a* ketubah.[40] Rabbi Moses Isserless (*Rema*) notes the broader

---

38 See *Gittin* 90a-b. Thus, according to Biblical law, exit from marriage differed fundamentally from entry into marriage: Though marriage and divorce in Judaism are private contractual rights rather than public rights, divorce did not require the consent of both parties even though marriage is entered into by mutual agreement.

39 This insight is generally ascribed to the 11th century Tosafist Rabbenu Tam in his view of the repugnancy claim (Heb.: *mais alay*). In fact it flows logically from the view of Rabbenu Gershom, who not only had to prohibit polygamy in order to end coerced divorce, but even divorce for soft fault.

40 Thus, for example, *Shulhan Arukh* (*Even ha-Ezer* 177:3) states that "a man who rapes a woman ... is obligated to marry her, so long as she ... wish[es] to marry him, even if she is crippled or blind, and he is not permitted to divorce her forever, except with her consent, and thus he does not have to write her a *ketubah*." The logic seems clear.

implications of this conclusion in the beginning of his discussion of the laws of pre-nuptial dower contracts (*ketubah*s):

> See *Shulhan Arukh Even ha-Ezer* 177:3[41] where it states that in a situation where one only may divorce with the consent of the woman, one does not need a *ketubah*. Thus, nowadays, in our countries, where we do not divorce against the will of the wife because of the ban of Rabbenu Gershom...it is possible to be lenient and not write a *ketubah* at all....[42]

In short, he believes that with regard to divorce, *a* ketubah *has no value at all* (although for several other reasons, the custom has always been to nonetheless have a *ketubah*). Rabbi Moses Feinstein reaches the same conclusion:

> The value of the *ketubah* is not known to rabbis and decisors of Jewish law, or rabbinical court judges; indeed we have not examined this matter intensely as for all matter of divorce it has no practical ramifications, since it is impossible for the man to divorce against the will of the woman, [the economics of] divorce are dependent on who desires to be divorced, and who thus provides a large sum of money as they wish to give or receive a divorce.[43]

Elsewhere Rabbi Feinstein writes:

> One should know that in divorce there is no place for evaluating the *ketubah*, since the ban of Rabbenu Gershom prohibited a man from divorcing his wife without her consent. Thus, divorce is dependent on who wants to give or receive the writ [of divorce] and who will

---

Since he cannot divorce her under any circumstances without her consent, the presence or absence of a *ketubah* seems to make no difference to her economic status or marital security. When they both want to get divorced, they will agree on financial terms independent of the *ketubah*, and until then, the *ketubah* sets no payment schedule. Should she insist that she only will consent to be divorced if he gives her $1,000,000 in buffalo nickels, they either reach an agreement or stay married.

41 The case of rape discussed in note 40.
42 *Shulhan Arukh, Even ha-Ezer* 66:3.
43 Moses Feinstein, *Iggerot Moshe, Even ha-Ezer* 4:91 (This responsum was written in 1980).

give or receive money as an inducement.... Only infrequently, in farfetched cases, is [the *ketubah*] relevant to divorce....[44]

Generally, parties to Jewish weddings in America intuit this. Indeed, for the last number of years, at every wedding at which I am invited to sit at the groom's table (*hatan's tisch*) while the *ketubah* is signed, I ask the husband:

If the marriage were to end by divorce, does the husband expect to pay his wife the value of the *ketubah* and return to her the assets that she brought to the marriage, or does the couple expect some other form of asset division in cases of divorce?

I am almost always told that the groom does not intend for the *ketubah* to control the division of assets. The fact that this is truly the intent of many couples is reflected in the American custom of *not* negotiating the dollar amounts in the *ketubah*, either in terms of how much money the woman actually brings into the marriage or how much the husband shall pay her upon divorce or his death, as was the custom in Europe many centuries ago. Thus, neither formal Jewish law nor the common practice of husbands and wives (*minhag ha-makom*) is to use the *ketubah* as the foundation document for determining the fair financial distribution of assets in cases of divorce. The simple fact is that, absent the arbitrary exercise of rabbinic authority (*shuda de-dayni*), the community has accepted some sort of equitable distribution and alimony as the appropriate practice instead.

To recapitulate, it is common commercial custom (*minhag ha-soharim*) or secular law (*dina de-malkhuta*) that provide the relevant rules for the financial settlements of divorce in place of the *ketubah*'s provisions,[45] as they do in many other legal matters small and large. This reality is obvious even to people far removed from America. As Rabbi Avigdor Neventzal, rabbi of the Jewish Quarter in Jerusalem, states:

---

44 Ibid, 4:92 (This responsum was written in 1982).

45 It is important to note, however, that the practice of resolving these disputes in secular court remains a clear violation of *halakhah*, which requires that these types of disputes be resolved in *beit din*. See *Hoshen Mishpat* 26:2. However, the fact that these disputes should be resolved in *beit din* does not in any way lead one to assert that *beit din* cannot accept the common commercial custom of using secular law as the basis to resolve this dispute. Indeed, R. Mordechai Willig's prenuptial agreement explicitly lists that possibility as an option.

In the laws of oaths, vows, sales and rentals, the intent of most people when they speak nowadays is that the terms "day," "month," and "year" follow the Christian calendar, to our embarrassment and shame, and not the Jewish calendar. So too, in many activities that are dependent on the state of mind of a person, their state of mind follows the secular law and not the Torah law.[46]

It is important to understand that this rationale, standing alone, validates Jewish divorces given in light of the 1992 *Get* Law, since it changes the nature of the penalty imposed by the *Get* law into either a self-imposed one (valid only *post facto/be-de'avad*) or a denial of benefit to induce the writing of a *get*, which is permitted *ab initio* (*le-khathillah*).

(In fact, some have argued that the 1992 *Get* Law is merely a maintenance and support law, even in asset division. They contend that the woman who will not receive a *get* will need greater support payments, both alimony and in a larger share of the marital assets for support, since she cannot remarry even after her civil divorce. New York State recognizes this fact in its equitable distribution law: no penalty to give a *get* is intended at all. Although Rabbi Elyashiv clearly disagrees, at least one significant halakhic authority[47] clearly states that when a man is ordered to pay higher support provisions until he writes a *get*, even if the higher payments are without any basis in Jewish law, the resulting *get* is not considered an illicitly compelled divorce and is valid.[48] However, many secular legal authorities argue that the asset division provision of the 1992 *Get* Law is in fact a penalty provision, and this approach is thus only half correct.[49])

---

46 Letter of Approbation to R. Neharia Moshe Gotel, *Hishtanut ha-Teva'im be-Halakhah* (5755), at 15.

47 R. Moshe Feinstein, *Iggerot Moshe, Even ha-Ezer* 4:106.

48 See Breitowitz, *Between Civil and Religious Law*, at 228–229. One can add that there certainly were *poskim* who ruled that even property illicitly taken from the husband may be used as leverage to induce the writing of a *get* where the property was not originally taken for the purpose of inducing the issuing of a *get*. As was noted by Professor Irving Breitowitz in his extraordinary book (n. 637 and at 214–217), many *aharonim* accepted this rationale. This viewpoint would validate the use of equitable distribution penalties even according to those who rule that the wife has no claim on the jointly held assets. This rationale is particularly proper if the 1992 *Get* Law is merely a support bill and not a penalty law.

49 Indeed, the strongest rationale for supporting the 1992 *Get* law as a before-the-fact rule would be to label it as a support and maintenance law, which many aver can never lead to coerced divorce. However, the secular purpose of the 1992 *Get* law remains unclear, and we all wait for some clarification from the New York Court of Appeals.

Third, Rabbi Joseph Kolon (*Maharik*) rules that there is no problem of a coerced *get* in a case where the husband has the alternative of paying the monetary penalty and the penalty is reasonable (as penalties under the *Get* law normally are). Small economic sanctions of the type typically used in this law are permissible.[50] This position is cited by *Rema* and other authorities as a significant factor *post facto*.[51]

An additional relevant factor is the size of the penalties imposed. I have spoken to a number of practitioners in New York State specializing in Jewish divorce law, and they confirm that the penalties imposed typically are very small, that it is rare for a penalty ordered under the 1992 *Get* Law to increase the total monthly payments by more than three percent, or to shift the distribution of assets by more than five percent. While five percent of one's assets can be a significant amount of money, Rabbi Efraim Margaliot notes that in order to determine whether any particular *get* is void because of financial coercion, the *beit din* has to investigate whether the amount forfeited is sufficiently great to compel this person to divorce and:

> [I]f it is an amount of money that is sufficiently small that most people would not divorce their wife to avoid this loss, it is obvious that even if this person asserts that he is of those who are weak of mind, and a lover of money and thus feels compelled to divorce his wife to save the expense, we do not listen to such a person.[52]

A similar approach can be found in the writings of Rabbi Feinstein.[53] One is not believed when one asserts financial coercion and only a small amount of money is involved. The same should logically be true for a small percentage of the marital estate, even if it is a large amount of money.

This is even truer if one accepts the approach of the authorities cited above who rule that government-ordered support payments (even when lacking any basis in Jewish law) can never create a situation where the *get* awarded to avoid paying them is invalid. According to this approach, one would have to determine how much of the court-ordered payments to the wife under the 1992 *Get* Law are support payments and how much are penalty payments, and then one must evaluate whether the amount of the

---

50 R. Joseph Kolon (*Maharik*), *Responsa* 63.

51 See R. Moshe Isserless (*Rema*), *Even ha-Ezer* 134:5 and R. Tzvi Hirsch Eisenstadt, *Pithei Teshuvah* 134:11–12.

52 R. Efraim Margaliot, *Responsa Beit Efraim (Tenyana), Even ha-Ezer* 70.

53 R. Moshe Feinstein, *Iggerot Moshe, Even ha-Ezer* 1:137.

penalty alone (independent of the support component) is large enough to be a coercive amount.

Fourth, it is possible that in any given case under the *Get* law, coercion is permissible according to Jewish law because of misconduct by the husband or wife, a situation that would classify the divorce as either mandatory or a *mitzvah*.[54] According to many opinions, the resulting *get* (even if coerced) is valid.[55] Certainly in such a case the presence of the coercion does not void the *get* according to Jewish law.

Fifth, Rabbenu Yeruham is of the opinion that economic duress never creates a situation of a coerced *get*.[56] The 1992 *Get* Law would thus always be permissible according to this approach. Rabbi Yoav Weingarten uses this as one side of a multifaceted case of doubt (*sefek sefeka*) to validate a *get* that might be coerced.[57] More significantly, Rabbi Elijah of Vilna appears to categorically accept the ruling of Rabbenu Yeruham and rule that whenever physical force is not threatened or used, there is no problem of a coerced *get*.[58]

Sixth, Maimonides (*Rambam*) rules that coercion is acceptable in any case where the woman states that her husband is repugnant to her.[59] Many divorces currently fit that bill; this is even truer for divorces initiated by the woman, where the *Get* law is otherwise most problematic. The 1992 *Get* Law would thus be permissible according to this approach in most

---

54 Either a *kofin* or *yotzee* situation; see *Shulhan Arukh, Even ha-Ezer* 119 for more on this.

55 See Rabbis Herzog and Leibes, cited in notes 23 and 32.

56 Rabbenu Yeruham, *Sefer Toledot Adam ve-Hava, Netiv* 24, *Helek* 1.

57 R. Yoav Weingarten, *Helkat Yoav, Dinai Ones* 5.

58 R. Elijah of Vilna, *Biur ha-Gra, Even ha-Ezer* 154:67.

> It is important to note that this view does not rise to the level of normative *halakhah*, and I want to note explicitly that it should be used only as one side of a multisided *sefek sefeka*, as numerous *aharonim* have done. While my reading of the Gra (as supporting the concept that economic duress does not create coercion) would put Gra in tension with most *aharonim* and *rishonim*, such a reading of the Gra is not unique to me (See R. Ovadia Yosef's comments in *Yabia Omer, Even ha-Ezer* 7:23 and 8:25). While the Gra in *Hoshen Mishpat* 205:18 is ambiguous on this issue, the Gra in *Biur ha-Gra, Even ha-Ezer* 154:67, that I cite, states:
>> Since he can flee to another city and *any situation where they do not do violence to his body is not called force.*
>
> Either way, of course, it is clear that this approach is a minority opinion that should be used only in combination with other rationales.

59 *Rambam, Ishut* 14:8.

cases. Rabbi Isaac Herzog uses this as one side of a multifaceted case of doubt (*sefek sefeka*) to validate a *get* that might be coerced.[60] More significantly, in a case where the woman's claim of repugnancy toward her husband is based on reasonable and provable grounds (*amatla mevu'eret*), many authorities accept Rambam's rule that coercion is permissible, at least *post facto*; some even rule this way *ab initio* (*le-khathillah*).[61] Perhaps most, and certainly many, divorces fall into this situation.

Seventh, for marriages entered into after the *Get* law took effect and with (presumed) knowledge of the law, the penalties found in the 1992 *Get* Law become a voluntarily pre-agreed penalty for withholding a *get*, which are (at least *post facto*) permitted by many authorities.[62] The same can perhaps be said for anyone who continues to reside in New York, even if married prior to 1992, and is aware of the *Get* Law, particularly if the principle that the law of the land is the law (*dina de-malkhuta dina*) appropriately governs the finances of the case.

In addition, even if one considers this a case of illicit coercion because the coercion comes from a secular court, the *get* might not be void. Rabbi Yitzhak Elhanan Spector rules that so long as the illicit coercion from a secular court is not used directly to compel the actual writing of the *get*, but is separated in time and manner from the husband's ordering the *get* to be written, and the husband at the time of the writing of the *get* states to a *beit din* that his actions are voluntary, it appears that there is no imminent coercion present and the *get* is not void.[63] That is exactly the case of the *Get* law.

---

60 Rabbi Herzog, note 23 above.

61 See the many sources cited in R. Ovadia Yosef, *Yabia Omer, Even ha-Ezer* 3:18, where he cites many authorities who accept that economic coercion may be used in a case of reasonable and provable repugnancy (either *post facto/be-de'avad* or *ab initio/le-khathillah*), including Rabbi Yosef himself.

62 R. Shimon Duran, *Tashbetz* 2:168; R. Yom Tom Ishbili (*Ritva*) as quoted in R. Joseph Karo, *Beit Yosef, Even ha-Ezer* 154; R. Moshe Isserless (*Rema*), *Even ha-Ezer* 134:5. While it is true that R. Ya'akov Beruchin, *Mishkenot Ya'akov* 38, is strict on this matter and argues with the *Rema*, a clear consensus agrees with the *Rema* in this regard, at least *be-de'avad*. Certainly in a case where the husband does not categorically state at the time of the *seder ha-get* that he is being coerced, which is a very rare circumstance, the *get* is valid; R. Mordekhai Jaffe, *Levush* 134 and R. Abraham Isaiah Karelitz, *Hazon Ish, Even ha-Ezer* 99:5, but see R. Yehiel Mikhcl Epstein, *Arukh Hashulhan, Even ha-Ezer* 134:26–29. (Were the husband to state that he was coerced, without a doubt the *beit din* would not write the *get*, although many *poskim* would permit such a *get* to be written.)

63 R. Yitzhak Elhanan Spector, *Be'er Yitzhak* 10(8).

The Reality of Divorce

Added to these many halakhic rationales are three empirical observations that also vastly reduce the scope of the problem:

First, there are many Jewish divorces issued where there is no coercion in fact presented by the *Get* law, since the couple have settled their claims fully independent of any secular law, including the 1992 *Get* Law. These divorces are completely nonproblematic with regard to Jewish law. Many uncontested divorces are of this type.

Second, even when a penalty is explicitly imposed by a judge under the *Get* law for withholding a *get*, if the amount is clearly related to the wife's support needs and is comparable to the amount that a *beit din* could have ordered as maintenance (*mezonot*) for the wife, then there is no halakhically improper coercion.[64]

While one could claim that most women who file for divorce are halakhically classified as "rebellious wives" (pl., *moredot*; sing., *moredet*), and thus are not entitled to any support at all, this assertion can readily be questioned.[65] One can imagine many cases where the woman files for divorce, but it is the husband who abandons the wife; indeed, in most cases in which I have been involved it is the husband who moves from the abode and ceases providing support. In those circumstances the wife is not typically a *moredet*[66] although she would be well advised to seek permission from a *beit din* before filing a request for support in secular court, lest she violate the prohibition of litigating in secular court.[67]

---

64 See R. Moshe Feinstein, *Iggerot Moshe, Even ha-Ezer* 4:106 (at the end) and 1:137. It is important to realize that Rabbi Feinstein (in 4:106) does not require that the secular award be lower than that mandated by Jewish law, only comparable. This assumes that the support provisions of the 1992 *Get* Law are truly support provisions and not merely penalty clauses in the guise of support. Their proper understanding is disputed by various secular legal scholars; see Breitowitz, *Between Civil and Religious Law*, at 213–229, esp. n. 634, 636, 640, 643 and 662.

65 More significantly, in a case where the woman's claim of repugnancy toward her husband is based on reasonable and provable grounds (*amatla mevu'eret*), many authorities accept Rambam's rule that coercion is permissible as correct either *lekhathillah* or *be-de'avad*. (See the many sources cited in R. Ovadia Yosef, *Yabia Omer, Even ha-Ezer* 3:18).

66 See *Even ha-Ezer* 77.

67 If my argument above is correct and, in fact, the common custom in our community is to determine separation agreements on the basis of secular law, a strong claim could

Even in the case of woman who is a *moredet*, a very strong case can be made that a husband has no right to *both* decline to support her *and* decline to divorce her. As Rabbi Eliezer Waldenberg notes:

> [When a woman is a *moredet*], she forfeits her *ketubah* rights and other financial claims against the husband. However, on the other side, the husband must [*hayyav*] divorce her and may not keep her connected to him.[68]

Rabbi Waldenberg states that the legal ruling (*psak*) of the Israeli Rabbinical Courts, with which he agrees, is to require support payments to be paid even to a *moredet* who is an adulteress when a reasonable time has elapsed and the husband has not ended the marriage by writing a *get*. Indeed, no less an authority than Rabbi Zvi Hirsch Eisenstadt (*Pithei Teshuvah*) notes that the accepted practice is to make the husband support his wife (until he gives her a *get*) specifically to encourage him to give a *get* and not to compel a woman to remain in a "dead marriage," even if the marriage "died" because of her misconduct.[69] Similar sentiments can be found in the name of many Jewish law authorities, including such luminaries as Rabbi Yehezkel Landau, Rabbi Akiva Eiger, Rabbi Moses Schreiber and Rabbi Meir Posner; it is the normative halakhic posture, even if it is contrary to the assertion of *Tosafot*.[70]

---

be made that the custom is to pay support even in a situation where the woman might halakhically be classified as a *moredet*, so long as secular law and custom are to provide support. This approach would validate the *Get* Law, even if the woman is a *moredet*. (My thanks to Professor Breitowitz, who first pointed this out.)

68 R. Eliezer Waldenberg, *Tzitz Eliezer* 18:58. This *psak* can also be found in *Piskei Din Rabaniyim* 1:238 and 9:171 as the *psak* of the rabbinical courts of Israel and is defended by Rabbi Herzog and others in the appendix to volume 2 of *Otzar ha-Poskim*. Particularly the analysis found in 9:171 supports the contention that the *moredet* issue is not significant, because a *get* should be given even to a *moredet*.

69 R. Tzvi Hirsch Eisenstadt, *Pithei Teshuvah, Even ha-Ezer* 154:4 and 7.

70 *Tosafot, Zevahim* 2b *s.v. stam*. The approach of *Tosafot* is rejected, or limited to a case where the woman does not want to be divorced, by a breadth of authorities, including R. Yehezkel Landau, *Noda Be-Yehuda, Tenyana Even ha-Ezer* 12; R. Akiva Eiger, *Derush ve-Hidush, teshuvah* at the end of the *ketavim* section; R. Moses Schreiber, *Hatam Sofer, Nedarim* 89a *s.v. berishona* (cited in the preface); R. Meir Posner, *Beit Meir, Even ha-Ezer* 117; R. Tzvi Hirsch Eisenstadt, *Pithei Teshuvah* 154 (4&7) and can be implied from R. Yehiel Mikhel Epstein, *Arukh Hashulhan, Even ha-Ezer* 178:25–26. See the short article by R. Yaakov Moshe Toledano in the appendix to

This well-accepted halakhic approach undercuts the *moredet*-based critique of the 1992 *Get* Law. In essence, there is an argument in the alternative that validates the *get* given to an alleged *moredet* who takes court ordered support payments under the 1992 *Get* Law. If the husband claims that the woman is a *moredet* and the marriage is thus over, the husband should give a *get* because of that fact, and support payments to encourage such are not without significant basis in Jewish law once the husband makes it clear that he is withholding a *get*—the only time the 1992 *Get* Law would be applicable. If the husband denies that the wife is a *moredet*, there certainly is no problem with ordering him to make support payments.

It is important to add that in any case where the 1992 *Get* Law is applied so that the woman clearly is entitled to financial support, and she receives roughly what she is entitled to according to Jewish law, there is no problem of illicit coercion in these payments, because she is entitled to the money. If the 1992 *Get* Law is understood as a maintenance and support provision (and not a penalty provision), then a *get* issued to avoid payment of the maintenance would be valid according to at least some authorities, as Rabbi Feinstein explicitly validates a *get* issued to avoid payment of support, even if such support provisions are contrary to the dictates of Jewish law.[71]

Finally, it is important to note that determining the factual reality is made vastly more complex by the nature of secular divorce law. There are many cases where a husband will consent to the imposition of significant penalty because he knows that he will give (or has already given) the *get* of his own will and thus void the penalty. There are also many cases where people agree to such a penalty provision merely to convince their spouse of their genuine desire to issue a *get* and avoid any *agunah* problems. Thus a significant factual problem is created in determining whether any coercion is present in any given case, since the mere presence of a penalty provision in the judicial divorce decree is not evidence of illicit coercion. So

---

Otzar ha-Poskim (2:16) who avers that the approach which requires a husband to support his wife who is a *moredet*, and thus not technically entitled to support, in order to encourage the writing of a *get* by the husband, is the normative *halakhah* without a doubt. Consider the simple remarks of *Hatam Sofer*:

> But, when a woman demands a *get*, since he cannot fulfill his obligation of marital relations, why should he gratuitously withhold a *get*? Even if she sinned and committed deliberate adultery, and is prohibited to return to the marriage, nonetheless, we should not let him withhold a *get* from her.

R. Moses Schreiber, *Hidushei Torat Moshe (Hatam) Sofer*, *Nedarim* 89a s.v. *berishona*.

too, the absence of a penalty provision in a judicial divorce decree does not mean no coercion was present, as the mere existence of the law in the legal code can sometimes create coercion in the negotiations that is not reflected in the public record documentation.[72] Indeed, in reality it is nearly impossible for any outside observer to distinguish cases where coercion is present in the settlement negotiations from cases where it is not.

Conclusion

Secular interference in internal matters of Jewish law that are contested within the Jewish community should generally be discouraged and opposed.The 1992 *Get* Law is not a positive development and raises the possibility of illicit coercion in Jewish divorces. Indeed, it is possible to create a case of divorce that involves a coercive significant penalty that lacks any of the permissive characteristics mentioned above. Ideally Jewish law requires that one investigate every single case of possible coercion to determine the facts on a case-by-case basis and not rely on generalizations.[73]

However, not all bad ideas lead to divorces (*gittin*) that are void (*pasul be-de'avad*) and I believe that there are many Jewish divorces issued in the shadow of the 1992 New York *Get* Law that are valid according to Jewish law. If one considers the "typical" divorce, one sees how relevant this point is. In such a case, there is considerable disagreement over the financial terms for dissolving the marriage, but both sides agree that the marriage is over. Perhaps at some point the husband states that if he does not receive suitable financial terms, he will consider not writing a *get*. The wife responds that if that occurs, relief will be sought under the 1992 *Get* Law. The husband drops that line of negotiation, as his lawyer advises him to do. Before the civil divorce is completed, the husband goes to a *beit din* and authorizes the writing of a *get*, which at that time he attests is done

---

71 See note 47 above.

72 In the economic literature this situation is referred to as "negotiating in the shadow of the law."

73 See R. Shabtai ben Meir HaKohen, *Siftei Kohen* (*Shakh*), *Yoreh Deah* 98:9, who states that correctable gaps in one's factual knowledge do not create legally significant "doubt" in Jewish law.

under his own free will and is part of an integrated settlement between the husband and the wife. Such a *get*, albeit "tainted" by the 1992 *Get* Law in some way, would appear to be valid.

Furthermore, there is a very strong halakhic policy that considers all Jewish divorces coming from recognized arrangers of divorce (*mesadrei gitten*) as valid. Few rabbis arrange Jewish divorces; those who do are experts in the field, and an attestation of a proper divorce from one of them thus deserves a very strong presumption of validity.[74] This is even truer in the presence of the numerous halakhic rationales and factual realities discussed above. These factors incline one, *post-facto*, to validate nearly all Jewish divorces given under the cloud of the coercion created by the 1992 New York *Get* Law.

Keeping a firm grasp on the facts and the reality is vitally important. During the year I was the director of the Beth Din of America, I was involved in arranging many *gittin* in New York and found that most parties were completely unaware of the 1992 *Get* Law or its implications. Fewer than 10 percent of the parties had heard of the law or were told by a judge or attorney to participate in a "Jewish divorce;" they came to be divorced according to Jewish law because they wanted to be divorced in God's eyes. It is important to understand how small a percentage of Jewish divorces the 1992 *Get* Law actually affects, and even in those few cases where it has an effect, how few of these *gittin* are actually invalid because of the 1992 *Get* Law. Other arrangers of divorce (*mesadrim*) at other Jewish courts (*batei din*) can confirm this picture of reality. I have reviewed all of the reported cases in New York since the *Get* law passed, and cannot find more than ten cases where the law was used or referred to by a judge to address the lack of a *get*. There are more articles about the *Get* law than cases using it!

Let me repeat my opening sentiments in conclusion. I believe the 1992 New York *Get* Law is a bad idea, because all coercive secular regulation to enforce Jewish law should be sought only to enforce Jewish law norms that are accepted by (nearly) all members of the halakhic community. The 1992 *Get* Law is not; the whole Orthodox community should be

---

74 R. Moshe Isserless (*Rema*), *Even ha-Ezer* 154 (*seder ha-get*) in the introduction to the appendix.

against it, because secular regulation of Jewish law should occur only be with the consent of the whole Jewish community.[75] However, not all bad laws lead to invalid Jewish divorces, and the 1992 *Get* Law does not lead to void Jewish divorces on a regular basis.

---

75 One additional point needs to be considered in discussing the 1992 *Get* Law. The possible relationship between the rule *sha'at hadehak kemo be-de'avad* ("a time of urgency is to be treated as if it is after the fact") and the 1992 *Get* Law also requires some exploration. Given the reality of the *agunah* problems in America, and the fact that not solving the problem in any given case can also lead to *mamzerut* (due either to women abandoning Orthodox Judaism and marrying anyway, or receiving a "Jewish divorce" from a "*beit din*" that claims to be releasing many *agunot* without a *get*), perhaps a less than ideal, but minimally acceptable solution is all that we can realistically aspire to, and the 1992 *Get* Law is such. Maybe it is halakhically better to rely on the many leniencies advanced by many *poskim* in support of validating *gittin* issued in light of the 1992 *Get* law as *sha'at ha-dehak kemo be-de'avad*, rather than maintaining the none-too-pleasant or successful status quo, which also leads to *mamzerut*. This is even truer given the recent public desecrations of God's name that have occurred relating to the use of physical force to address the *agunah* problem. That calculus would require the approval of the foremost halakhic authorities of our times.

Glossary

This glossary begins with an introduction to Jewish law (*halakhah*) and its methodology and continues with short explanations of other Jewish law terms used in this book. The final section contains a glossary of legal terms.

JEWISH LAW TERMS

Jewish law or *Halakhah*: Jewish law (called *halakhah* in Hebrew) is the term used to denote the entire subject matter of the Jewish legal system, including public, private, and ritual law.

A brief historical review will familiarize the new reader of Jewish law with its history and development. The Pentateuch (the five books of Moses, the *Torah*) is the historical touchstone document of Jewish law, and along with the oral law are the cornerstones of Jewish law: The Prophets and Writings, the other two parts of the Hebrew Bible, were written over the next 700 years, and the Jewish canon was closed around the year 200 B.C.E. From the close of the canon until 250 C.E. is referred to as the era of the *Tannaim*, the redactors of Jewish law, whose period closed with the editing of the *mishnah* by Rabbi Judah the Patriarch. The next five centuries was the epoch in which the two Talmuds (Babylonian and Jerusalem) were written and edited by scholars called *Amoraim* ("those who recount" Jewish law) and *Savoraim* ("those who ponder" Jewish law). The Babylonian Talmud is of greater legal significance than the Jerusalem Talmud, and is a more complete work.

The post-talmudic era is conventionally divided into three periods: the era of the *Geonim*, scholars who lived in Babylonia until the mid-eleventh century; the era of the *Rishonim* (the early authorities), who lived in North Africa, Spain, Franco-Germany, and Egypt until the end of the fourteenth century; and the period of the *Aharonim* (the latter authorities), which encompasses all scholars of Jewiàh law from the fifteenth century up to this era.

From the period of the mid-fourteenth century until the early seventeenth century, Jewish law underwent a period of codification, which led to the acceptance of the law code format of Rabbi Joseph Karo, called the *Shulhan Arukh*, as the basis for modern Jewish law. The *Shulhan Arukh* (and the *Arba'ah Turim* of Rabbi Jacob ben Asher, which preceded it) divided Jewish law into four separate areas: *Orah Hayyim* is devoted to daily, Sabbath, and holiday laws; *Even ha-Ezer* addresses family law, including financial aspects; *Hoshen Mishpat* codifies financial law; and *Yoreh Deah* contains dietary laws as well as other miscellaneous legal matter. Many significant scholars—themselves as important as Rabbi Karo in status and authority—wrote annotations to his code which made the work and its surrounding comments the modern touchstone of Jewish law. The most recent complete edition of the *Shulhan Arukh* (Vilna, 1896) contains no less than 113 separate commentaries on the text of Rabbi Karo. In addition, hundreds of other volumes of commentary have been published as self-standing works, a process that continues to this very day.

Adam Hashuv: Literally: "a prestigious person." This term is used to denote the person in a community whose authority covered those areas where practical Jewish law, economic issues, and communal consensus was needed to authorize an action.

Agunah: An estranged wife denied a divorce conforming to Jewish law due to either a missing or recalcitrant husband.

Aharonim: See Jewish law, above.

Amoraim: See Jewish law, above.

Apostate: A heretic; one who rejects his religion.

Arevut: The concept that all Jews are responsible for each other.

Arkhaot: Secular court.

Ashkenazim: Jews of predominantly European origin.

Bedi'avad: What the Jewish law is after-the-fact or in a time of need.

Beit Din: A court invested with the authority to issue legal decisions under Jewish law.

Dayyan: A judge in a rabbinical court.

Dina de-Malkhuta Dina: The rule within Jewish law which obligates observance of secular law in certain monetary matters.

Geonim: See Jewish law, above.

Get: A Jewish divorce.

Get Me'useh: A coerced divorce, which is not valid. Jewish law mandates that divorces be given and received with free will.

Heter Iska: A document that recasts a loan into a partnership, thus bypassing the Jewish law prohibitions related to interest-charging.

Hillul ha-Shem: Improper behavior causing desecration of the Lord's name; in a broader sense, conduct resulting in Judaism being viewed in a negative light.

Ketav Seruv: A document issued by a Jewish court in a case where a person will not appear before it. This document provides for sanctions against one who defies the court and permits the plaintiff to litigate in secular court.

Ketubah: A prenuptial agreement mandated by Jewish law, specifying the duties of the couple in the case of death or divorce, as well as the various obligations within the marriage itself.

Kippah: A head-covering for males, impressing upon its wearer and others awareness of the Lord. (Yiddish synonym: *yarmulke*.)

Le'khathillah: What the Jewish law should be in ideal circumstances.

Migo: Jewish law's rule that since a defendant could have put forth a provable fully-exonerating (but not true) response to an allegation, his unprovable—but claimed true—defense should be accepted.

Mesirah: The common term used to refer to situations where one informs on a fellow Jew to the secular government in violation of Jewish law.

Mezonot: Maintenance, typically referring to support payments by a husband to his estranged wife or by a parent to a child.

Mitzvah: Commandment, obligation, or good deed.

Noahide Laws: The seven mandates that Jewish law rules applicable to all humans ("children of Noah"). They consist of the obligation to enforce laws and the prohibitions against idol worship, taking God's name in vain, murder, prohibited sexual activity, theft, and eating flesh from a living animal.

Orekh Din: Lawyer; advocate in Jewish law.

Pesharah: Compromise

Responsum: Response to a question on a specific matter by a Jewish legal scholar.

Ribbit: Term for usury in Jewish law.

Rishonim: See Jewish law, above.

Rodef: One who pursues another in order to kill him, and can himself be killed.

Savoraim: See Jewish law, above.

Sephardim: Jews of predominantly Arabian and North African countries.

Sefek Sefeka: A case of double doubt. There are circumstances where Jewish law rules that the confluence of circumstances can create cases where two debatable leniencies might be applicable to one case simultaneously, thus establishing a case of double doubt leading to a permissive ruling. The reverse is possible also.

Shtar Hov: A note of indebtedness.

Tannaim: See Jewish law, above.

Tinokot Shenishbu: Literally, "kidnapped children." This term denotes one who was raised without any knowledge of the Jewish tradition, and for the purposes of many issues, is considered an unintentional violator of Jewish law.

To'en (pl. to'anim): One who represents another in a matter in front of a Jewish court, *beit din*.

Tokhahah: Literally, "admonition." Informing a fellow Jew of a behavior that needs to be modified to conform to Jewish law.

Yarmulke: See *kippah*.

Zebla: This term is an acronym for the Hebrew phrase "each side picks one judge," and refers to the process used by litigants to create a Jewish court made up of judges chosen by each party.

LEGAL TERMS

A.B.A.: The American Bar Association, which is the umbrella organization of attorneys in the United States.

Ab Initio: A Latin translation of the Hebrew term *le'khathillah*.

Alternative Pleadings: Issuance by a party in a legal action of two or more inconsistent allegations.

Arbitration: Proceeding by which, with the consent of the opposing parties, a third party (but not a court) resolves a dispute.

Counterclaim: A claim, more frequently by a defendant, made in response to an opposing party's claim.

Demurrer: A response to a claim, charging it with a deficiency that should either freeze or end the proceedings.

De Minimus: Minimal (Latin).

De Novo: A full review of a legal decision. Literally, "from the beginning, anew" (Latin).

Legatee: A party designated to receive property in a will.

Litigation: An action surrounding a lawsuit.

Living Will: A legal directive by a person expressing his wishes should he one day be in need of medical care and incapable of directing his own treatment.

Perjury: Knowingly putting forth a false statement in a legal proceeding.

Post-facto: A Latin translation of the Hebrew term *bede'avad*.

Power of Attorney: An instrument delegating a person the authority to effect the legal actions of another.

Probate: A process by which the legal and financial affairs of a decedent are administered.

Standard-fee Agreement: Payment based on a set amount stipulated by parties in contract with each other, in contrast to payment based on hours worked.

Usury: The charging of interest.

Writ of Mandamus: A common-law order, issued by a judge directing a government official to either do, or not do, a specific act.

Bibliography

(Publication information for works that have been reprinted numerous times is not provided.)

COMMENTARIES ON SHULHAN ARUKH AND TUR

This list of authorities cited does not include commentaries found in the standard edition of the Vilna *Shulhan Arukh*, the new edition of *Hoshen Mishpat* (sections 1–58) published by *Morashah leHanhel* (Jerusalem, 1994), or the new *Tur* published by *Makhon Yerushalayim* (Jerusalem, 1994).

Raphael Alkova, *Karnei Re'em* (Brooklyn, 1992).

Raphael Alnaqua, *Pa'amonei Zahav* (Jerusalem, 1912).

Hayyim Benveniste, *Knesset ha-Gedolah* (Jerusalem, 1992).

Hayyim Benveniste, *Sha'arei Knesset ha-Gedolah* (Jerusalem, 1992).

Yehiel Mikhel Epstein, *Arukh ha-Shulhan* (Hoboken, 1991).

Yaakov Meshullam Ginsburg (ed), *Halakhah Pesukah al Hoshen Mishpat* (Makhon Harry Fischel, Jerusalem, 1988).

Moshe Isserles, *Darkei Moshe ha-Shalem, Orah Hayyim* (Jerusalem, 1993).

Abraham Isaiah Karelitz, *Hazon Ish* (*Hoshen Mishpat*) (Jerusalem, 1954).

Samuel Katz (ed.), *Kovetz ha-Poskim al Hoshen Mishpat* (Brooklyn, 1969).

Israel Meir Kagan, *Mishnah Berurah*.

Tzvi Hirsch Shapira, *Darkhei Teshuvah* (New York, 1951).

Mordecai Shimon, *Matteh Shimon* (Salonika, 1797).

Shmuel Shor, *Minhat Shai* (Jerusalem, 1911).

Yaakov Hayyim Sofer, *Kaf ha-Hayyim* (Jerusalem, 1905).

Israel Wolf, *Sha'ar ha-Mishpat* (Brooklyn, 1979).

Mordecai Yaffe, *Levush* (New York, 1962).

COMMENTARIES ON TALMUD AND MISHNAH

This list of authorities cited does not include commentaries found in the Vilna edition of the Talmud.

Betzalel Ashkenazi, *Shittah Mekubetzet*.

Akiva Eiger, Commentary on the Talmud (*Niddah*).

Yaakov Ettlinger, *Arukh la-Ner* (*Niddah*).

Abraham Isaiah Karelitz, *Hazon Ish* (*Sanhedrin*).

Shlomo Luria, *Hokhmat Shlomo* (*Niddah*).

Yosef Shapira, *Hiddushei Mahari Shapira* (*Niddah*) (Jerusalem, 1981).

Yom Tov Lippman Heller, *Tosafot Yom Tov*.

COMMENTARIES ON MAIMONIDES

This list of authorities cited does not include commentaries found in the standard edition of Maimonides.

Isser Zalman Meltzer, *Even ha-Azel* (Jerusalem, 1962).

Meir Simcha of Dvinsk, *Or Sameah* (Jerusalem, 1992).

COMMENTARIES ON BIBLE

This list of authorities cited does not include commentaries found in the standard edition of Mikraot Gedolot.

Baruch HaLevi Epstein, *Torah Temimah* (New York, 1928).

BOOKS

Abraham S. Abraham, *Nishmat Avraham* (Jerusalem, 1993).

David Abudarham, *Abudarham ha-Shalem* (Jerusalem, 1963).

Sinai Adler, *Devar Sinai* (Jerusalem, 5760).

Jerold S. Auerbach, *Rabbis and Lawyers: The Journey from Torah to Constitution* (Indiana, 1990).

Ezra Batzri, *Dinei Mamonot* (Makhon HaKetav, 1982).

Yaakov Blau, *Berit Yehuda* (Jerusalem, 1979).

Yaakov Blau, *Pithei Hoshen* (Jerusalem, 1982).

J. David Bleich, *Time of Death in Jewish Law* (New York, 1991).

J. David Bleich, *Contemporary Halakhic Problems* (Ktav, 1979).

Irving Breitowitz, *Between Civil and Religious Law: The Plight of the Agunah in American Society* (Greenwood, 1994).

Hayyim Cohen, *Divrei Geonim* (Jerusalem, 1970).

Feivel Cohen, *Kuntres Midor L'dor: Laws of the Torah Relating to the Writing of a Will and the Distribution of One's Estate* (Targum, 1983).

Menachem Elon, *Ha-Mishpat ha-Ivri* (3rd ed., Magnes Press, 1988).

Menachem Elon, *Jewish Law: History, Sources, Principles* (JPS, 1994).

Shlomo Englander, *Kelala Deribbita* (Benei Brak, 1973).

Azaryah Figo, *Giddulei Terumah* (Jerusalem, 1988).

Isadore Grunfeld, *The Jewish Law of Inheritance* (Targum, 1987).

Judah HeHasid, *Sefer ha-Hasidim* (Jerusalem, 1970).

Yosef Elijah Henkin, *Kol Kitvei ha-Rav Henkin* (New York, 1989).

Moshe Hershler & Eliyahu Hershrik, *Torat Ribbit* (Jerusalem, 1992).

Israel Meir Kagan, *Hafetz Hayyim*.

Dov Katz, *Tenuat ha-Musar* (5th ed., Jerusalem, 1974)

Eliezer ben Joel ha-Levi, *Sefer Raavyah* (Jerusalem, 1966)

Oded Lipa Levfar, *Mishpetei ha-Migo* (2nd ed., Benei Brak, 1993).

Aaron Levine, *Economics and Jewish Law* (Ktav, 1987).

Aaron Lichtenstein, *The Seven Laws of Noah* (2nd ed., New York, 1986).

Yitzhak ben Aba Mari, *Sefer ha-Ittur* (Jerusalem, 1970).

Nahum Rakover, *Ha-Shelihut ve-ha-Harsha'ah ba-Mishpat ha-Ivri* (Jerusalem, 1972).

Hershel Schachter, *Nefesh ha-Rav* (Jerusalem, 1994).

Benzion Schareschevsky, *Dinei Mishpahah* 348–375 (3rd. ed., Jerusalem, 1983).

Shmuel Shilo, *Dina de-Malkhuta Dina* (Jerusalem, 1974).

Haym Soloveitchik, *Pawnbroking: A Study in the Interrelationship between Halakhah, Economic Activity and Communal Self-Image* (Magnes, 1985)

Nahum Stefansky, *Ve'aleihu Lo Yibol* (Jerusalem, 1999).

Moshe Sternbuch, *Ta'am Ribbit* (Jerusalem, 1990).

Rabbenu Tam, *Sefer ha-Yashar, Helek ha-Teshuvot* (Berlin, 1898)

Abraham b. Nathan ha-Yarhi, *Sefer ha-Manhig* (Jerusalem, 1978)

Rabbenu Yeruham, *Sefer Toledot Adam ve-Hava* (Jerusalem, 1983).

Shaul Yisraeli (ed), *Ha-Torah ve-ha-Medinah* (Tzomet, 1990, 2nd ed.) (This is a collection of articles from the periodical *Ha-Torah ve-ha-Medinah*, 1948–1956, that was republished in book form).

RESPONSA

Jacob ben Aaron, *Mishkenot Ya'akov* (Jerusalem, 1960).

Samuel Aboab, *Devar Shmuel* (Jerusalem, 1967).

Moshe Alshekh, *Responsa* (Venice, 1605).

Yom Tov Ishbili (*Ritva*), *Responsa* (Safed, 1975).

Yekutiel Asher Zalman Enzel, *Mariaz Enzel* (Jerusalem, 1983).

Tzvi Hirsch Ashkenazi, *Hakham Tzvi* (Furth, 1767).

Nissim Abraham Ashkenazi, *Nehmad le-Mareh* (Salonika, 1831).

Shlomo Zalman Auerbach, *Minhat Shlomo* (Jerusalem, 1985).

Yair Hayyim Bacharach, *Havvot Yair* (Jerusalem, 1968).

Ezra Batzri, *Sha'arei Ezra* (Jerusalem, 1981).

Yehoshua Pinhas Bombach, *Ohel Yehoshua* (New York, 1979).

Abraham Boorstein, *Avnei Nezer* (Jerusalem, 1959).

Yaakov Breisch, *Helkat Yaakov* (Jerusalem, 1992).

Zvi Hirsch Chajes (*Maharatz Chayes*), *Torat Nevi'im* (in *Kol Kitvei Maharatz Chajes*, Jerusalem, 1958).

Saul Dweck, *Emet me-Eretz* (Monroe, 1992).

Shmuel di-Medina, *Maharshdam* (New York, 1959).

Shimon Duran, *Tashbetz* (Tel Aviv, 1964).

Yaakov Emden, *She'elat Ya'avetz* (Lemberg, 1887).

Yaakov Ettlinger, *Binyan Tziyyon* (Jerusalem, 1989).

Moshe Feinstein, *Iggerot Moshe* (New York, 1959).

Tzvi Pesach Frank, *Har Tzvi* (Jerusalem, 1976).

Yehuda Leib Grauburt, *Havalim ba-Neimim* (2nd ed., Toronto, 1968).
Shimon Greenfeld, *Maharshag* (Jerusalem, 1959).
Hayyim Ozer Grodzinski, *Iggerot Ahiezer* (Benei Brak, 1989).
Shammai Gross, *Shevet Kehat*i (Benei Brak, 1986).
Aryeh Grossnass, *Lev Aryeh* (London, 1958).
Kalfon Moshe ha-Cohen, *Sho'el ve-Nishal* (Jerusalem, 1989).
Ovadia Hadaya, *Yaskil Avdi* (Jerusalem, undated).
Hayyim Halberstam, *Divrei Hayyim* (Brooklyn, 1980).
Mordecai ben Judah ha-Levi, *Darkhei Noam* (Venice, 1697).
Hayyim David ha-Levi, *Mekor Hayyim* (Jerusalem, 1975).
Joseph Hazan, *Hikrei Lev* (Jerusalem, 1987).
Yitzhak Isaac Herzog, *Hekhal Yitzhak* (Jerusalem, 1972).
Yitzhak Isaac Herzog, *Tehukah le-Yisrael al pi ha-Torah* (Jerusalem, 1989).
Azriel Hildesheimer, *She'elot u-Teshuvot Rabi Azriel* (Tel Aviv, 1976)
David Tzvi Hoffmann, *Melammed Le-Ho'il* (New York, 1954).
Meyer Issaacson, *Mevasser Tov* (Jerusalem, undated).
Moshe Isserles, *Responsa* (Brooklyn, 1976).
Menahem Mendel Kirschbaum, *Menahem Meshiv* (Lublin, 1939).
Menasheh Klein, *Mishneh Halakhot* (Brooklyn, 1977).
Joseph Kolon (*Maharik*), *Responsa* (Jerusalem, 1993).
Abraham Isaac Kook, *Orah Mishpat* (Jerusalem, 1985).
Abraham Isaac Kook, *Etz Hadar* (Jerusalem, 1984).
Jonah Landsofer, *Me'il Tzedakah* (Jerusalem, 1968).
Yitzhak Isaac Liebes, *Beit Avi* (New York, 1972).
Shlomo Luria, *She'elot u-Teshuvot Maharshal* (Lemberg, 1859)
Benyamin ben Mattityahu, *Binyamin Ze'ev* (Jerusalem, 1989).
Hayyim Menahem, *ve-Sameh Lev* (Jerusalem, 1978).
Israel Meyer Mizrachi, *Peri ha-Aretz* (Istanbul, 1732).
Jacob Molin, *Responsa Maharil Hahadashot* (Jerusalem, 1977).
Yom Tov ben Moshe Zahalon, *Maharit Zahalon* (Jerusalem, 1985).
Ephraim Oshry, *Responsa from the Holocaust* (Boston, 1977).
Hayyim Palache, *He-Hafetz Hayyim* (Jerusalem, 1977).

Aaron Parhi, *Perah Matteh Aharon* (Amsterdam, 1707).

Yitzhak bar Sheshet Profiat, *Teshuvot Rivash* (Jerusalem, 1993).

Moshe Preschel, *Va-Yeshev Moshe* (Munkacs, 1904).

Yaakov Reisher, *Shevut Yaakov* (New York, 1961).

Judah ben ha-Rosh, *Zikhron Yehudah* (Berlin, 1846)

Joseph Rozin, *Tsofnat Paneah* (New York, 1954),

Moshe Schick, *Maharam Schick* (New York, 1991).

Hayyim Shapira, *Minhat Elazar* (New York, 1991).

Isaac Judah Schmelkes, *Beit Yitzhak* (New York, 1958).

Shalom Mordecai Schwadron, *Maharsham* (Jerusalem, 1974).

Moses Schreiber, *Hatam Sofer* (Jerusalem, 1989).

Yitzhak Elhanan Spector, *Be'er Yitzhak* (Brooklyn, 1968).

Betzalel Stem, *Be-Tzel ha-Hokhmah* (Jerusalern, 1992).

Moshe Sternbuch, *Teshuvot ve-Hanhagot* (2nd ed., Jerusalem, 1992).

Yekutiel Teitelbaum, *Avnei Tzedek* (New York, 1958).

Yoel Teitelbaum, *Divrei Yoel* (Brooklyn, 1982).

Joseph Trani, *Mabit* (Jerusalem, 1990).

Samuel Turk, *Peri Malka* (Brooklyn, 1988).

Meir Ben Zion Chai Uze'il, *Mishpetei Uze'il* (Jerusalem, 1969).

Eliezer Waldenberg, *Tzitz Eliezer* (Jerusalem, 1985).

Yoav Weingarten, *Helkat Yoav* (Jerusalem, 1962).

Dov Baer Weidenfeld, *Dovevei Mesharim* (Jerusalem, 1983).

Yitzhak Yaakov Weiss, *Minhat Yitzhak* (New York, 1989).

Yitzhak Wolf, *Nahalat Binyamin* (Amsterdam, 1682).

Shmuel Wosner, *Shevet Ha-Levi* (Bnei Brak, 1970).

Asher ben Yehiel (*Rosh*), *Responsa* (Jerusalem, 1994).

Shlomo ben Yitzhak (*Rashi*), *Responsa*.

Ovadia Yosef, *Yehavveh Da'at* (Jerusalem, 1987).

Ovadia Yosef, *Yabia Omer* (Jerusalem, 1986).

Binyamin Zilberg, *Az Nidberu* (Bnei Brak, 1971).

David ben Solomon ibn Zimra, *Radvaz* (Warsaw, 1892).

BOOKS OF COMMANDMENTS

Moshe ben Yaakov mi-Kutzi, *Sefer Mitzvot Gadol* (*Semag*).
Aaron Halevi, *Hinnukh* (Jerusalem, 1992).
Moshe ben Maimon (*Rambam*), *Seferha-Mitzvot*.
Eliezer me-Mitz, *Yereim*.
Yitzhak ben Yosef mi-Corbeil, *Mitzvot Katan*.
Baruch ben Yitzhak, *Sefer ha-Terumah* (Jerusalem, 1988).
Rav Aha mi-Shabha, *She'iltot* (Jerusalem, 1961).
Naphtali Tzvi Yehuda Berlin, *Ha'amek She'alah* (Jerusalem, 1961).
Joseph Babad, *Minhat Hinnukh* (Jerusalem, 1992).

ENCYCLOPEDIAS

Shlomo Yosef Zevin, ed., *Encyclopedia Talmudit* (Yad HaRav Herzog).
Encyclopedia Judaica (Keter, 1973).
Hezekiah di-Medini, *Sedei Hemed* (Brooklyn, 1959).
Yitzhak Isaac Herzog, *Otzar ha-Poskim* (Jerusalem, 1946).

ARTICLES

Yehudah Amichai, "A Gentile who Summons a Jew to Beit Din", *Tehumin* 12:259–265 (1991).
Yehuda Amital, "Rebuking a Jew: Theory and Practice," *Jewish Tradition and the Non-Traditional Jew*, 119–138 (J.J. Schacter, ed. 1992).
Jennifer Bagby, "Justifications For State Bystander Intervention Statutes: Why Crime Witnesses Should Be Required to Call For Help," *Indiana Law Review* 33:571 at 572 (2000).
Naphtali Bar-Ilan, "Edut al Tenuat Derakhim be-Beit Mishpat," *Tehumin* 10:179–189 (1990).
Tzvi Yehuda Ben-Yaakov, "Checks: Their Essence and Legal Status," *Tehumin* 13:422–470 (1993).
Mordecai Biser, "Can an Observant Jew Practice Law? A Look at Some Halakhic Problems," *The Jewish Law Annual* XI:101–135 (1994).
J. David Bleich, "Extradition," *Tehumin* 8:297–303 (1988).

J. David Bleich, "Jewish Law and the State's Authority to Punish Crime," *Cardozo L.R.* 12:829–857 (1991).

J. David Bleich, "Hasgarat Poshea Yehudi she-Barah le-Eretz Yisrael," *Or ha-Mizrah* 35:247–269 (1987).

J. David Bleich, "Jewish Law and the State's Authority to Punish Crime," *Cardozo L. R.* 12:829, 830 (1991).

J. David Bleich, "Survey of Recent Halakhic Literature: Checks," *Tradition* 24(1)74–83 (1989).

Dov Bressler, "Arbitration and the Courts in Jewish Law," *J Halacha & Contemporary Society* 9:105–117 (1985).

Michael Broyde, "The Establishment of Maternity and Paternity in Jewish and American Law," *National Jewish L.R.* 3:117–152 (1988).

Michael Broyde, "Tradition, Modesty and America: The Obligation of Women to Cover their Hair," *Judaism* 40:79–87 (1991).

Michael Broyde, "The Definition of Fire in Halacha: A Theoretical Discourse with Some Practical Insights," distributed by *Rabbinical Council of America*, October 1993.

Michael Broyde, "The Obligation of Jews to Seek Observance of Noahide Laws by Gentiles: A Theoretical Perspective," in *Tikkun Olam: Jewish Responsibilities to Society* (D. Shatz and C. Waxman, eds. Northvale, 1997).

Michael Broyde, "Child Custody: A Pure Law Analysis," *Jewish Law Association Studies VII* 1–20 (1994).

Michael Broyde, "Forming Religious Communities and Respecting Dissenter's Rights: A Jewish Law Approach to a Tort Law Problem," in John Witte, Jr., ed., *Religious Human Rights in the World Today: Legal and Religious Perspectives* (Martinus Nijhoff, 1995).

Michael Broyde & Michael Hecht, "The Gentile and Returning Lost Property According to Jewish Law: A Theory of Reciprocity," in the *Jewish Law Annual* XIII 31–45 (2000).

Michael Broyde, "On the Practice of law," *J. Halacha & Contemporary Society* 20:5–45 (1990).

Michael Broyde & David Hertzberg, "Enabling a Jew to Sin: The Parameters," *J. Halacha & Contemporary Society* 19:5–33 (1990).

Evan Caminker, "The Constitutionality of Qui Tam Actions," *Yale L.J.* 99:341–467 (1989)

She'ar Yashuv Cohen, "Ma'amad Orkhei Din ba-Halakhah," *Torah she-B'al Peh* 22:64 (1981).

Alfred Cohen, "On Maintaining A Professional Confidence," *J. Halacha & Contemporary Society* 7:73–87 (1984).

Alfred Cohen, "Privacy: A Jewish Perspective," *J. Halacha & Contemporary Society* 1:53–102 (1981).

Judah Dick, "Jewish Law and the Conventional Last Will and Testament," *J. Halacha & Contemporary Society* 2:5–18 (1982).

Menachem Elon, "Extradition in Jewish Law," *Tehumin* 8:263–286, 304–309 (1988).

Gedaliah Felder, "Secular Courts," *Sefer ha-Yovel le-Rav Yosef Dov ha-Levi Soloveitchik*, 399–411 (Mosad HaRav Kook, 1984).

David Fried, "Too High a Price for Truth: the Exception to the Attorney-Client Privilege for Contemplated Crimes and Frauds," *North Carolina L.R.* 64:443–499 (1986).

Dov Frimer, "The Role of a. Lawyer in Jewish Law," *J. Law & Religion* 1:297–305 (1983).

Israel Tzvi Gilat, "Is the Best Interest of the Child a Major Factor when Parents Conflict on Custody of a Child," *Bar Ilan Law Studies* 8:297–349 (1980).

Jessica R. Givelber, "Imposing Duties on Witnesses to Child Sexual Abuse: a Futile Response to Bystander Indifference," *Fordham Law Review* 67:3169–3205 (1999).

Yechiel Grunhaus, "The Laws of Usuary and Their Significance in Our Times," *J. Halacha & Contemporary Society* 21:48–59 (1982).

Chaim David Gulevsky, "Questions on the Custody of Children," *Sefer Kavod Harav: Essays in Honor of Joseph B. Soloveitchik* 104–132, (New York, 1984).

Gregory Hankin, "Alternative and Hypothetical Pleadings," *Yale L.J.* 33:365–403 (1933).

Yehudah Hertzl Henkin, "Mutav Sheyihyu Shogegim ve-al Yiheyu Mezidim be-Zeman ha-Zeh," *Tehumin* 2:2727–280 (1991).

Yosef Elijah Henkin, "The Law of the Land is the Law," *Hapardes* 17:54–58 (1954).

Jerome Hornblass, "The Jewish Lawyer," *Cardozo L.R.* 14:1639–1655 (1993).

Ulrich Huber, "Creditor Equality in Transnational Bankruptcies," *Vanderbilt Journal of Transnational Law* 18:741–783 (1986).

Howard Jachter, "The Use of a Video Teleconference for a Get Procedure," *J. Halacha & Contemporary Society* 28:5–17 (1994).

Howard Jachter & Michael Broyde, "Fire, Light and Electricity in Positive Cornmandments According to Jewish Law," *J. Halacha & Contemporary Society* 25:89–127 (1993).

Aaron Kirschenbaum, "Representation in Litigation in Jewish Law," *Dine Israel* 6:25–30 (1975).

Aaron Kirschenbaum, "The Good Samaritan: Monetary Aspects," *J. Halacha & Contemporary Society* 17:83–92 (1989).

Aaron Kirschenbaum, "'Covenant' with Noahides Compared with Covenant at Sinai," *Dinei Israel* 6:31–48 (1975).

Aaron Kirschenbaum, "The Bystander's Duty to Rescue in Jewish Law," *J. Religious Ethics* 8:204–226 (1980).

Simcha Krauss, "Litigation in Secular Courts," *J. Halacha & Contemporary Society* 3:35–54 (1982).

Norman Lamm, "Loving and Hating Jews as Halakhic Categories," *Tradition* 24:98–122 (1989).

Norman Lamm, "Self Incrimination in Law and Psychology: The Fifth Amendment and the Halakhah," *Faith and Doubt* 247–289 (2nd ed., Ktav, 1986).

Sanford Levinson, "Identifying the Jewish Lawyer: Reflections on the Construction of Professional Identity," *Cardozo L.R.* 14:1577–1612 (1993).

Sharone Levy, "Balancing Physical Abuse by the System against Abuse of the System: Defining "Imminent Danger" Within the Prison Litigation Reform Act of 1995," 86 *Iowa L.R.* 361 (2000).

Gerald Lynch, "The Lawyer as Informer," *Duke L.J.* 1986:491–547 (1986).

"Oaths and Affirmations," *American Jurisprudence 2d* 58:1043 (1994).

Melissa Philbrick, "Agreements to Arbitrate Post-Divorce Custody Disputes," *Columbia J. Law & Social Problems* 18:419–462 (1985).

Nachum Rabinovitch, "All Jews are Responsible for One Another," *Jewish Tradition and the Non-Traditional Jew*, pp. 177–204 (J.J. Schacter, ed).

Nahum Rakover, "Jewish Law and the Noahide Obligation to Preserve Social Order," *Cardozo L.R.* 12:1073–1136 (1991).

"Rape in Prison," *The New York Times*, April 22, 2001, Section 4; Page 16; Column 1.

Steven Resnicoff, "A Commercial Conundrum: Does Prudence Permit the Jewish 'Permissible Venture [Heter Iska]'?", *Seton Hall L.R.* 20:77–129 (1989).

Steven Resnicoff, "Bankruptcy: A Viable Halachic Option?" *J. Halacha & Contemporary Society* 24:5–54 (1992).

Steven Resnicoff, "The Corporate Paradigm and Jewish Law," *Wayne State Law Journal* 43:1685–1818 (1997).

Hershel Schachter, "Dina Di'Malchusa Dina: Secular Law as a Religious Obligation," *J. Halacha & Contemporary Society* 1:103–132 (1981).

Menachem Mendel Schneerson, "Sheva Mitzvot Shel Benei Noah," *Hapardes* 59:(9)7–11 (1985).

Gedaliah Dov Schwartz, "The 1992 New York 'Get Law'," *J. Halacha & Contemporary Society* 27:26–34 (1994).

Gedaliah Dov Schwartz, "The Abused Child—Halakhic Insights," *Ten Da'at* (Spring 1988).

Abraham Sherman, "Ma'amad Beit Din Penimin shel Tenuah al pi Halakhah," *Tehumin* 14:159–164 (1994).

Eliav Shochatman, "The Essence of the Principles Used in Child Custody in Jewish Law," *Shenaton le-Mishpat ha-Ivri* 5:285–320 (1978).

Eliav Shochatman, "Ma'amad ha-Halakhti shel batei ha-Mishpat biMedinat Yisrael," *Tehumin* 13:337–370 (1993).

Arthur Silver, "May One Disinherit Family in Favor of Charity?" *Tradition* 28(3):79–92 (1994).

Peter Smedresman & Andreas Lowenfeld, "Eurodollars, Multinational Banks, and National Laws," *New York University L.R.* 64:733–804 (1989).

Judah Stern, "Ribis: A Halachic Anthology," *J. Halacha & Contemporary Society* 4:46–69 (1982).

Harry Subin, "The Criminal Lawyer's 'Different Mission': Reflections on the 'Right' to Present a False Case," *Georgetown J. Legal Ethics* 1:125–153 (1987).

Yechiel Tauber, "Secular Court," *Kovetz Meshiv ba-Halakhah* 10:9–10 (1993).

Gordon Tucker, "The Confidentiality Rule: A Philosophical Perspective with Reference to Jewish Law and Ethics," *Fordham Urban L.J.* 13:99–112 (1984).

Patrick Tuite, "ABA Ethics Opinion Refines Standards on Fees and Billing," *Chicago Daily Law Bulletin* 140:(24)6 A 12.

Ronald Warburg, "Child Custody: A Comparative Analysis," *Israel Law Review* 14:480–503 (1978).

Jack Weinstein, "The Informer: Hero or Villain?—Ethical and Legal Problema," *New York L.J.* (Nov. 8, 1982) 1, col. 3.

Shaul Yisraeli, "Extradition," *Tehumin* 8:287–296 (1988).

Shaul Yisraeli, "Extradition," *Tehumin* 8:287–296 (1988).

Eric Zimmer, "Men's Headcovering: The Metamorphosis of this Practice," in *Reverence, Righteousness and Rahamanut: Essays in Memory of Rabbi Dr. Leo Jung* 325–351 (J.J. Schacter, ed., Northvale, 1992).

CASES, STATUES, AND CODES

Aloni v. Nakash, Israel High Court of Justice (Supreme Court) 852/86, 869/86.

Eastman Kodak v. Kavlin, 978 F.Supp 1078 (S.D. Florida, 1997).

In re The Liverpool Household Stores Ass'n, 59 Law. Rep. 616, 617 (England, 1890).

Mapp v. Ohio, 367 U.S. 643 (1961).

Nix v. Whiteside, 475 U.S. 157 (1986).

In re Vrdolyak, 137 Ill.2d 407, 560 N.E.2d 840 (1990).

People v. Drelich, 506 N.Y.S.2d 746 124, A.D.2d 441 (2d App. Div. 1986).

People v. Fentress, 425 N.Y.S.2d 485 (Sup. Ct. 1980).

Ran-Dav's County Kosher, Inc., v. New Jersey, 608 A.2d 1353 (N.J., 1992).

New York Domestic Relations Law §236B(5).

42 USC § 2000bb-1 ("The Religious Freedom Restoration Act").

Uniform Commercial Code (New York, 1994).

Canon of Judicial Ethics (American Bar Association, 1994).

Model Code of Professional Responsibility (American Bar Association, 1994).

The American Bar Association Standing Committee on Ethics and Professional Responsibility Formal Opinions (American Bar Association, 1994).

Table of References for the Bible, Talmud, Post-Talmudic Codes, Commentators and Responsa

This section contains a table of reference to the various works cited in this book, organized by the name of the work. The left side of each column is always the page or section within the work discussed, and the right side of each column is the place in this book where that work is discussed or cited. Works referred to in passing are not always indexed.

Bible

Exodus
21:1	38
21:15	50
22:7–8	9, 17
22:24	51, 143
23:7	74

Leviticus
19:14	15, 19, 49
19:16	21
19:17	27
25:36–37	51, 143

Deuteronomy
16:20	164

Isaiah
58:7	11
51:20	83

Proverbs
31:8	9, 17
14:34	112

Mishnah

Ethics of the Sages (*Avot*) 1:8   7, 8, 10, 10–12, 18, 73

Jerusalem Talmud

Sanhedrin 3:1   9

Terumot 8:4   104

Babylonian Talmud

Avodah Zarah
6b	51, 52
14a	51

Bava Batra
117	93
133b	125, 128

Bava Kamma
92b	39
115b–117b	80, 82, 84, 86

Bava Metzia
58b	74
75b	51, 143
83b–84a	101, 104, 112

Eruvin 82a   134

Gittin
7a	82
35a	69
88b	47
90a-b	176

Ketubot
17a	151
50a	125
52b	11, 14
59b	134
65b	134
93a	64
122b	134
123a	134

Kiddushin 29b   50

Moed Katan 17a   50

Nedarim 21a-b   149

Niddah 61a   102, 103, 116, 117, 190

Pesahim 22b   50

Sanhedrin
56a	56
75a	27

Shevuot 30b–31a   10, 74

Sotah 10b   74

Talmudic Commentaries

Arukh la-Ner
Niddah 61a   120

Asefat Zekenim
Niddah 61a   120

Eiger, R. Akiva
Niddah 61a   117

Hiddushei Mahari Shapira
Niddah 61a 52

Hiddushei Anshei Shem
Avodah Zarah 4a 52

Hokhmat Shlomo
Niddah 61a 117, 120

Kitzur Piskei ha-Rosh
Niddah 9:5 118

Meiri
Avot 1:8 10–11
Bava Batra 133b 125
Ketubot 50a 125
Niddah 61a 117
Yevamot 65b 30

Mordecai
Bava Kamma 117 83
Betzah 689 30

Nahmanides
Avodah Zara 6b–7a 53

Rabbenu Nissim
Avoda Zarah
6b 53
15a 52
Sanhedrin 46a 104

Rabbenu Asher
Tosafot ha-Rosh
Niddah 61a 102, 103
Bava Kamma 8:17 39
Sanhedrin 3:2 9, 42
Teshuvot ha-Rosh
17:1 83

Rashbam
Bava Batra 174b 14

Rashba
2:393 16
1:1105 96

Rashi
Avot 1:8 11, 13

Bava Kamma 116b 84
Gittin 9b 103, 120
Niddah 61a 102
Sanhedrin 75a 27
Yevamot 65b 30

Ritva
Bava Metzia 83b 104
Ketubot 52b 14
Yevamot 65b 30

Shiltei Giborim
52b 13

Tosafot
Avodah Zarah
6b 53
15a 52
22a 52
Bava Metzia 61a 146
Eruvin 62a 44
Hagigah 13a 53
Niddah 61a 102, 117
Sanhedrin 20b 112
Zevahim 2b 184

Rambam and Commentators

Mishnah Torah
Deot
5:6 71
7:1–7 73
Gerushin 2:20 171
Gezelah ve-avedah
11:3 86
Hovel u-Mazek
8:5 44
Ishut
14:8 181
21:17–18 134
Malveh ve-Loveh
4:2 53, 133
Melakhim
3:10 104
10:10 44
Nahalot 6:11 125, 128

Rotzeah 2:4 112
Sanhedrin
18:6 116
26:7 46
Shevuot 12:12 69

Books of Commandments

Maimonides, Sefer ha-Mitzvot
Negative 299 50, 52
Positive 205 30

Sefer ha-Hinnukh
232 19
239 30
585 24

Minhat Hinnukh
231:2 52
232:3 52

Sefer Mitzvot Gedolot
11 30

Sefer Mitzvot Katan
114 30

Sefer Yereim ha-Katzar
37 30

Yereim
223 30

Tur and Commentaries

Tur
Even ha-Ezer 82 135
Yoreh Deah 161 146
Hoshen Mishpat
17 8, 9
388 42

Beit Yosef
Hoshen Mishpat
26 39, 45
66 44
388 104

Index

Darkei Moshe
Orah Hayyim 8:4   67, 71

Bah
Hoshen Mishpat
17   12, 13
Yoreh Deah
232   149

Shulhan Arukh

Even ha-Ezer
65:1   157
66:3   177
77   183
79:1–2   12
82:6–8   134
93:1–2   11
96:1–2   12
119   181
134   167, 180, 182
154   167, 187
177:3   176, 177
Hoshen Mishpat
1:5,6   61
2:1   61
4:1–2   74, 75
7–8   42
8:5   61
11:1,5   61
12:1–3   154
13:1   153
16:13   61
17:1   120
17:5–9   8
17:9   9, 13
18:3   61
26:1–3   37–40, 45,
            47, 61, 178
28:11   69, 74
66:82   13
100:3   61
104:1   64
231:2   158
236:1   60
266:1   86, 105, 108
282:1   128
290:13   136
331:1–2   158
333:5   159
337:19   159
348:8   48
369   63, 82, 105
375:1–3   24
388   84–88
Orah Hayyim
156:1   69
551:1   60
608:2   30, 31
Yoreh Deah
39:1   94
151:1   54, 58
159:1,2   142
160:1   143, 147
160:16   146
168–9   147
232:2   149
237:1–3   69
245:17   161
253   83
328:12   32
334   61
334:48   32

Commentators on Shulhan Arukh

Arukh ha-Shulhan
Hoshen Mishpat
13:1–7   9, 42
17:1–15   9, 10, 13
22   153
26:1–3   38
388:7   91
Orah Hayyim
2:10   70, 72
608:7   29
Yoreh Deah
232:2, 3   150
334:42   32

Arukh ha-Shulhan he-Atid
Melakhim
7:1–4   44

Ba'er ha-Golah
Hoshen Mishpat
388   85, 91, 101

Beit Shmuel
5:18   56, 57
65:1   151

Beit Yitzhak
Yoreh Deah
49   98

Be'ur ha-Gra
Orah Hayyim
8:2   71
425:10   21
608:4   30
Yoreh Deah
39:1   94
151:8   56, 57
157:5   24
Even ha-Ezer
154:67   181

Birkei Yosef
Yoreh Deah
151   56, 57
Orah Hayyim
608   32

Dagul me-Revavah
Yoreh Deah
151   55–57

Darkei Teshuvah
157:1   104
157:53   84, 92, 102

R. Akiva Eiger
Hoshen Mishpat
3:1   153
26:1   37

Havat Daat			*Minhat Shai*		388:20	80, 85
160:1	143	Yoreh Deah 173	144	388:22	86
161:1	146	*Mishkenot Yaakov*		388:45	85, 87

Havat Daat
160:1 143
161:1 146

Hazon Ish
Hoshen Mishpat
16 65, 164
Even ha-Ezer
99:2 170, 182
Rambam Melakhim
10:10 44
Sanhedrin
15(4) 38

Helkat Mohokek
65:1 151

Kaf ha-Hayyim
2:13–16 70

Karnei Re'em
Hoshen Mishpat
88:1 47

Kesef ha-Kodashim
17:9 13, 18
26 40

Knesset ha-Gedolah
Hoshen Mishpat
17:19 16
Yoreh Deah
157 71

Levush
Yoreh Deah
151:3 56, 57

Magen Avraham
347:7 56, 57
608:3 28

Mahatzit ha-Shekel
Orah Hayyim
163:2 56, 57

Matteh Shimon
Hoshen Mishpat
123:4 15

Minhat Shai
Yoreh Deah 173 144

Mishkenot Yaakov
Yoreh Deah 16 94

Mishnah Berurah
608:1–4 29–32

Netivot ha-Mishpat
9:16 10
17:16 10
22:14 153

Pithei Teshuvah
Hoshen Mishpat
17:15 13
Yoreh Deah
157:4 24
334:19 32

Sema
26:1, 11 37
331:2 158
369:21 63, 67
388:5 84
388:13 86

Sha'ar ha-Mishpat
17:9 13
26:1 45

Shai la-Moreh
Edut 2:1 47

Shakh
Yoreh Deah
98:9 186
151:6 54
161:3 146
168:16 147
323:3 149
Hoshen Mishpat
22:15 153
66:82 13
73:39 65, 105
123:32 13
388:13 84

388:20 80, 85
388:22 86
388:45 85, 87

Turei Zahav (Taz)
Yoreh Deah
157:7–8 104
334:23 32, 33
388:3 86

Modern Halakhah Codes

Dinei Mamonot
1:5 (11) 42
1:256–265 14, 15
1:439–441 15
3:140–198 125
4:25n.1 95
5:5(n. 4–5) 83, 144

Berit Yehuda
2:7 146
6:1–2 146, 147
7:24 143
15:16–18 144, 145
30:16 142
33:1–6 145, 147

Pithei Hoshen
1:6(n.12) 43
1: 4 (n. 63) 65
5:4 80, 81, 83,85,
99, 108, 113
5:12 96
7:4 96

Halakhah Pesukah al Hoshen Mishpat
17:9 10, 13–16
22:2 153

Kovetz ha-Poskim on Hoshen Mishpat
17:9 9
26:1 37–41
136(pp.) 153

178–180(pp.)	39	*Darkhei Noam*			3:136	21	
207(pp.)	154	Hoshen Mishpat			4:23	120	
217–218(pp.)	61	42	16		5	112	
250–251(pp.)	40	*Devar Shmuel*			*Helkat Yoav*		
Otzar ha-Poskim		41	15		Dinei Ones 5	181	
2:11–13(appendix)	170	43	15		*Hikrei Lev*		
Divrei Geonim		*Divrei Hayyim*			Hoshen Mishpat		
52:15	3, 39, 41	Even ha-Ezer			2:155	144	
77:9	40	2:26	161		*Rabbi Azriel*		
77:19	3, 39	*Dovevei Mesharim*			*Hildesheimer*		
Torat Ribbit		1:97	125		2:253	71	
18:18–19	144	*Emet me-Aretz*			*Iggerot Ahiezer*		
22:3	147	46	43		1:25	126	
23:1–3	147	*Etz Hadar*			*Iggerot Moshe*		
Ta'am Ribbit		38	44		Even ha-Ezer		
1:1–4	142	184	44		1:104, 105	126	
160:1, n.3–4	143	*Har Tzvi*			1:137	137, 170, 175,	
Responsa		Kuntres Milei				180, 183	
Alshekh, R. Moshe		de-Brakhot			3:44	170, 171	
38	102, 134	Hoshen Mishpat			3:90	57	
Avnei Nezer		3	71		4:106	129, 183	
461:4	31	*Hatam Sofer*			4:61	56, 127	
Az Nidberu		Hoshen Mishpat			4:91	177	
3:74	1	1:1	40		4:92	178	
Be-Tzel ha-Hokhamah		176	24		Hoshen Mishpat		
4:371	40	Yoreh Deah			1:8	38, 109	
Be'er Yitzhak		19	70		1:92	67, 110, 113	
Even ha-Ezer		220	69		1:93	71	
10	182	227	69		2:11	42	
Beit Avi		6:14	120		2:15	147	
2:144	38	Likkutim			2:29	109	
4:169	137, 174	14	112		2:49	126	
Binyamin Ze'ev		*Havalim ba-Neimim*			2:50	125	
50	9	Even ha-Ezer			2:62	64, 106	
Binyan Tziyyon		55	137, 175		2:92	111	
1:15	70	*Havvot Yair*			5:9	110	
Appendix 24	126	137	55		388:12	109	
		Helkat Yaakov			Orah Hayyim		
		2:160	65		2:25	70, 71	
					3:2	70	
					4:2	70	

4:79	52	Mariaz Enzel		Orhot ha-Mishpatim	
Yoreh Deah		72	43	46:2	41
1:68	52	Me'il Tzedakah		Paamonei Zahav	81
1:71	70	53	9, 15		
1:72	30, 56			Panim Meirot	
2:33	71	Mekor Hayyim		2:155	93
2:40	71	1:22	43		
2:62–63	142			Perah Mateh Aharon	
		Melammed le-Ho'il		1:60	126
Lev Aryeh		1:34	52	Peri ha-Aretz	
1:53	126	2:59	146	Hoshen Mishpat	
		2:56	71, 72	1:13	37
Mabit		Menahem Meshiv			
1:309	137, 174, 175	1:54	10	Radvaz	
				5:1579	52, 59
Maharam Schick		Meshiv Ba-Halaha	58		
Yoreh Deah		Mevasser Tov		Rashba	
50	104	1:85	1, 154	1:1105	96
161	144			2:393	16
Hoshen Mishpat		Mishneh Halakhot		3:29	104
42	125	2:11	43	5:238	28
		5:214	46	6:244	164
Maharashdam		6:277	65, 106	Rema, Responsa	
Hoshen Mishpat		7:255	38, 43, 46	10	44
2:215	159	7:285	106	52	45
55:6	113				
		Minhat Shlomo		Responsa from the	
Maharik		9–13	3	Holocaust	
63	180	44	127	108	118
Maharil		Minhat Yitzhak		Sefer Ikkarei ha-Dat	
123	112	1:233	125	Orah Hayyim	
		4:52	44	21	26
Maharit Zahalon		7:64	144		
1:16	134			Sha'arei Ezra	
2:232	134	Mishpetei Uziel	47	1:333	1
Maharshag		Nahalat Binyamin		Shai la-Moreh	
Yoreh Deah 5	142	30	71	Hoshen Mishpat 88:1	47
Maharshal		Nehmad le-Mareh		She'elat Ya'avetz	
19	86	3:100	15	2:9	116, 120
72	71			1:39	144
		Ohel Yehoshua			
Maharsham		2:115	39, 43	Shevet ha-Levi	
1:224	126			Yoreh Deah	
2:215	159	Orah Mishpat		58	102
4:105	40	Hoshen Mishpat	1		

Shevet Kehati
3:322   16, 46

Shevut Yaakov
1:64   9

Shoel ve-Nishal
Hoshen Mishpat
5:2   15

Tashbetz
1:1   172
1:147   125
1:61   39
2:168   172
2:290   34
3:168   113
3:133   57
4   38, 41, 172

Rashi, Teshuvot
20   30
88   86

Teshuvot ve-Hanhagot
1:730   132
1:795   40
1:822   43
1:850   82
2:701   65

Tsofnat Paneah
184   142

Tzitz Eliezer
7:50   69
11:93   153
12:82   1
13:81   21, 67
17:37   29
18:67   43
19:52   92
19:58   133

Va-Yeshev Moshe
22   43

Ve-Samach Lev
2:60   38

Yabia Omer
Hoshen Mishpat
2:1   57
Even ha-Ezer
3:18   182, 183
4:15   71
4:52   71
Orah Hayyim
3:21   131
4:15   71
4:52   71

Yaskil Avdi
Hoshen Mishpat
6:8   38
Orah Hayyim
1 (appendix)   71
6:8   1

Yehavveh Da'at
1:10   70
3:38   59, 70
3:67   59
4:1   71
4:65   38, 42, 44, 45

Zikhron Yehudah
20   71

Miscellaneous Works

Abudarham ha-Shalem
41   71

Ha'amek She'alah
2:3   44

Ha-Torah ve-ha-Medinah
1:44   1
7:10   1
7:89   43

Sefer ha-Yashar le-Rabbenu Tam

Helek ha-Teshuvot
2   167

Hafetz Hayyim
Rekhilut 9:1–15   74
Lashon Hara 10:1–17   74

Rabbenu Yeruham, Sefer Toledot Adam ve-Hava
Netiv 24, Helek 1   181

Maharatz Chayes
Torat Nevi'im Ch. 7   113

Nefesh ha-Rav
Hoshen Mishpat
267–269   106, 153

Nishmat Avraham
4:86, 93, 94   56

Piskei Din Rabani'im
13:259–274   154, 184

Sedei Hemed
6:26 (p.3)   117
9:36 (p.6)   19

Sefer Hasidim
413   28
1124   57

Sefer Raavyah
2:145   71

Sefer ha-Manhig
1:84, 87   71

Sefer Ha-Ittur
Shekhiv Mera
40:109   125

Sefer ha-Terumot
300   15

She'iltot
Numbers 12:9   102, 117, 120

Cases, Statutes, and Model Codes

Cases
In re Vrdolyak, 137 Ill.2d 407, 560 N.E.2d 840 (1990)	160
Mapp v. Ohio, 367 U.S. 643 (1961)	119
Nix v. Whiteside, 475 U.S. 157 (1986)	121
People v. Fentress, 425 N.Y.S.2d 485 (Sup. Ct. 1980)	23
Ran-Dav's County Kosher, Inc., v. New Jersey, 608 A.2d 1353 (N.J., 1992)	169
Eastman Kodak v. Kavlin, 978 F.Supp 1078 (S.D. Florida, 1997)	79

Codes
18 US.C. §1001	89
42 U.S.C. §9607-08	66
42 U.S.C. §2000bb-1	72
New York Domestic Relations Law §236B(5)	166
Uniform Commercial Code §3-408	145

Model Laws
Model Rules of Professional Conduct, Rule 1.6	22, 23
Model Rules of Professional Conduct, Rule 1.3	115
Model Rules of Professional Conduct, Rule 3.4	19
Model Code of Professional Responsibility DR7-102 (A)(4)	74
Model Code of Professional Responsibility DR 4-101	22
Model Code of Professional Responsibility, Canon 7	15

Ethical Opinions
Washington D.C. Rules of Professional Conduct, Rule 1.3(a)	115
Canon of Judicial Ethics, Canon 3(b)(5)	10
Formal Opinion of the American Bar Association, 93	157, 159, 160

Subject, Person and Work Index

Listings for rabbinic authorities can be found either according to the authority's last name, the name of the classical work written, the acronym used by the authority, or, in the case of Talmudic Sages, their first name. Thus, to find the places in this book where the medieval scholar R. Joseph Kolon, author of the responsa known as *Maharik*, is referred to, one would need to check the index under either "*Maharik*" or "Kolon, R. Joseph".

In addition, it would be useful to check the earlier section that is a detailed table of references for the Bible, Talmud, post-Talmudic codes, commentators, and responsa for pages where specific portions of a work are cited. Thus, it would be more fruitful to start with that section to determine at which page *Shulhan Arukh*, *Even ha-Ezer* 65:1 is dealt with.

No authorities are listed under the initial word "rabbi" in this index.

A.B.A., see *American Bar Association*
Abandonment 3, 176
Aboab, R. Samuel 15
Abraham, R. Abraham S. 56, 129
Abudarham 71
Acquittal 116
Adam hashuv 18
Administrative law 67, 154
Admonishment 27–33, 129
Adret, R. Shlomo ben (*Rashba*) 16, 17, 28, 67, 68, 96, 104, 106, 163, 164, 173
Adversarial system 18, 115
Advice 7, 8, 10, 11–16, 18, 19, 31, 50, 73, 81, 131, 132, 148, 151
Advocacy 8–10, 14–19
Affirmation 69–72
Agudath Israel of America 3
Agunah 132, 166, 168, 185, 188
Aiding in a violation, see *lifnei iver*
Alimony 37, 175, 178
Alkova, R. Raphael 47
Alshekh, R. Moshe 102, 134
Alternative pleadings 75
Amichai, R. Yehudah 40

Amatla mevo'eret 182, 183
American law 10, 17–19, 46, 48, 64, 75, 79, 87–89, 115–117, 121, 122, 144, 145
American Bar Association 3, 22, 157
Amital, R. Yehuda 29, 30, 33, 132
Amoraim 52, 189
Anti-semitism 88, 113
Apostate 39, 40, 54, 56, 86, 142
Arbitration 38, 34, 136, 153, 155
Arbitration, mandatory 154
Arevut 27, 31
Arkhaot, see also *secular court* 37, 38, 46, 63, 67
Arrangers of the law 7, 8
Arukh ha-Shulhan 9, 10, 13, 29, 32, 38, 42, 70, 72, 88, 90–92, 95, 150, 153
Arukh la-Ner 120
Ashkenazi, R. Abraham 15
Ashkenazi, R. Betzalel 104
Assisting in a violation, see also *lifnei iver*
Assisting the guilty 115–122

Auerbach, R. Shlomo   3, 84, 93, 94
Avnei Nezer   31, 172
Avnei Tzedek   65
Az Nidberu   1
Babad, R. Joseph   52
Bacharach, R. Yair Hayyim   55
Bad advice   19, 50, 132, 148
Bah   12, 13, 92, 149
Bankruptcy   63–66
Batzri, R. Ezra   1, 14, 15, 42, 83, 95, 96, 97, 108, 125, 144
Be-tzel ha-Hokhmah   40
Be'er Yitzhak   182
Beit din   7, 8, 15–17, 19, 37–44, 45, 46, 58, 60, 61, 64, 65, 81, 85, 88, 109, 113, 129, 133, 135–137, 153–155, 166, 168, 170, 178, 180, 182, 183 186–188
Beit Hillel   151
Beit Shammai   151
Beit Yosef   39, 44, 104, 112, 147, 182
Beit Avi   38, 137, 174, 175
Benveniste, R. Hayyim   15, 16, 71
Berit Yehudah   142–147
Berlin, R. Naphtali Tzvi Yehuda   44
Billing   1, 139, 141,157–161
Billing travel time   159–161
Binyan Tziyyon   70, 126
Biser, Mordecai   1, 3, 16, 17, 19–21
Blau, R. Yaakov   43, 65, 96, 97, 99, 113,142–145, 147, 158
Bleich, R. J. David   21, 40–42, 60, 66, 67, 91, 94, 95, 104, 112, 116, 120, 127, 129, 141, 145, 174
Bombach, R. Yehoshua Pihas   39, 43
Bonds   146
Boorstein, R. Abraham   32, 172
Breish, R. Yaakov   21, 76, 108, 111–113
Breitowitz, Irving   132,167–169, 179, 183
Bressler, R. Dov   153

Broyde, Michael J.   3,31, 50, 56, 61, 70, 86, 107, 131, 134, 166
Business ethics   157
"Case of the Kettle"   75
California   22, 23
Carminker, Evan   66
Chajes, R. Zvi Hirsch   113
Champertry   14
Child custody   131, 133–137
Child support   134, 137
Children   29, 83, 92, 131, 134–136, 164, 171, 174
Christian society   2
Clients   21–23, 25, 27–33, 42, 46, 48, 49, 56, 58, 60, 65–67, 74–76, 125–129, 132, 151, 158, 159
Cohen, R. Feivel   126, 127
Cohen, R. Se'ar Yashuv   15
Cohen, R. David   116, 121
Cohen, R. Alfred   24, 25, 167
Cohen, R. Hayyim   37, 39, 40
Collective responsibility   27–29, 31, 33
Common law   7, 22, 46, 68, 69, 75, 75, 163, 174
Compromise   136, 153–155
Contemporary Halakhic Problems   21, 116, 141, 174
Corporation   28, 31, 64, 65, 142, 143
Corruption   88
Counsel   7, 9, 11, 13, 15, 17, 19, 60, 132
Counterclaim   42
Credibility   8, 74, 119
Creditors   63, 64
Criminal procedure   119
Criminal law   79–122
Cross-examination   8
Custom   32, 40, 41, 60, 70, 91, 101, 155, 157–161, 175, 177, 178, 183, 184
Darkhei Noam   16
Dayyan, see also *beit din*   9, 13

Defendant 9, 38–40, 42–43, 46, 48, 52, 75, 76, 115, 116–122, 154, 155
Defense attorney 115–122
Demurrer 75
Devar Shmuel 15
Dick, R. Judah 125, 126
Dina demalkhua dina 19, 25, 63–65, 82, 90, 101–103, 105–107, 109, 119, 137, 138, 160, 173, 175, 178, 182
Dinei Mishpahah 166
Dinei Mamonot 14, 15, 42, 83, 95, 125, 144
Divorce, coerced, see also *duress* and *get me'usah* 137, 138, 166–188
Divorce, uncontested, see also *divorce, coerced* 183
Divrei Geonim 3, 39–41
Duran, R. Shimon 38, 39, 113, 125, 172, 182
Duress 87, 96, 99, 118, 167, 181
Eiger, R. Akiva 37, 117, 153, 184
Eleazar, Rabbi 103, 104, 112
Elon, Menachem 1, 37, 91, 169
Elyashiv, R. Yosef Shalom 93, 168, 169, 179
Emden, R. Yaakov 116, 120, 144
Eminent scholarly person, see *adam hashuv*
Encyclopedia Judaica 2, 4, 142
Encyclopedia Talmudit 3, 11, 56
Environmental Protection Agency 63, 66
Epstein, R. Baruch 9, 17
Ettlinger, R. Yaakov 70
Europe 2, 91, 92, 178
Examining witnesses, see *witnesses* and *cross-examination*
Expense reimbursement 158
False defense 74–76, 121, 136
Family law 131–137, 174, 175, 190

Fear of heaven 71, 112
Feinstein, R. Moshe 30, 38, 42, 52, 56, 57, 60, 64–67, 70, 71, 106, 108–110, 113, 125–127, 142, 143, 147, 170, 173, 175–177, 179, 180, 183, 185
Felder, R. Gedaliah 42, 44, 58, 59
Frank, R. Tzvi Pesach 38, 44, 71
Fried, David 23
Frimer, Dov 15
Gartner, R. Tzvi 173
Ge'onim 39, 189
Gentiles 27, 39, 43, 46, 47, 56, 64, 83, 84, 90, 101–103, 112, 142
Germany 33, 189
Get me'useh, see *divorce, coerced*
Goldstein, Yair 31
Gossip, see *lashon hara*
Gra (R. Elija of Vilna) 21, 24, 30, 56, 57, 71, 94, 181
Grauburt, R. Yehuda Leib 174, 175
Grodzinski, R. Hayyim Ozer 126
Gross, R. Shammai 16, 46
Grossnass, R. Aryeh 126
Grunfeld, R. Isadore 126
Grunhaus, R. Yehiel 141
Guilty, assisting the 117–122
Hadaya, R. Ovadia 1, 38, 71
Hafetz Hayyim 13, 73, 74
Har Tzvi 44, 71
Hatam Sofer 24, 40, 69, 70
Havalim ha-Neimim 137, 145
Hazan, R. Joseph 144
Hazon Ish 38, 44, 65, 154, 170, 182
Head covering 70, 71
Hecht, R. Michael 29, 86
Hehasid, R. Judah 57
Helkat Yaakov 21, 65, 112, 120
Heller, R. Yom Tov Lippman 13
Henkin, R. Yehudah Hertzel 31
Henkin, R. Joseph 41, 65, 106, 132, 133, 164, 166, 170

Hertzberg, R. David	31, 56	Kashrut	169
Herzog, R. Yitzhak Isaac	38, 126, 170, 181, 182, 184	Katz, Dov	33
		Ketav seruv	40
Heter iska	31, 141	Ketubah	11, 12, 176–178
Hikrei Lev	144	Kiddush ha-Shem	86, 108, 164
Hildesheimer, R. Azriel	71	Kippah	70
HIllul ha-Shem	86, 87, 93, 105, 107, 108, 164	Kirschenbaum, Aaaron	1, 21, 24, 27, 48, 142
Hinnukh	19, 24, 30, 52	Klein, R. Menasheh	3, 43, 46, 65, 106
Hirsch, R. Samson R.	7, 72		
Hoffmann, R. David Tzvi	52, 71, 72	Knesset Ha-gedolah	16, 71
Hokhmat Shlomo	117, 120	Kofin	170, 181
Holocaust, Responsa from the	118	Kolon, R. Joseph	180, 181
Hornblass, Jerome	3	Kook, R. Abraham Isaac	44, 153
Idol worshipers	47	Krauss, R. Simcha	37
Iggerot Moshe	30, 38, 42, 52, 56, 57, 64, 67, 70, 71, 106, 109–111, 113, 125–127, 137, 142, 147	Labor law	67
		Lamm, R. Norman	33, 116
		Landau, R. Ezekiel	54, 58, 59, 147, 184
Iggerot Ahiezer	126		
Illicit coercion	167, 168, 170, 171, 173, 182, 185, 186	Landsofer, R. Jonah	9, 15
		Lashon hara	73, 90
Immigration law	67	Law of the land is the law, see *dina de-malkhuta dina*	
Informing	80–94, 101–114		
Inheritance	125–129	Legal ethics	5, 10, 14, 22, 23, 121
Interest charging, see *usury*		Levine, R. Aaron	150
Internal Revenue Service	63, 110, 119	Levush	56, 57
		Lichtenstein, R. Aaron	56
Ishbili, R. Yom Tov, see *Ritva*		Liebes, R. Yitzhak Isaac	38, 125, 174, 181
Isserles, R. Moshe see *Rema*			
Jachter, R. Howard	3, 136	Lifnei ivver	27, 45, 48–57, 60, 70, 127, 129, 132, 143, 147, 148
Jacob ben Asher, R. see *Rosh*			
Jerusalem Talmud	9, 102, 104, 189	Litigant, Gentile	39, 43
Jewish business ethics	157	Litigation	1, 13, 14, 16, 18, 35, 37, 38, 40, 41, 42, 45–49, 58, 60, 63, 66, 65, 53, 76, 100, 137, 141, 154
Jewish divorce, see also *get*	132, 165, 166, 170, 175, 180, 187, 188		
Jewish court, see *beit din*		Living will	128–130
Joshua, Rabbi	103, 104, 112	Luria, R. Shlomo	71, 117, 120
Judge, see *dayyan*		Lying, see *truth telling*	
Kaf ha-Hayyim	70	Mabit	174, 175
Kaminetsky, R. Yaakov	80	Magen Avraham	28
Karelitz, R. Abraham Isaiah	38, 44, 65, 154, 170, 182	Maharam Schick	104, 125, 144
		Maharatz Chayes	113
Karnei Re'em	47	Maharik	180, 181

Maharshag	142
Maharsham	40, 126, 159
Maharshdam	113
Maimonides	10, 16, 44, 46, 52–55, 71, 73, 86, 116, 125, 128, 134, 135, 145, 171, 181, 183
Me'il Tzedakah	9, 15
Mediation	153
Mesirah	79–104
Menahem, R. Chaim	38
Mevasser Tov	1, 154
Mezonot	183
Migo	75, 76
Minhat Yitzhak	44, 125, 144
Minhat Hinnukh	52
Minhat Shlomo	3, 127
Mishnah Berurah	29–32
Mishneh Halahkhot	38, 43, 46, 65, 106
Model Rules of Legal Ethics	19, 22–25
Model Code of Legal Ethics	22, 23, 74
Modern Legal Ethics	14, 100
Motzi shem ra	73
Nahmanides	44
Nathan, Rabbi	50–52
Nefesh ha-Rav	106, 153
Negotiations	76, 115, 139, 149–151, 186
New York *Get* Laws	138, 166–188
Nishmat Avraham	56, 129
Noahide	27, 44, 50, 55–57, 103
Oath-taking	35, 69–71, 76
Oaths	69, 72, 149, 150, 179
Orekh Din	7, 8, 16, 17
Oshry, R. Ephraim	118
Perjury	12, 16, 19, 74–76, 116, 121
Pithei Hoshen	43, 65, 81, 96, 99, 100, 113
Plaintiff	11, 38, 39, 41–43, 45, 46, 48, 49, 52, 58, 66, 74–76, 96, 129, 150, 154, 155
Power of attorney	128
Peri Megadim	22, 56
Pre-nuptial agreement	177, 178
Preschel, R. Moshe	43
Probate	60, 127, 129
Professional confidences	21–24, 67
Profiat, R. Yitzhak bar Sheshet	81, 158
Prophylactic rules	119
Prosecutor	79, 81, 95, 96, 98, 100, 103, 108, 113, 114
Public causes of action	63
Public law, see *Public causes of action*	
Puffery	149
Punishment	88, 93–98, 102–104, 108–114, 118, 120, 121, 142
Prison	79, 84, 94, 96–98, 109
Pursuer, see *rodef*	
Raavyah	71
Rabbenu Nissim, see *Ran*	
Rabbenu Asher, see *Rosh*	
Rabbenu Tam	167, 176
Rabbenu Yeruham	181
Rabinovitch, R. Nachum	31
Radvaz (R. David ben Solomon Ibn Zimra)	52, 59
Rakover, Nahum	1, 14, 15, 44, 103
Rambam, see *Maimonides*	
Ran (Rabbenu Nissim)	52–56
Rashba, see *Adret, R. Shlomo*	
Rashi (R. Shlomo Yitzhaki)	11, 13, 16, 30, 38, 102, 103, 117, 120
Rebuke	27–33, 129
Recalcitrant husband, see also *agunah*, *get*, and *divorce*	166, 168
Rekhilut	73
Rema (R. Moshe Isserles)	39, 44, 45, 54–56, 58, 61, 64, 71, 85–87, 101, 105, 106, 113, 145–147, 149, 166, 176, 180, 182, 187
Resnicoff, Steven	31, 107, 141
Ribbit, see *usury*	
Ritva (R. Yom Tov Ishbilli)	14, 30, 44

Rodef 82, 83, 90, 98, 99, 113
Rosanes, R. Judah 53, 133
Rosh (Rabbenu Asher) 9, 39, 42, 82, 83, 93, 97, 102, 117, 119, 120
Salanter, R. Israel 33
Savoraim 189
Schachter, R. Hershel 107, 108, 118, 153
Schareschevsky, Benzion 166
Schick, R. Moshe 104, 125, 144
Schneerson, R. Menachem Mendel 56, 57
Schreiber, R. Moshe 24, 40, 112, 120, 69, 70, 184, 185
Schwab, R. Shimon 16, 17
Schwadron, R. Shalom Mordecai 40
Schwartz, R. Gedaliah Dov 92, 168
Secular law 63, 65, 67, 79, 82, 88, 92, 101, 102, 105–109, 111, 113, 116, 120, 131, 141, 154, 157, 163, 168, 173, 174, 178, 179, 182, 183, 185
Secular government 63–67, 69, 79–83, 87, 88, 90–95, 99–105, 108–121, 131
Secular society 89, 120, 148
Secular courts, see also *arkhaot* 3, 4, 37, 38, 40, 42–45, 47–49, 60, 61, 63, 69, 111, 136, 137
Securities and Exchange Commission 63
Sedei Hemed 19, 54, 143
Sefek sefeka 30, 181, 182
Sefer ha-Yashar 167
Sefer ha-Manhig 71
Sema 37, 67, 85, 86
Sha'ar ha-mishpat 13, 45
Shakh (R. Shabtai b. Meir) 13, 15, 30, 33, 54–59, 65, 84–87, 93, 105, 106, 111, 146, 149, 153, 186
She'elat Ya'avetz 116, 120, 144
She'iltot 102, 117, 120

Shevet Kehati 16, 46
Shittah mekubetzet 104
Shmelkes, R. Yitzhak 98–100
Shocatman, Eliav 1, 38, 135
Shulhan Arukh 8–13, 24, 39, 42, 46, 54, 60, 61, 63, 64, 69, 74, 75, 80, 82–87, 94, 95, 100, 105, 107–109, 111–113, 128, 134, 135, 142, 143, 147, 150, 153, 154, 158, 159, 161, 176, 177, 181, 190
Silver, Arthur 125
Sirkes, R. Joel, see *Bah*
Smedresman, Peter 144
Sofer, R. Yaakov Hayyim 70
Soloveitchik, Hayyim 141
Soloveitchik, R. Joseph B. 106
Spector, R. Yitzhak Elhanan 182
Sternbuch, R. Moshe 40, 43, 65, 82, 132, 42, 143, 144
Subin, Harry 121
Summary judgment 75
Support payments 134, 137, 175, 179, 180, 184, 185
Supreme Court 119
Swearing 69–71
Talmud 39, 46, 50–52, 56, 76, 80, 82, 84, 91, 92, 96, 103, 104, 116, 129, 134, 149
Tannaim 189
Tarfon, Rabbi 102, 116, 120
Tashbetz 38, 39, 41
Taxes 45, 67, 85, 87, 89, 101, 105, 110, 119, 128, 150
Taz (Turei Zahav) 32, 33, 85, 86, 104
Teitelbaum, R. Yoel 106
Teomim, R. Joseph (*Peri Megadim*) 22, 56
Tenuat ha-Musar 33
Teshuvot ve-Hanhagot 40, 43, 65, 82
Tinokot shenishbu 28
To'anim 15

Tokhahah, see *rebuke*
Torah 3, 17, 84, 93, 94, 98, 108, 118, 119, 125, 179, 189
Tosafot 44, 52–56, 58, 102, 112, 117, 119, 120 146, 147, 148, 173, 184
Tosafot Yom Tov 13
Trani, R. Joseph 137, 174, 175
Truth-telling 73–76
Tuite, Patrick 159
Tur 8, 9, 12, 15, 16, 39, 92, 95, 135, 146, 147, 149
Tzitz Eliezer 1, 21, 29, 43, 67, 69, 92, 133, 153, 184
United States Constitution 70
Usury 27, 36, 51, 141–148
Waldenberg, R. Eliezer Yehudah 1, 21, 29, 43, 67, 69, 90–92, 94, 133, 153, 184
Warburg, Ronald 135
Weidenfeld, R. Dov Baer 125
Weingarten, R. Yoav 181
Westlaw 24
Willig, R. Mordechai 178
Wills 125–129
Witnesses 8, 19, 35, 47, 51, 69, 70, 72–75, 79, 81, 87, 89, 95, 98, 108, 113, 114
Wolf, R. Yisrael 45
Wolf, R. Yitzhak 71
Wolfram, Charles 14
Wosner, R. Shmuel 101–105
Writ 63, 177
Yabia Omer 37, 71, 131, 181–183
Yarmulke, see *kippah*
Yaskil Avdi 1, 38, 71
Yehavveh Da'at 38, 42, 44, 45, 59, 70, 71
Yisraeli, R. Shaul 91
Yitzhaki, R. Shlomo, see *Rashi*
Yohanan, Rabbi 11, 12, 14
Yosef, R. Ovadia 37, 38, 42, 44, 45, 59, 70, 71, 131, 181, 182
Zahalon, R. Yom Tov 134
Zebla 42
Zimmer, Eric 71

About the Author

Michael J. Broyde is Professor of Law at Emory University School of Law and the Academic Director of the Law and Religion Program at Emory University. His primary areas of interest are Law and Religion, Jewish law and ethics, and comparative religious law. Besides Jewish law and family law, Professor Broyde has taught Federal Courts, Alternative Dispute Resolution, Secured Credit, Bankruptcy and other courses. He received a juris doctor from New York University and published a note on the Law Review. He clerked for Judge Leonard I. Garth of the United States Court of Appeals, Third Circuit. In addition, Professor Broyde is ordained (*yoreh yoreh ve-yadin yadin*) as a rabbi by Yeshiva University and is a member (*dayan*) of the Beth Din of America, the largest Jewish law court in America. He was the Director of that court during the 1997-1998 academic year while on leave from Emory.

Professor Broyde published more than sixty articles in various aspects of law and religion and Jewish law, including "Error in the Creation of Marriage and its Relationship to the Talmudic Text, it is better to be married than to be single," *Techumin* 22: 231-242 (2003). He has also published a number of articles in the area of Federal courts, including an article in the *Harvard Journal of Law and Public Policy* on the impeachment process. His first book, *The Pursuit of Justice and Jewish Law*, was published by Yeshiva University Press and his second, *Human Rights and Judaism*, by Aronson Publishing House. He is the author of a recent article in the *Connecticut Law Review* entitled "Cloning People: A Jewish View;" His most recent book is *Marriage, Divorce and the Abandoned Wife in Jewish Law: A Conceptual Understanding of the Agunah Problems in America*, 2003.

Other Books from Yashar

The Right and the Good: Halakhah and Human Relations (Revised Edition)
by Daniel Z. Feldman

Rabbi Daniel Z. Feldman explores the vital role that the masters of Jewish thought have ascribed to laws of interpersonal relations. The author explains—with style and grace—what Jewish law really has to say about ethics and human relationships. He answers the skeptics who dismiss *halakhah* as anachronistic "ritual" and gives new sense, meaning and relevance to traditional observance. Feldman gives a detailed, scholarly overview of the laws of ethics, citing a wide range of rabbinic opinions in a highly readable work accessible to all. Tough questions often yield different answers.

Gray Matter volume 2
by Chaim Jachter

Rabbi Chaim Jachter selects Jewish law topics of relevance and interest to contemporary Jews and, in his characteristically clear and readable style, comprehensively surveys the issues and the varying views of contemporary scholars. Torah authorities from a broad spectrum of Jewry are included in these broad studies. Topics covered range from how and when to save lives on Shabbat including whether one may return from the hospital, the complex *Agunah* cases that emerged from the World Trade Center tragedy, when *halakhah* causes infertility, the use of lawyers in a *Beit Din*, and much more. This book contains the first extensive English discussion of the contemporary theoretical and practical issues involved in building and maintaining *mikvaot*.

Moral Issues of the Marketplace and Jewish Law
by Aaron Levine

Dr. Aaron Levine uses the real-world case study method he pioneered to confront moral dilemmas of the marketplace in the light of American law, secular business ethics, and Jewish law. Rabbi Levine covers the full range of Jewish law in the business world: professional ethics; fair competition; marketing ethics; labor relations; privacy issues; public policy; and ethical issues in the protection of property. From a deep understanding of the workings of applied *halakhah*, coupled with a keen sense of economics and the realities of today's complex business environment—this straightforward, hard-hitting book takes on some of the key issues of the day.

www.YasharBooks.com